LUBAVITCHERS AS CITIZENS

LUBAVITCHERS AS CITIZENS

A Paradox of Liberal Democracy

JAN FELDMAN

CORNELL UNIVERSITY PRESS

ITHACA AND LONDON

First published 2003 by Cornell University Press

Printed in the United States of America

Library of Congress Cataloging-in-Publication Data

Feldman, Jan L. (Jan Lynn), 1955–
  Lubavitchers as citizens : a paradox of liberal democracy / Jan L. Feldman.
      p. cm.
Includes bibliographical references and index.
  ISBN 0-8014-4073-4 (cloth : alk. paper)
  1. Hasidim—North America—Political activity.   2. Jews—North America—Politics and government—20th century.   3. Habad—North America—Political aspects.   4. Liberalism—Religious aspects—Judaism.
5. Democracy—Religious aspects—Judaism.   6. United States—Ethnic relations.   I. Title.
  BM198.54 .F45   2003
  323'.042'088296—dc21   2002013044

Cloth printing   10 9 8 7 6 5 4 3 2 1

To my dear parents, Stanley and Frances Feldman:

As it is written, "From those who have taught me I have gained wisdom, indeed your testimonies are my counselors."

PIRKEI AVOT 4:1

To my beloved children, Jeremiah (Yirmeyahu Aryeh), Danit (Devorah Rachel), Gabriel (Tzvi Hirsch), and Zev Amos: Akavya ben Mahalalel said, "Know from where you came, and to where you are going, and before whom you are destined to give accounting."

PIRKEI AVOT 3:1

CONTENTS

PREFACE

First, let me be clear about what I am not trying to achieve. I am not trying to make a general case about religious subgroups and democracy. I certainly do not want to conclude from my study of Lubavitch that all non-liberal groups are capable of serving democratic purposes. Nor am I making a case for Lubavitcher essentialism. Rather, I am describing a specific group's behavior from which some important conclusions about liberalism and democratic citizenship can be drawn.

Second, I make no pretense about being a completely objective and detached social scientist. Such a stance, were it even possible, would be undesirable. My study is a form of political ethnography, but while many researchers in this mode worry about "identity management problems," I have no need to support a self-conscious distinction between "them" and "me."

My close affiliation with Lubavitch goes back seventeen years to the pre-Gorbachev Soviet Union where I first encountered its members taking enormous risks to revive the remnants of Jewish life. My continuing relationship with Lubavitch has enhanced my ability to make their story accessible. Without this insider perspective, deciphering the Lubavitcher world of meaning would be quite impossible. This is not to say that members of the community would give an outsider a cold or hostile reception. On the contrary, they are, for the most part, a very warm and welcoming group of people. On the other hand, they are very sensitive about the fact that many outsiders, particularly journalists (and, in a recent case, a best-selling author), have, in their view, misrepresented and sensationalized the practices of the community. My guess is that there was no malicious intent here; rather, these outsiders simply did not, or could not, make sense of the Lubavitch world. As a participant-observer, I could enter this world without yielding my social scientific training. My vantage point allowed me to see their world and the secular one from each other's perspective.

My findings are based on several years of research on the Lubavitch community in the United States as well as on the sabbatical year I spent as a visiting professor in the Department of Judaic Studies at McGill University. During this year, I lived in the heart of Lubavitch Montreal, one block from the Yeshiva Tomche T'mimim, the center of the community's religious, academic, and social life. There is no doubt that my four children, ranging in age then from six to twelve, gave me entree into the community and an instant rapport with the mothers on the block. My children were properly attired, sporting the traditional haircut, the distinctive black velvet *kippot* (skullcaps), and *tzitzis* (fringes) dangling from under their shirts. My oldest son became *hanachos tefillin* (the small ceremony in which a boy, shortly before he becomes Bar Mitzvah, puts on *tefillin*, or phylacteries, for the first time) and Bar Mitzvah in the community, having prepared intensively for months with a young *bocher* (rabbinical student) from the yeshiva.

The adjustment to urban life was made easier for my children by the thrill of having flocks of instant friends on the street. In Vermont, the stringent requirements of Sabbath *don'ts* remove them from the activities and games of their peers, but they did not feel even slightly onerous in our adopted neighborhood, where Sabbath was a joyous flurry of friends and noise. For children who have stood out because of their skullcaps, fringes, and dietary requirements, it was an enormous novelty to jettison their minority status and melt blissfully for the first time into the crowd.

Being in a sizable community allowed us to participate in the cycle of holidays and festivals, the *simchas* or celebration of happy events. We prayed (*davened*) in one of the Lubavitch shuls (synagogues), and I attended *shiurim* (classes) and women's discussion groups and school fund-raisers. I was asked to speak at the annual women's convention. I visited the Beit Din, the religious court, the Va'ad Ha'ir, and the separate boys' and girls' schools. One of the most intensely emotional experiences for Lubavitchers is a visit to the *Ohel*, the grave of Rebbe Menachem Mendel Schneerson and his father-in-law, the previous Rebbe. I joined a contingent from the community on a pilgrimage to Brooklyn, the site of the Ohel, on what was considered a momentous occasion—the fiftieth anniversary of the date that the Rebbe took up his position. I won't deny that I left the Montreal community with some real regret, having developed true affection and respect for the community and its individual members. My oldest son is now enrolled in yeshiva in Montreal, because the Lubavitch school in Vermont, where my younger children study, only goes through grade seven.

In addition to living according to the rhythms and activities of daily life in the community, my findings are based on dozens of target interviews. These interviews were based on a set of twenty-three questions that were intended to direct rather than confine the discussion. While I did not treat these questionnaires as an authoritative source of hard facts, they served quite well as markers of what the respondents took to be important about the community. I spoke with rabbis, students, housewives, midwives, teachers, jewelry makers, garment makers, doctors, psychologists, school principals, wig makers, hatmakers, businessmen, accountants, computer programmers, provincial and municipal politicians, party activists, elected officials at the municipal and provincial level, and civil servants.[1]

A number of my colleagues warned me that any "ultra-Orthodox" group would be both impenetrable and inscrutable, particularly to a woman. They anticipated that the custom of *tsnius* (modesty), which requires the strict separation of the sexes, would make interviewing men difficult if not impossible. In fact, in my case, strict formulas and rules actually facilitated the interview process by structuring the interaction.

The advantage of rules that are well known and impersonal is that the nature of a relationship is already defined. Adhering to the rules allowed us to relax and get down to the business at hand without the awkwardness involved in sizing up one another. I felt more at ease and trusted the authenticity of the responses of Lubavitcher men much more than when I conducted research for my doctoral thesis at the Pentagon, or when, during a sabbatical year, I interviewed coal miners in the Donbass region of the Ukraine. There, the posturing and formulaic gallantry of men in the presence of any woman made interviewing difficult, even comical.

Ironically, it was harder to get the undivided attention of women simply because they were always occupied with their children, but since I often had my own children in tow, I quickly got used to working around interruptions. In a small community (about three hundred families) word quickly got around about my project and I no longer had to sell people on participating. I always left an interview with a list of additional people to speak with. This level of cooperation might have been a bad sign if it had indicated some sort of official clearance or permission, or if people had been coached to present a uniform and rosy picture of the community. In fact, I found that people were very candid and perfectly willing to be critical of aspects of the community life or institutions, such as the schools or teachers that displeased them. Moreover, the answers that my questions elicited were anything but uniform and suggested a high degree of independent thinking.

I was also warned that the "ultra-Orthodox" are wary of secular academics. Although they are certainly wary of the press, based on experience, several Lubavitchers are professors in secular institutions such as McGill and Concordia and the Rebbe studied engineering at the Sorbonne, so my profession is not considered that unusual. There is a good-natured tendency to belittle secular academics, and Lubavitchers enjoy a bit of academic bashing now and then, the same as everyone else. Nor was it considered noteworthy that I am a female academic. Having a career outside of the home is not uncommon for women in this community, although it is assumed that a mother of four small children, such as myself, would be working only out of necessity. Moreover, political science doesn't arouse any particular emotion because Jewish law and custom have nothing to say about it. On the other hand, had I announced an intention to research Kaballah I would certainly have raised eyebrows; such study is considered inappropriate for women (Madonna's well-publicized forays into Jewish mysticism notwithstanding), not to mention inadequately prepared men.

Another challenge a researcher faces in studying the community has to do with sorting out the difference between verifiable facts and "common knowledge" claims, some of which have been so often repeated as to become embellished or exaggerated versions of the truth, bordering on hagiography. This is particularly problematic when information about the seventh Rebbe, Menachem Mendel Schneerson, is sought. I want to be clear here: What some outside observers condemn as hagiographic misrepresentations of his life are not deliberate or conscious deceptions, but are fully in keeping with an ancient Jewish tradition of respecting, even venerating, sages and scholars. This tradition continues among Chassidim and among Sephardic Jews and often involves imbuing the sage in question with exceptional, even miraculous, intellectual abilities and powers, traceable to his childhood, before anyone knew that he would become a Rebbe.

I constantly encountered this reverential attitude toward Menachem Mendel. Much of it was deserved, particularly regarding his prodigious intellect and his remote yet approachable, modest, and undeniably charismatic demeanor. But the tendency to romanticize the Rebbe can be maddening for a researcher who expects modern individuals to be aware when they are inflating the good and ignoring the bad, thereby creating a superhuman hero who can do no wrong. Moreover, what outsiders regard as the stuff of legend and lore is likely to be regarded as unassailable truth by many community members.

Additionally, a researcher has to come to grips with the fact that there is a public side and a private side to the life of this community. There is an element of secrecy that could be equated with censorship, but it is not the result of a deliberate subterfuge. Emphasizing the positive and downplaying the negative is customary.

Perhaps the best example is the way that the community, in its literature and accumulated oral lore, represents the life of Menachem Mendel in his youth, or pre-Rebbe, days. He spent his student years in Berlin and Paris and was apparently rather comfortable in the outside world. Photographs show a man with a trimmed beard, dapper attire, and French newspapers in hand. This would be seen, in any other man, as somewhat unseemly, or *unchassidische*, behavior. Moreover, the photos of his wife reveal a sophisticated, stylish woman with partially uncovered hair and a definite ease in the world. There is no attempt to censor or suppress these photos, though the details of the couple's early life together are shrouded in mystery. What is interesting and very revealing is that Lubavitchers have turned the young Rebbe's modernity into an advantage by using it to illustrate the distinction between the character of a Rebbe and that of an ordinary man. While the rest of us would clearly run great spiritual risks were we to engage in worldly activities, a Rebbe cannot only skirt dangers, he can transform them into holiness. Unlike the average person, he can come into contact with aspects of life that would taint a person of lesser character. The average person does not possess his spiritual purity, and therefore should certainly not emulate his reading of secular newspapers. (Young people circulate the story that the Rebbe was hiding holy texts behind the newspaper.)

More important than whether claims about the Rebbe or his life or his powers hold up to careful scrutiny is the significance and meaning of these claims to the community. For instance, researchers have pointed out with great indignation that there is no hard evidence that the Rebbe Menachem Mendel ever graduated from the Sorbonne, as is universally accepted by the community.[2] Whether he graduated or, for that matter, ever even attended, the fact that his followers make him out to have been a star student in the sciences and engineering speaks to their recognition of the esteem granted by the outside world to academic credentials and scientific knowledge. For understanding the community, this fact may be in itself an important truth. In the final analysis, I did not find it particularly disturbing that Lubavitcher publications and oral lore gloss over or even ignore some issues or controversies. Challenging the truth claims of the Lubavitchers about their beloved Rebbe was not part of my project.

I came to know many people as friends, confidants, neighbors, co-workers, and citizens. I found Lubavitchers to be complex people who live not in two worlds but in one world with two dimensions, two clocks, and two calendars. Their role in life is to unite the two dimensions, sacred and profane, by infusing practical, ordinary, daily activities of life at home and at work with G-dliness. They believe to a person that we are obligated to make a home for G-d in the world, and that we will imminently leave *golus,* or exile (physical and spiritual), for *geulah* (redemption). They expect this eternal Sabbath to be ushered in by the messiah (Moshiach).

Joshua ben Perachaya said, "Provide yourself with a teacher; acquire for yourself a friend" (Pirkei Avot 1:6).

In researching and writing this book, I have had the good fortune to have found both, and often in the same person. The spiritual and practical guidance of Rabbi Yitzhok Raskin and his wife Zeesy Raskin through the years is beyond measure. In addition, Yisroel and Rachel Jacobs have been a continuing source of both friendship and inspiration.

While it would be impossible to thank all of the people who were willing to be interviewed or who showed my family hospitality during our year in Montreal, I would like to acknowledge the special kindness of the members and rabbis of the Montreal Torah Center. They gave us a spiritual home. In particular, I benefited enormously from the wisdom of Rabbi Moshe New and his wife, Nechama New. I am especially indebted to Rabbi Shmuel and Chaya Zalmanov and to Miriam and Tanya Landa for their friendship and insights. In addition, I am greatly indebted to Rabbi Yitzhok Sputz, principal of Yeshiva Tomche T'mimim, for his kindness to my oldest son, and to Meyer and Nomi Gniwisch for providing him a loving home and keeping a watchful eye on him when I returned to Vermont, thereby allowing him to continue his studies at yeshiva.

With great affection and admiration I want to acknowledge Rivka Cymbalist. The chance meeting that turned into an enduring friendship I count as my great good fortune. You and your husband Gedalia have been our trusted confidants and advisors in many matters. Rivka, while our children gave you the label "the fun Mom," I appreciated your serious reflections, direct manner, intensity, wisdom, and sincerity as much as your snowball-throwing prowess. May we, in the merit of our collective striving and in the merit of our children, be privileged to see the final redemption in our times.

I also want to thank my friends and colleagues, Pat Neal, Thomas Mazza, and Robert Taylor, for their thoughtful and kind comments on this manuscript. Bob, your unstinting encouragement and friendship contributed to the successful completion of this project.

I am grateful to the Department of Judaic Studies at McGill University for hosting me during my sabbatical year and for their generous provision of facilities and support.

Finally, I want to acknowledge the generous financial support by Jerry D. Jacobson for the Political Science Department of the University of Vermont and for this project in particular.

NOTE ON SPELLING
AND TRANSLITERATION

Because it is sometimes awkward or even impossible to convey a meaning in translation, I have used a number of Yiddish and Hebrew words in the text. I provide a rough translation in parentheses following the word. There is no standard guide for transliterating Yiddish and Hebrew, and I encountered various spellings of the same word. On one poster, for instance, I noticed three different renderings of the word *Moshiach* (messiah). I initially decided that I would adopt the spellings used in the Lubavitch presses, but even those were not standardized. Finally, I decided to use the spelling that produced the pronunciation closest to that used by my Lubavitcher acquaintances. This choice also has its problems, since pronunciation varies between the older, European-born generations and the younger, native Canadian and American generations. Even within generations, different countries and regions are reflected in speech patterns and accents. In this case, I stuck with the spelling that conformed to the most prevalent pronunciation. Accordingly, while many scholars write Hasid or Hasidic, I have written Chossid or Chassidic. In a more theoretical discussion in the text, I might have used Shabbat for Sabbath, but in relating someone else's words, I may have used Shabbos, as it is most often spoken in the latter way and written in the former.

I have also used *G-d* because the name of G-d is not written out by many observant Jews because of the strong prohibition against attempting to represent or define, and therefore limit, G-d. Many religious Jews use *Hashem*, which means "the name," in order to speak of G-d. The prohibition is also related to the making of idols, which even writing G-d's name would represent.

LUBAVITCHERS AS CITIZENS

CHAPTER ONE

Does Democracy Need Liberals?

The public philosophy of the United States and Canada, liberalism, is ambivalent about diversity, sometimes seeing it as a healthy by-product of democracy, at other times as a threat to it. One specific type of diversity, that constituted by nonliberal religious groups, seems more than other types to test the extent to which the state is willing to honor its expressed commitment to toleration and neutrality with respect to citizens' views of the good life. In this arena, where the values of a particular subgroup may collide with the values of the majority, liberalism's putative commitment to tolerate diversity may be overridden by its apprehension about the impact of a nonliberal subgroup's demands on the stability of the liberal democratic regime.

Framed in this way, this apprehension becomes submerged in the more general question of what values and virtues are necessary to the survival of democracy. Here, it becomes one strand of an ongoing and lively discussion prompted by the loss of confidence in most circles that private vices automatically become public virtues when refracted through the prism of the economic and political marketplace. Democracy might be a *low-maintenance* political regime, but it is becoming clear that it is not a *no-maintenance* one. This realization has led to a revival of interest in normative concepts of citizenship. What does it mean to be a good citizen? Must private and public values correspond? If so, does a democracy have a legitimate interest in shaping the private values of its citizens?

It is commonly asserted, and intuitively persuasive, that democratic political institutions require the support of a democratic political culture. This being the case, common sense would seem to support some form of government intervention, most likely in the form of public education, into the process of value formation of its citizenry. It is no surprise that having noticed a correlation between democratic values and liberal values, many political theorists treat the two as virtually synonymous. For them, the statement "democratic political institutions require the support of democratic values" can just as accurately be rephrased as "democratic political institutions require the support of liberal values." But this assertion, in addition to being insufficiently tested, casts needless suspicion on some nonliberal enclaves in American and Canadian society, which, despite their rejection of such liberal values as individual autonomy and critical rationality, hold tight to democratic values.

This is a study of a particular religious enclave, a subset of Chassidic Judaism known as Lubavitch or ChaBad. It is intended to test the proposition that democratic values and behaviors depend on a liberal mindset. The characteristic liberal mindset might include:

1. critical rationality, or the willingness to scrutinize all beliefs and truth claims, treating them as provisional until *proven* according to *objective* standards;

2. universalism, or the willingness to put aside parochial or particular loyalties in favor of attachments to more general principles *common* to all of humanity; and

3. individual autonomy, or the willingness to treat the individual as the basic unit of analysis and the final arbiter of all of his or her choices, values, and commitments.

Chassidim, including Lubavitchers, reject this liberal mindset, yet they seem to function reasonably well as democratic citizens, without resembling either Pericles or Diogenes. This is not to say that all nonliberal groups are equally benign and should be accorded full approval and the right of unscrutinized and unimpeded activity among us. Nor would I want to claim that liberal values are irrelevant to democracy simply because some nonliberal groups demonstrate the capacity to operate democratically despite their illiberal attitudes. What Lubavitchers allow us to investigate is the common assumption that liberal and democratic attitudes and behaviors are inextricably linked. Perhaps if more legal and political theorists were to take a close look at some of the groups that they find so troubling, they might feel less alarmed about the threat that these groups pose to democracy. Lubavitchers, generally speaking, make an excellent test case because they are articulate, informed, politically active, democratic, and nonliberal.

Lubavitch is an example of what Robert Cover[1] would have referred to as a nomic group, a self-legislating island of traditional authority with its own enduring and distinctive narrative and world of meaning. This nomic group is resistant to change, insular, hierarchical, and patriarchal; in short, it is a stark contrast to the dominant liberal culture. Unlike the Amish or Hutterites, with whom they are often compared, Chassidim do not depend on rural isolation for survival as a group. Chassidim function remarkably well in urban settings despite the attractions and distractions of liberal secular life, which they cannot escape.

Unlike religious movements that possess a "theological impulse to tyrannize over others,"[2] this group does not attempt to use the state to promote its conception of the good beyond the borders of its own community. Yet its members are politically active in ways that occasionally make their neighbors edgy and make themselves controversial among legal and political theorists. Chassidim have been called a "liberal paradox" in that they vote, run for office, serve on local school boards and commissions, yet their Rebbe allegedly delivers a bloc vote like a political machine because the individual voters cannot think for themselves.[3] It is claimed that Chassidim do not violate the laws of the liberal state, but they certainly violate the spirit of liberalism. And unlike the Amish who are not good citizens, Hasidim are "bad citizens." In the same vein one theorist asks, "Why should the United States accommodate subgroups like the Hasidim and Amish which reject principles of justice fundamental to the American regime?"[4] Another condemns the Satmar Chassidim, claiming that "as an enclave group Satmar is not healthy for democracy especially when they exercise political power."[5] This is because their internal values are not liberal. Yet another theorist, referring to Chassidim, charges that "so-called nomic communities are likely to reveal a high frequency of Constitution-flouting."[6]

Ironically, Chassidim are characterized as bad citizens not for being politically passive or disengaged but for being politically active. What would count as civic virtue and good citizenship if exercised by a mainstream liberal group is likely to be condemned as bad citizenship when exercised by a nonliberal group. There is no reason to believe these nonliberal citizens enter the political realm in bad faith, seeking to subvert the very laws that give them a political voice. If it is not their behavior that comes under fire, it is the way they deliberate about political issues. It is often alleged that such citizens are incapable of informed, rational, autonomous political deliberation. They are assumed to march in lockstep to the polls to cast their leader's vote. They are seen as refusing to be bound by the accepted standard of "reasonable public speech" because they may refer to Torah, the core of Jewish law, for guidance. This is regarded as a breech of political civility. Finally, they are perceived as rejecting our fundamental principles of justice and democracy when they reject liberal values. We put the burden of proof on them to demonstrate that their "otherness" is not a threat to us. This habit typically produces willful or accidental misperceptions, which, in turn, commonly generate hostile feelings toward groups that we find culturally opaque. This has led to all sorts of inaccurate and unfounded claims about Lubavitchers.

For instance, an unwillingness to try to understand the unique relationship between a Rebbe and his Chossid (follower) led one *New York Times* reporter to ineptly compare the seventh Lubavitcher Rebbe to Mao at the height of the Cultural Revolution.[7] The inability of a *Chicago Tribune* reporter to understand Lubavitchers led him to mischaracterize their traditions in a dramatically denigrating way. Instead of lauding a Lubavitcher initiative that established a kosher slaughterhouse and thereby revived the dying rural town of Postville, Iowa, the reporter chose to emphasize the self-isolation of the Lubavitcher families as well as the seemingly contradictory claim that they had imposed their alien culture upon the townsfolk. Failure to understand the principle of *tsnius* (modesty), which keeps Lubavitcher men and women from staring directly into the eyes of any member of the opposite sex, Jewish or otherwise, led the same reporter to claim that "the women are not allowed to make eye contact with the locals."[8] This phenomenon whereby the observer from the dominant society is freed of the responsibility of understanding and accurately portraying his subjects has many parallels in liberal society and scholarship. It is left to the minority group to make its culture comprehensible to the majority and to square its values with those of the majority, and hence, the state.

Depending on our own perception of the Lubavitcher community, we might choose to condemn this community simply because it is an anachronism, a throwback to an unenlightened era, a cultural dinosaur as extinct as the giant reptiles that roamed an earth that Chassidim refuse to believe is older than 5,763 years. Alternatively, we might treat them as a living, breathing postmodern critique of liberalism, in which the quaint daily life of its members serves to deconstruct Enlightenment rationalism. A more sympathetic viewer might see in Lubavitch and other Chassidim a countercultural reminder that liberalism, as a way of life, may not have all the answers. This viewer is likely to applaud these few islands that resist the corrosive, homogenizing forces of consumerism and mass culture. In a postmodern world that is devoid of enchantment and a sense of "home," Chassidim may represent to them the enviable reestablishment of sacred space in the midst of a fragmented and alienated world. But what all of these approaches have in common, be they romantic, sincerely sympathetic, condescendingly indulgent, or downright hostile, is the statist approach. They evaluate the group not on how its members understand their interaction with the society and the state, but on outsiders' judgments about whether the group contributes positively to society, culture, and democracy. According to Nomi Maya Stolzenberg, "The persistence of Jewish communal expression should sensitize us to the limitations of the American constitutional principles of tolerance."[9]

Lubavitcher Chassidim, numbering only about 250,000 members worldwide, may seem fairly marginal to American life and political theory. One need not be overly concerned that they will have much of an impact on politics in the United States or Canada, except in small, localized contexts. As for the "demonstration effect," their lifestyle is altogether too stringent to appeal to many outsiders. Yet such groups are conceptually central to contemporary scholarly preoccupations, occupying the intersection of at least five important strands of liberal thought: civic republicanism, feminist theory, communitarianism, multiculturalism, and the study of the relationship between legal and normative orders.

Civic Republicanism and Normative Citizenship

Concern that we may not be producing citizens of sufficient skill and activism to keep our democratic institutions afloat has prompted a revival of interest in classical or republican citizen virtues. If democratic behavior relies on democratic norms, then a fairly high degree of congruence between private and public norms might be essential to the survival of democracy. This would mean, in turn, that nonliberal private associations like Lubavitch might have negative political consequences for the state. Theorists such as Amy Gutmann and Steven Macedo believe that nonliberal values indeed produce a destabilizing effect on our political institutions.[10] It is of paramount importance to them that the state be involved, through the public schools, in the transmission of appropriate values to our youth. Not surprisingly, education is frequently at the center of the tug-of-war between parental and state authority, often involving religious families that believe the state is interfering with their right to transmit their values to their children.

The "civic virtue" theorists have raised the bar with respect to what constitutes good citizenship. They fear that democratic institutions will succumb to elite rule, filling the civic vacuum left by the retreat of citizens into the private realm. The only force that seems to jolt citizens out of their lethargy and free-ridership is their obsessive concern with their self-interest and with their rights. These concerns, while not necessarily counterproductive to democracies, are not in keeping with the civic orientation that these theorists believe is essential to democracy. They would require that children be taught not merely to respect the law and understand the mechanics of government; they would additionally foster in children the attributes of the liberal mindset. Their premise is that liberalism and democracy are so intertwined and interdependent as to be essentially synonymous.

There are varying degrees of militancy with respect to how far government should go in inculcating liberal values. Benjamin Barber advocates not only mandatory civic education but mandatory service in the community as well.[11] Some regret that liberalism supplies only limited resources for influencing the internal attitudes of nonliberal groups. Others, however, see benefits for democracy in various, even nonliberal, forms of associational life. While Robert Putnam[12] favors associations that are internally both liberal and democratic, he does not rule out the possibility that groups whose norms and purposes are not liberal might still serve as incubators of democratic habits and building blocks of democratic regimes. Relaxing the connection between liberalism and democracy even further, Nancy Rosenblum and Benjamin Barber believe that associational life in almost all of its forms may contribute to democracy.[13] Any group, short of those that advocate the violent overthrow of the government or the deprivation of other citizens' civil rights, habituate their members to the norms of cooperation and mutual respect, and thus tame their antidemocratic urges. Barber and Kent Greenawalt[14] are even more lenient toward religious groups because they see them as so crucial to the coherence and solidarity of civil society that we have good reason to embrace them even when they reject liberal norms.

If Lubavitchers hold to the "family values" and the traditional, G-d-fearing mentality that any American political candidate would claim as his own, and they carry these values into the political realm, why wouldn't they represent the very ideal of civic republicanism? That Lubavitchers have become increasingly politically active has made liberal theorists such as Jeff Spinner, Christopher Eisgruber, and Ira Lupu uncomfortable because Lubavitchers' political activism is perceived as being directed at preserving the autonomy of the group rather than the well-being of its individual members. Liberal theorists who would inject civic republican virtues back into public life still view political activism through a liberal lens. It might be nice if individuals would be more civic and publicly oriented, capable of pursuing a common good as opposed to being blatantly and crassly self-interested in their political behavior, but the model still involves individual citizens and an abstract collectivity called the polis or state. It doesn't account for individuals who conceive of themselves primarily as members of a substate collective and direct their political activity toward promoting the well-being of their group rather than the individual or the state.

That the political behavior of Lubavitch may not differ remarkably from that of the myriad interest groups to which we have become accustomed does not impress their detractors. Members of interest groups pool their individual political resources in pursuit of their individual self-interest, while members of nonliberal groups like Lubavitch, despite casting their votes as individuals, are perceived as subservient to the will and well-being of the group. They are neither pursuing their individual self-interest nor are they consciously pursuing a grand common good for the entire polis. In short, they do not conform to Waldron's "Rousseauian" or "Benthamite" voter[15] or to Flathman's "high" or "low" citizen.[16] They are neither private man nor public man, neither bourgeois nor *citoyen*. In a political regime that conceives of the individual, rather than the group, as both the bearer of rights and the unit of representation, there is no comfortable political or conceptual niche for Lubavitchers.

Feminist Theory

For liberal feminist theorists, Lubavitch represents a classic case of patriarchal religion in which male domination is exercised under the guise of absolute, eternal, immutable religious truths, making Lubavitcher women either victims or dupes. Susan Okin[17] criticizes Judaism from the perspective of an outsider, but Jewish feminists such as Judith Plaskow are as vehemently critical of Orthodox and Chassidic Judaism as are non-Jewish feminists, and for many of the same reasons.[18] These feminists have a difficult time making sense of the seeming paradox that not only do the vast majority of Lubavitcher women express contentment with their lives but a large portion of them are *ba'alot teshuva*, or voluntary returnees to Judaism.

Many returnees have consciously and deliberately fled liberal, secular society, even though they were usually success stories of women's emancipation, that is, young, educated professionals. Their reasons for becoming Lubavitchers almost always include their disappointment over what they regard as the unfulfilled promises and fraudulent claims of liberal feminism. Their views are more in keeping with the critiques offered by radical feminists. In contrast, they laud Jewish values as protective rather than oppressive, supportive of family life, and respectful of women. It is not uncommon for Lubavitcher women to speak of their sense of dignity and power within the community, not despite the separation of the sexes but because of it. They

point to the many examples of heroic women in Jewish history who are celebrated for having intervened politically and militarily on behalf of their people. They assert that Orthodox, particularly Chassidic, Judaism is about the
least macho of cultures. All the male virtues have to do with scholarship and
gentleness, and masculine prowess is measured by how much Talmud a man
has mastered. Here, when a baby boy is eight days old, his parents recite a
prayer that he should grow up to be a scholar. Here, athleticism, fast cars, and
business acumen are all subservient to Torah learning. Here, a firm handshake
is considered rude and aggressive. This may be the only community in which
the boy with the thickest glasses gets the girl.

For Lubavitcher Chassidim, liberalism represents the secular masculine
ethos of individualism, aggressiveness, ambition, and self-gratification, while
Judaism represents the feminine ethos of collectivity, caring, and responsibility. While liberal feminists find women's role in the Lubavitch community
to be stultifying and oppressive, radical feminists are more sympathetic to
the claim that women are truly free when they create their own world. Celebrating women's distinctive abilities, values, contributions, and traits, rather
than attempting to break into and achieve equality in the traditional male
world, may constitute a valid form—or perhaps the only authentic form—
of liberation from male domination. The Lubavitch community may be an
approximation of the radical feminist ideal, and the liberal feminist's worst
nightmare. Resolving the ambivalent position that Lubavitcher women occupy in liberal feminist thought requires that liberals be willing to take a stand
on what does or does not count as objective happiness.

If liberal feminists maintain the strict neutrality with respect to individuals' determinations of the good life for which liberalism is often applauded, they will be forced to rely on the reports that Lubavitcher women
offer about their satisfaction with their lives. Then they will have to concede that these are happy women, and, by implication, that this may be a
good life. But if liberal feminists are unwilling to concede that happiness
and oppression are in the eyes of the beholder, they must repudiate the neutrality principle and defend a particular view of the good life as superior to
other freely chosen, competing conceptions. In short, they need to defend
the assertion that a life lived according to liberal values is more fully human or more conducive to human flourishing than a life lived according to
nonliberal values. The only remaining alternative is to focus on the component of free choice, arguing that for women who appear to willingly and
consciously embrace nonliberal lives, their capacity for free choice has been
subverted or blighted. Their consciousness can comfortably be dismissed
as "false."

The Subgroup Question

The Communitarian Critique of Liberal Individualism

If Lubavitchers understand themselves primarily in the context of their group, they would seem to conform to the communitarian model. Communitarians reject liberalism's fixation on the individual, self-interested voter. Though moved by some of the same concerns as the civic republicans, communitarians lay much of the blame for declining civility and political participation at the feet of liberalism itself. It is excessive, not insufficient, inculcation of liberal values that is threatening democratic institutions. Active since the 1980s, this group criticizes classical liberalism for denying the inherent sociability of humans. The Hobbesian model of atomistic, aggressively competitive, and self-seeking individuals simply does not ring true to them. Instead, they understand humans as embedded in groups and cultures, which provide a context in which individuals discover, rather than choose, their values.

While an individual may ultimately reject the values and norms of his or her community, this is not a casual choice. Our culture and our values are understood by communitarians to be integral to our personalities. In this context, the Lubavitch community might represent the ideal of associational life, exhibiting the virtues of solidarity, self-help, vitality, and intimacy. In this unified, coherent world, each generation transmits to the next an entire world of meaning, which constitutes the parameters of choice. The concerns of some liberals about excessive insularity or impermeable boundaries might be dismissed by communitarians in the light of the obvious benefits of the group to its members. Small allowances for the nonliberal values of a cultural or religious group might be made because communitarians see a rationale for keeping an array of distinctive groups alive: If cultures provide the context of individual choice, then the wider the array of groups, the bigger the menu of values and lifestyles from which to choose.

Yet Lubavitch is unlikely to be heralded by communitarians as their ideal. Communitarianism, in many respects, represents a variation on the liberal theme. It shares with liberalism the acceptance of the individual as the basic unit of society, parting company with liberalism primarily on the issue of the boundaries of the self and the source of its identity. Lubavitch is likely to represent a tainted or flawed community because it does not exist to serve or further the individuation or self-actualization of its members. It is not simply a context or backdrop against which an individual discovers his or her values and then decides whether they are personally suitable. The Lubavitch community is something quite different from an aggregate of individuals united in a collective search for self. When tethered to civic or republican virtues, associational life is applauded by communitarians. But they feel some discomfort when subnational affiliations, in addition to being sources of identity and values that are then projected outward, become recipients of ultimate loyalty as well.

Cultural Pluralism, Diversity, and Group Rights

Perhaps Lubavitch and similar nonliberal enclaves in Canadian and American society are best studied under the rubric of multiculturalism and diversity. Perhaps they can be truly celebrated as a legitimate part of the varied rainbow of cultural life in North America. Whether diversity serves democratic purposes or is simply an inescapable nuisance of contemporary pluralist societies is a matter of debate. Canadians are more lenient than Americans about the internal norms of various cultural, ethnic, and religious minorities. Canadians, for a variety of legal and historical reasons, are in the vanguard of group rights theory. Americans, on the other hand, are much more likely to see diversity as a threat to, rather than a benign product of, democracy. As the first nation to declare itself officially multicultural, Canada jettisoned the idea that national unity requires a unified culture, whereas the creation of a unified culture through the "Americanization" and assimilation of immigrants was an explicit objective of American educational policy well into the twentieth century. Contemporary theorists of normative citizenship are mindful of the centrifugal pull of multicultural affiliations, but many continue to promote the possibility of distilling a unified core of political–cultural values that can achieve widespread, if not universal, consensus.

Related to concerns about shared core citizenship values in the face of multiculturalism, theorists worry about the impact of multiculturalism on our understanding of the unit of political representation. They worry about meeting the competing demands that might be generated if minority cultures were to be given formal political recognition. Some fear that legitimizing group-based politics would fuel resentment and competition among groups, especially if entitlements are granted on the basis of demonstrating a history of oppression at the hands of the majority. This would create a fragmented polity of adversaries rather than citizens. In addition to concerns about the political dynamics that might be created by fostering group-based politics, Americans are uncomfortable with ascriptive groups. This discomfort makes sense against an historical backdrop in which race, ethnicity, sex, and religion were the basis for legalized discrimination. But even when groups or categories are created by the members themselves in order to promote solidarity or shared identity, they are viewed with suspicion because they inevitably, by establishing criteria of belonging, discriminate against outsiders. There is a palpable ambivalence in the group rights and cultural diversity literature reflecting this tension between inclusivity, which is regarded positively, and its flip side, exclusivity, which is regarded negatively.

It is also feared that by recognizing groups for political purposes, the political rights of the group may end up taking precedence over the autonomy of its individual members. While many theorists acknowledge that interest groups and political parties may be the best vehicles for representing individual interests, they see the state as a better guarantor of individual liberty and rights than any subnational entity. Since individuals rather than groups are rights bearers under the U.S. Constitution, protections against the possibility that a group might interfere with, rather than protect, a member's civil or political rights must be enforced. To this end, many legal and political theorists suggest that a higher level of scrutiny be directed at groups that do not hold liberal values; they presume that there's a greater likelihood such groups will discourage free exit. Martha Minow contends that Americans subject the practices of minority religions and cultures to a much higher degree of scrutiny than they do those of more mainstream associations.[19]

Lubavitchers value their autonomy, but not for nefarious purposes of enforcing group solidarity or impeding exit. Autonomy, as they understand it, is part and parcel of the First Amendment right of association, in their case, for the purposes of religious practice. Lubavitchers have not sought group representation in any formal sense. Yet, as a community, they cannot fully erase the imprint of their political experiences. They are the product of a long history of European corporatism. Although Lubavitchers are mindful of the superiority of democratic procedures and are aware that they have benefited from democracy's accountability, responsiveness, and respect for individual rights, they understand that corporate status has certain advantages for a tiny minority. In the context of a massive electorate and majority rule, the political impact of a small group, when it must rely for its political voice on the aggregate of the votes of its individual members, is diluted to negligibility.

It is true that Lubavitchers employ a host of "boundary maintaining" tactics that are intended to ensure the survival of the group. Political activism is one of these tactics. Lubavitchers are politically sophisticated and more likely to vote than their non-Jewish neighbors in both Montreal and New York. But their political activism often comes under fire in those quarters where it might be expected to win praise, namely, among proponents of participation in the democratic system.

Those who grouse about the political tactics or motives of Lubavitch might be comforted by the idea that drawing such groups into politics might be an effective way of defusing their "danger" to the system. Michael Walzer and Nancy Rosenblum contend that any interaction with the outside world will unavoidably have a reciprocal influence on the group, forcing its behavior into the realm of the acceptable. By entering the political and legal spheres, groups such as Lubavitch cannot escape liberal influences. Evaluating the interaction of the Satmar Chassidim and the legal system in a recent controversy involving the creation of a separate Satmar school district in New York, Kenneth Karst noted that a cultural group's participation in politics is a step along the path toward assimilation.[20] Even groups that possess dangerous ideologies and objectives will eventually be rendered politically innocuous, according to this view.

In fact, contact with the liberal, secular world has tended to harden Lubavitchers' attachment to their traditional values. Yet, members of the Lubavitch community clearly understand that they must be able to employ the language of liberalism with their children and prospective members, if only to be able to mount persuasive arguments against liberal, secular values. Likewise, to succeed in their far-reaching objectives of group survival as well as such smaller, nitty-gritty objectives as fixing the crack in the sidewalk, Chassidim must engage the polity according to its own rules. The acceptance of democratic norms, in my view, is unlikely to cause Lubavitchers to internalize liberal values. Lubavitchers demonstrate, therefore, that a group that does not share liberal values may nevertheless share democratic values.

Multiple Sources of Norms and Laws

This relatively new area of study concerns the relationship between legal and normative orders. Pioneered by Canadian scholar Roderick A. Macdonald and by U.S. scholars such as Robert Cover, Martha Minow, Nomi Maya Stolzenberg, Robert Lipkin, and Marc Galantar, the central idea is that there may be multiple contenders for the authority to generate laws.[21] Polynomia, or a society in which multiple legal traditions coexist, might represent a legitimate and morally enriching form of social diversity. In this context, Lubavitch can be considered an instance of a nomic community locked in a struggle with the state for jurisgenerative superiority, or the right to interpret the Constitution. Here, the conflict is most often over the reading of the First Amendment. Lubavitch, like many other religious groups, emphasizes the free exercise clause and freedom of association, while the U.S. courts currently emphasize the establishment clause. Are we willing to recognize the value and legitimacy of these challenges by nomic groups to the court's interpretive monopoly?

Instead of adopting a statist perspective, as most strands of political theory do, we could reverse the lens and look at political life from the vantage point of individuals living the embodied normative life of their community on an everyday basis.[22] How Lubavitch or other nomic groups view the state may reveal more about the state than what it says about itself. For instance, many liberal theorists depict the liberal state as neutral with respect to substantive definitions of the good life. Yet for theorists of legal or normative pluralism, this is far from the case. Liberalism simply fails to acknowledge that it stacks the deck for or against certain lifestyles. What is intended by the state, and perhaps felt by the majority, to be facially neutral policy, can be experienced as anything but neutral by members of many religious, ethnic, racial, or cultural minorities.

My own experience suggests a dynamic interaction between Chassidim and their environment. While retaining their exacting traditions, they are anything but isolated from the secular, liberal world. But what Lubavitchers and other Orthodox Jews regard as a several-thousand-year-old, ongoing, proactive attempt at religious and cultural self-preservation, against a backdrop of various and shifting majority cultures, contemporary Americans tend to view as defensive tribalism. What Lubavitchers see as a way of life in accordance with internal values and laws, outsiders tend to see as a response or reaction to external, threatening forces, including democracy. The political activities of Lubavitchers are therefore likely to be interpreted as a choice of fight rather than flight, as opposed to a genuine affirmation of the rights and duties of citizenship.

Still, Lubavitch deviates from Cover's pure model nomic group in that it has not been particularly defiant. On the contrary, its members are noted for being law-abiding and for accepting, even seeking, compromises. But like Cover's true nomoi, Lubavitchers grant ultimate and definitive authority to their law, Torah, rather than to the Canadian or U.S. Constitutions. At first glance, Cover's model seems to be a better fit for Lubavitch in the United States and Canada than the other models or approaches we have looked at briefly. The problem is that Cover conceived of his nomoi as existing in a constant state of principled opposition—permanent outlaws and voluntary outcasts, gleefully thumbing their noses at conventional interpretations of the Constitution. Lubavitchers are not seeking confrontation with the state. They would not relish living as Cover's nomic heroes. They simply want to live according to their own lights and they feel confident that they can do this, for the most part, within the confines of the law and the democratic system.

In short, Lubavitcher Chassidim are not captured by any single strand of political theory, which is part of the reason their continued presence and political activism should be of interest to theorists working in a variety of areas of liberal and democratic studies. They are both very much like, and very much unlike, the rest of us. They have interesting things to say about themselves as citizens, from the inside, and about liberal culture and politics, from the outside. They are not prophets, but theirs is a "healthy cry in the wilderness" that we might do well to heed.

Why Study Lubavitch?

Recent legal controversies have made Chassidim and other traditional religious groups the focus of discussions about church-state relations, about groups and associations within democracy, and about the civic virtues of democratic citizens. What these studies have in common is the statist perspective, meaning that they are primarily concerned with how elastic and tolerant the liberal state can afford to be with respect to citizens and groups that challenge the norm. This project is the product of my attempt to square the concerns expressed by many liberal theorists about the nonliberal, and therefore presumably undemocratic, tendencies of some religious enclaves with my own intimate and long-term relationship with one particular group, Lubavitcher Chassidim. On a more personal level, it is also a product of my attempt to square my feminism and nonpartisan humanism acquired during my 1970s adolescence with my strong attachment to Lubavitch.

The notion that all nonliberal groups are incapable of exercising responsible democratic citizenship is widely held but empirically unsubstantiated. The extensive literature in law and political theory journals reflects almost no firsthand experience with Chassidim from a closer vantage point than the courtroom. The handful of academics who have made personal contact with Chassidim are primarily sociologists such as Shaffir, Davidman, Belcove-Shalin, and Kaufman or historians like Kranzler, Hertzberg, and Mintz. While many of these sociological, historical, and ethnographic studies are very valuable glimpses into a different way of life, it is time for an empirical political study that allows one of these groups to speak for itself about politics, democracy, liberalism, and citizenship. The objective of this study is to fill a void in the literature on liberalism and democratic citizenship by providing a close look at a nonliberal community living within the larger liberal democracies of Canada and the United States. While these liberal democracies are not of one mind about the treatment of nonliberal nomic groups, they share a tendency to conflate liberal and democratic values. Accordingly, they are most likely to demonstrate their acclaimed virtue of tolerance when they are asked to accommodate those requests that do not strain their liberal commitments.

Beyond my personal reasons for selecting this particular community for my study, the Lubavitch communities of Canada and the United States present a good opportunity to test several assumptions about the connection between liberal values, democratic values, and the behavior of citizens. Lubavitchers are accessible, being concentrated in large urban areas, and widespread, having established a multitude of small communities worldwide. Almost all members of the community speak English in addition to Yiddish, Hebrew, and, in Montreal, French. Lubavitch is the largest and most visible of the Chassidic groups, and by far the most politically active—that is, proactive as opposed to merely reactive. It is also the most "in step" of the Chassidic groups in its dress, language, and comfort with modern science, technology, politics, and culture. Lubavitchers are also more accustomed to contact with outsiders. Their ambitious and expensive outreach programs necessitate ongoing fund-raising ventures outside of their own communities, which in turn necessitate the cultivation of social skills and polish.

Responding to Outside Influences

In part because of their constant interaction with the wider world and the related necessity of explaining themselves to outsiders, and in part because of the success of their outreach program, which has drawn in countless secular Jews, Lubavitch has had to be more adaptable than other Chassidic groups. This is an extremely sensitive point. The need to balance complete loyalty to Torah (from which nothing may be added or subtracted) with the realities of contemporary life creates ongoing dilemmas. No Lubavitcher would accept a trade-off between Torah law (Halakhah) and convenience. Even when there is a great need consonant with justice, there is no support for bending or modifying established law. But this does not preclude innovations and interpretations that leave law otherwise intact. This is in keeping with the position of Rabbi Nachman of Breslov: "You may expound the Torah and innovate in any area you wish. The only condition is that you may not use your interpretations to innovate or change any law."[23]

In dire circumstances, such as during the first and second Temple period, when the verbal transmission of Torah was threatened by invasion, occupation, and exile, the general prohibition against writing down the Oral Torah was overturned and it was gradually recorded as the Babylonian and the Jerusalem Talmud. Similarly, in order to revive the spiritual life of Russian Jews demoralized by economic privation and political oppression, the founder of the Lubavitch movement, Rabbi Schneur Zalman of Liadi, violated the longstanding prohibition against publicizing the esoteric or mystical aspects of Torah to the common person.

Another example of innovation in keeping with both Torah and extraordinary needs or crises is the contemporary emphasis on the education of women. In Lubavitch circles, girls and women may now engage in full-scale Torah studies, and they are formally taught a good deal of Talmud and even the esoteric texts that used to be restricted to men. Additionally, the coming of age of girls, or the ancient rite of Bat Mitzvah, is now celebrated publicly. This is a good example of the kind of innovation that does not change the law. Although this was certainly a concession to the Reform and Conservative branches that were the first to offer public and egalitarian Bat Mitzvahs, Lubavitch still does not call girls to the Torah. The transition to womanhood is marked in a more private way, fully in keeping with their understanding of the law.

Perhaps the most poignant example of how Lubavitch has agonized over the need to keep to both the letter and the spirit of the law has to do with the laws of divorce. The dilemma raised by the *agunah,* or a woman chained to a husband who will not grant her a divorce, will be discussed in detail in a later chapter. It is a clear case of how Lubavitchers undertake to resolve a glaring problem created by contemporary circumstances without changing authoritative Torah law. In short, Lubavitchers do respond to the outside world. They care what the outside world thinks of them. They selectively adopt positive features from the surrounding culture. At times they use what they regard as its negative features to reinforce their own values through invidious comparison. Although Lubavitchers seek to avoid personal encounters with the ugly side of secular life, they can get their fill of stories vicariously through such sources as the *Dr. Laura Show,* which is a running litany of out-of-control teenagers, shattered families, perverse values, excessive materialism and pleasure seeking, and the ravages of drugs.

Discussing the latest broadcast of this radio program serves as another boundary-maintaining mechanism (in addition to providing a bit of a voyeuristic thrill). Dr. Laura's credibility in the community is high not only because she shares the community's outrage toward elements of contemporary popular culture but because she has several times spoken respectfully and affectionately of Lubavitch values and traditions on her show. In short, the Lubavitch community has evolved in response to outside forces, but always within the limits of Torah precepts. The community's political behavior is simply another example of how this particular group of Chassidim has selectively adopted skills from the outside world in order to survive.

Who Is a Lubavitcher?

One of the challenges of researching the Lubavitch community is defining who it encompasses. For instance, one might legitimately ask how many members belong to Lubavitch. It is no easy task to quantify membership. The community itself must rely on estimates, in part because they count families instead of individuals and do not have regular congregations or collect membership dues. But the most significant impediment, which makes determining who is and is not a member nearly impossible, is the amorphous definition of what constitutes "being a Lubavitcher." There are no tests, formal requirements, list of attributes, dramatic sudden conversions, or "born again" revelations. There are no ceremonies such as those that mark a Catholic novitiate's; no pledging ritual like those that mark induction into a fraternity; no issuing of uniforms, cards, or the like. There is no credo that one must subscribe to, nor does birth into the community alone identify one as a member. Finally, there is no committee or authority that decides who is or is not a Lubavitcher.

Because it is the only Chassidic group that actively recruits members among nonobservant Jews, a significant number are *ba'alei teshuva* (returnees to the faith). This community more and more resembles a voluntary association as opposed to an ascriptive group. There is no recipe or orderly process whereby a person makes the transition to full-fledged membership. Some returnees adopt the stringent life in one sudden, complete gesture. Others move gradually. They may begin by lighting Shabbat candles, then start keeping the dietary laws (*kashrut*), then the laws of family purity (*taharat ha mishpacha*), then they may begin to keep the laws of Shabbat. At some point, largely of their own choice, they may begin to dress according to the Lubavitch style, then perhaps take up residence in the neighborhoods where Lubavitch congregate. They may enroll their children in Lubavitch schools and psychologically identify themselves as Lubavitchers. Usually, membership in the community is a matter of self designation. Once a person identifies himself or herself as Lubavitch, no one will challenge them.

I can think of a couple of instances in which the question "Is he or isn't he?" was asked, not out of idle curiosity but because possible marriage partners were being discussed. One party to the discussion answered that he must be because he prays at yeshiva, and the other party to the discussion answered that his trimmed beard, secular education, and light gray suit might indicate otherwise. But in the absence of a compelling reason, such as finding a suitable marriage partner, it is considered not merely bad manners to discuss a person's commitment but a violation of the very serious prohibition against *loshon hara* (an evil tongue). Any discussion of a person's religious observance is likely to bring up his shortcomings, which is a violation of the principle, even if they are accurately presented.

The Torah warns against gossip repeatedly because it can so easily divide a community. Moreover, it is part of Lubavitch thinking that each of us is deficient in some way. The difference between the most observant person and the least is just a matter of degree; every person has a long way to go in a never-ending process of taking on more mitzvahs. One speaks of his or her own personal struggle to reach a higher *madraiga* (spiritual level), but one never speaks of someone else's status.

In addition to the prohibition against loshon hara, the strong principle of modesty inhibits returnees from declaring that they are truly Lubavitchers. Almost everyone will publicly understate their own progress, emphasizing how far they have to go rather than how far they have come. These customs further complicate a researcher's attempt to quantify formal membership in the community in precise terms. I am particularly aware of this because of my ambivalence about my identity and status. My children, on the other hand, simply take for granted that we are Lubavitchers because they see their lives as conforming to the practices of the community that are visible to them.

Ultimately, the community has neither the means nor the desire to establish firm criteria of membership, which means that the community's boundaries are a more fluid than those of other Chassidic groups. The concern that these new members may dilute the stringent requirements of Chassidic life is overridden by the fact that these new members tend to be very scrupulous in their observances. Finally, to allay the concerns of those political theorists who worry about the possibility of exiting from religious enclaves, where there is the possibility of entering, by definition there is the possibility of exiting. Though the latter is exercised extremely rarely (there are no figures available as to which members—those born in, or those entering as adults—are more likely to leave), the permeability of the boundaries make Lubavitch more like a voluntary association than other Chassidic groups.

There are ample reasons to study the Lubavitch. They are a remarkable and interesting people who seek holiness in the midst of the mundane. In an age that is witnessing something of a spiritual revival, encountering people who succeed in meshing their spiritual and material lives is refreshing. These are remarkably practical and down-to-earth people who follow economic and political news, go camping, swim (the local municipal pool has separate hours for men and women to serve the Jewish and Islamic communities), play ice hockey on Saturday nights after Shabbos, gossip with neighbors, and even tune their car radios occasionally to catch a bit of the baseball game. Seeming contradictions abound. Ancient texts are studied on the Internet and talked about on the telephone. Beards get brushed to the side to accommodate the smallest of cell phones. Yeshiva boys (*bocherim*) compare their electronic pocket organizers, which allow them to e-mail their parents in Australia, Calgary, or Detroit. One of the fleet of aging vans that line the streets has, between the two bumper stickers announcing the imminent arrival of the Moshiach, a third that declares "This car climbed Mt. Washington." A McGill microbiologist with a Harvard Ph.D. believes that the Earth is 5,763 years old because Torah says so. A businessman sends the Rebbe an e-mail (the letter is placed on his grave) when he needs advice on a business matter or a son's prospective marriage. A mother of thirteen children who runs her household with the efficiency of the CEO of a large corporation writes a note to the Rebbe with a question or request, and randomly inserts it into a book of the Rebbe's *Igros Kodesh* (collected letters). She is sure she will find a response intended for her personally on the page where her letter was placed. Dozens of rabbinical students return to their dorm on a cold December night to find it, and all of their possessions, destroyed by fire. Instead of complaining about their misfortune, they find evidence of G-d's miraculous powers in a photograph of the Rebbe found uncharred amid the ashes. To these people, the remarkable and the ordinary, the practical and the spiritual, the scientific and the theological all coexist comfortably. If Lubavitchers as individuals can combine what seem to outsiders to be incompatible and even contradictory positions, it is not altogether surprising that they can hold very democratic attitudes without holding liberal ones.

CHAPTER TWO

Chassidim: History, Customs, Beliefs, and Organization

Chassidus is Divine intelligence, an understanding which shows man how small he is, and how great he can become.

HaYom Yom Iyar 19

From a Hasidic perspective, maintaining devout faith is more significant than having a sense of what the secular world terms reality.

Jerome Mintz, *Hasidic People*

Lubavitch is one of more than thirty courts, or *hoyfen,* that make up the Chassidic world. The Chassidic movement is of fairly recent origin, founded less than three hundred years ago by Israel Ba'al Shem Tov, or the "Master of the Good Name," also known by the abbreviated form "Besht." Neither the Ba'al Shem Tov nor his followers attempted to change the substance of Jewish law. Rather, their innovations were carried out on two fronts: in the style of worship, and in revealing the esoteric, hidden, and mystical texts of Judaism to the common person. All of the various Chassidic courts or groups are spiritual descendents of the Ba'al Shem Tov, Lubavitch included. Schneur Zalman of Liadi, the third Rebbe after the Ba'al Shem Tov, was the founder and first Rebbe of Lubavitch.

Chassidim did not challenge or tamper with the fundamental obligation of each Jew to carry out the 613 mitzvot, or 365 negative commandments and 248 positive commandments, listed in the Torah. These commandments spell out the great and small ethical, social, economic, ritual, and family relations on which hinge the spiritual well-being of each individual and the community. This compendium of law covers the totality of daily existence. It consists of the written portion, sometimes abbreviated TaNaKh for Torah, Neviim (prophets), and Ketuvim (writings). Torah, or Chumash, consists of five books: Bereshis (Genesis), Sh'mot (Exodus), Vayikra (Leviticus), Bamidbar (Numbers), and Devarim (Deuteronomy). These five books are divided into fifty-four portions or *parshas* that are read chronologically each Sabbath to complete the reading of the Torah in a yearlong cycle. Following each parsha is a *haftorah* (a section from the writings of one of the prophets or Neviim).

In addition, there is the Oral Torah (Torah Sheh Ba'al Pei), which is believed by Orthodox Jews to have been received complete, along with the written Torah, by Moses at Sinai.

The Oral Law or Talmud, which was recorded in Jerusalem and Babylon in the early centuries after the fall of the Temple, consists of Mishnah, or a portion of law in Hebrew, and Gemara, or the rabbinic explanations and discussion of the law in Aramaic. Talmud is divided into six general categories specifying proper observances and conduct in the following areas: agriculture and *brochos* (blessings); Shabbos and holidays; marriage and divorce; damages, property, and justice; the Beit Hamikdash (the Temple) and *kashrut* (laws pertaining to clean and unclean foods); and laws of purity and *mikvah* (ritual bath). The Babylonian Talmud also includes later commentary by Rashi, Tosafists, and Maimonides.

For Chassidim, there is nothing contradictory about the fact that Torah and Talmud are divine and authoritative and the fact that they have been developed, extended, and interpreted by sages. Consistent with the view that "nothing can be added or subtracted from the Torah" is the view that, beneath the surface, there is much that can be revealed, elaborated, and made accessible. As it is said, "The Torah has seventy faces." This is the context in which the additional homiletic writings, including *agadot*, *midrashim*, and rabbinical *responsa*, that have accumulated through the ages are understood.

In addition to these exoteric (*niglah*) writings that were meant to be public knowledge, in the sixteenth century Kaballah (the esoteric writings on Torah) appeared. According to Chassidim, Yitzhok Luria the "Arizal" discovered what was revealed much earlier by Shimon Bar Yochai as the Zohar (Splendor), the central work of Kaballah. Many contemporary non-Chassidic scholars believe that Luria was the author of these writings. Kaballah represents the esoteric (*nistar*), inner, hidden, mystical side of Torah.

Chassidim fostered a spiritual revival, which could not have come at a more critical time in Jewish history. The disastrous pogroms carried out in the area that is now Ukraine by the Cossack Hetman Bogdan Chmielnicki between 1648 and 1650 were soon followed by the Russian and Swedish invasion of Poland, in which Jews were considered enemies by both sides. Meanwhile, the Thirty Years War (1618–1648) made life tenuous for the Jews of central Europe. These upheavals had repercussions for both the economic and spiritual life of the community. Not only did the community suffer a huge loss in terms of its population but it sank into economic ruin and spiritual despair. With the destruction of the *kahal* or *kehillah* (the self-governing communities) that had previously been able to structure and shield Jewish life, there was no collective body to bear the cost of providing education, dispensing charity, mediating disputes, or interceding with the state on behalf of the Jewish community.

Where once Jewish learning had been so widespread that nearly the entire male population was literate, the ability to immerse oneself in Torah and Talmud learning now became limited to a wealthy minority. The Jews' economic impoverishment was matched by their spiritual impoverishment, making many people susceptible to the appeal of false messiahs such as Shabbetai Zevi (1626–1676) and, fifty years later, Jacob Frank. The rabbinic authorities blamed Kaballah and its mystical teachings for both the Shabatean and Frankist heresies and for provoking the Catholic Church, with the result that the study of these texts fell into disrepute.

It was in this unpropitious setting that the youthful Ba'al Shem Tov, a contemporary of Jacob Frank, was living a relatively isolated existence as an itinerant laborer, digging clay and lime in the Carpathian Mountains. Around 1736, Israel Ba'al Shem Tov revealed himself as a healer, a preacher, and, very soon, as a leader. In 1740, he moved with his wife to Mezhibozh in the Ukraine where he began to attract disciples. His followers were called Chassidim, or pious ones, but the actual word, Chossid, comes from the Hebrew root that consists of the three letters H–S–D, or *hesed,* which translates as grace or loving-kindness. The revolutionary aspect of the Ba'al Shem Tov's teaching is summed up in these three letters. The Chassidic movement's innovation lies in the claim that simple folk, without having mastered the intricacies of Talmud, could establish a personal relationship with G-d through the combination of fulfilling Torah *mitzvot* (commandments) and joyous enthusiasm. Each individual has a specific spiritual mission, his or her own special talents and abilities, and should therefore work in the service of G-d according to his or her capacities. Each individual is equally important to G-d and to the redemption of the community. Each mitzvah performed will hasten the arrival of the messianic age. Therefore, each person, regardless of his economic status or learning, should regard himself, as the great philosopher Maimonides had urged, as if the whole world hung in the balance, awaiting his mitzvah to tip the scale in favor of the good.

In addition, the Ba'al Shem Tov rejected the asceticism of his contemporaries. Drawing upon the declaration that "the whole world is full of his glory" (Isaiah 6:13) he emphasized that G-d is present in all of creation and that the physical beauty of this world should not be ignored but recognized as infused with holiness. In revealing the inner or mystical dimension of the Torah, Chassidus intends to demonstrate the spiritual essence of all matter. But, unlike non-Jewish forms of mysticism that emphasize contemplation,

Chassidus teaches that it is only through the physical performance of an act that the "spark" of G-dliness is revealed. When a physical object is used in the fulfillment of a mitzvah, it becomes holy. It ceases to be merely physical when it is dedicated to a higher purpose, as in a coin given for charity or a candle lit for Shabbat.

By directing oneself toward the fulfillment of these commands, a Jew can change and refine his or her natural faculties or character. The highest achievement, according to Chassidic teachings, is to become *bittul* (to put yourself completely at the service of G-d). This makes you a partner in G-d's purpose in creating the world. It is through this sublimation and purification that humans "make a home for G-d in the lower world." The mitzvot outlined in the Torah constitute a blueprint for making this world G-d's home.

The word *mitzvah* stems from *tzavta* (connection or attachment). In the act of fulfilling mitzvot, Chassidus holds, a Jew binds him or herself to G-d. What distinguishes a Chossid from a merely pious or observant Jew is that the Chossid goes beyond fulfilling the letter of the law and seeks to attach himself to G-d. G-d is not fully knowable to humans. Therefore, meditation alone cannot apprehend him. Action, specifically the physical performance of a mitzvah, is the vehicle for attaching oneself to G-d. This is why he creates so many opportunities (613) for achieving a connection with him.

The Ba'al Shem Tov, impressed during his wanderings by the fervent piety and generosity of the Jews he met, believed that the untutored can be as pious as the scholar. He used stories and parables to teach that the presence of G-d permeates and sustains all of creation. This view contrasted with the view of the great early Torah scholar, Hillel (himself a simple laborer who had acquired his learning late in life): *lo am-ha-aretz Hasid* ("an ignorant man cannot be pious"). It also contradicted the yeshiva-based traditional Judaism that had emphasized for centuries the close textual study of Torah and Talmud, an emphasis that favored intellectual rigor over emotional fervor.

Structure and Customs

The *hoyf* (court) is the distinctive organizational innovation of Chassidic life, which persisted until the disruptions of the First and Second World Wars and Bolshevism. Today, the reconstructed Chassidic courts, primarily in North America and Israel, retain the same town names and the same language and dress of their forebears. While most Chassidim have acquired the language of their new homeland, they still speak Yiddish or Hungarian or Polish, depending on the town of origin of their court. By outward appearance, they are unchanged as well. With some variation in hat or coat styles, they still wear the dress of eighteenth-century Eastern European noblemen after whom they originally modeled their attire. Some still wear knee breeches, though Lubavitch wear long pants. All wear long black coats called *kappotas* (which Lubavitchers reserve for Shabbos); all wear the distinctive sidelocks called *payos* (which Lubavitchers keep short). All men keep their heads covered at all times with a yarmulke or kippa and a broad-brimmed black hat or a fur hat called a *shtreimel*. Lubavitchers wear black fedoras. Men also wear *tallit katan* (an undergarment of white cotton or wool with a blue stripe) and *tzitzis* (long dangling fringes), which are knotted precisely according to instructions in the Torah.

The primary purpose of these distinctive articles of attire is to remind the wearer that he is constantly in the presence of his creator and of the mitzvot that he must fulfill throughout the day. But the clothing, intentionally or unintentionally, also creates a boundary by setting the Chossid apart from the rest of society. Even if he were inclined to misbehave, say, by entering a bar, his clothing would call attention to him and hopefully cause him to think twice before he acted. Lubavitchers have adopted more mainstream clothing, wearing long pants and short payos, but like other Chassidim, their beards, kippot, fringes, fedoras, and black suits still serve as a signal to one another and to distinguish them from the general public.

The monotony of the uniform attire is broken in subtle ways by the tilt of the hat, the way the brim is turned up, and its make. A boy gets his hat about two months before he becomes Bar Mitzvah, at his *hanachos tefillin* (first donning of his *tefillin*—the box containing Torah portions that is bound to forehead and arm by leather straps each morning except on Shabbat and holidays). Boys know which make of hat is preferred. My son begged (unsuccessfully) for a Borcelino, which is regarded as the top-of-the-line model. Before their Bar Mitzvah, little boys are free to dress casually as long as they wear their kippa and tzitzis. Until his first haircut at the age of three, a boy is not required to wear kippa or tzitzis, and, with the exception of a mop of hair or long ponytails, he is indistinguishable from other little boys.

Chassidic women are not always recognizable at a glance, but they also dress distinctively. With some variation according to the customs of individual courts, women are bound by the precepts of Torah that, although they do not spell out the details of attire, dictate that women obey the principle of *tsnius* (dignity or modesty). This principle applies both to men and women, and not only to dress but to demeanor and speech. Just as one should behave modestly and not call attention to oneself through loud or vulgar lan-

guage or boasting, one should dress in a way that does not draw the attention or arouse the desire of the opposite sex. Accordingly, women wear below-
the-knee-length skirts and high-necked, long-sleeved shirts. Most wear
opaque stockings, even in the summer. Pants are not worn, nor are clingy or
revealing clothes. These rules are unwritten, but fairly strictly adhered to
from the age of three on. In addition, after marriage women cover their heads
with a scarf, hat, or wig. There is no injunction to be drab, particularly on
Shabbos. On the contrary, men are expected to buy their wives pretty clothes
and jewelry if they have the wherewithal, and women and girls are encouraged to be attractive, though excessive emphasis on one's appearance is
frowned upon. (My boys were taught that men may spend a maximum of
two minutes a day in front of the mirror, a rule nearly impossible to honor
for my teenaged son.)

Separation of the sexes is practiced by all Orthodox Jews, but it is more
strictly adhered to by Chassidim. In addition to separate schooling of boys
and girls, there is almost no contact with the opposite sex in social settings.
A *mechitza* (wall, curtain, or screen) separates men and women at prayer or
celebrations. Dating only occurs for the purposes of deciding whether two
young people who have been introduced are compatible marriage partners.
There is no random dating for social reasons and almost no opportunities are
created for boys and girls to mingle informally. Most families, when inviting
yeshiva *bocherim* (students) for a Shabbos meal, will send their daughters to
a neighbor's house, just as they will send away their sons when they invite
seminary girls. This seems to be fine with boys and girls, both of whom feel
considerable discomfort and awkwardness in each other's presence. On the
other hand, they forge deep, lifelong friendships with members of their own
sex. While in Montreal, my family frequently shared a Shabbos meal with a
family that has five boys. My solitary daughter willingly fled the company of
eight boys, joining our neighbor's more "girl-friendly" table, a family up the
block with eight daughters.

Boys apparently find the close proximity of girls so unnerving that when
the Lubavitcher community opened its new campus for young women two
blocks from the yeshiva (rabbinical college), the principal of the yeshiva re-
quested that the principal of the women's seminary direct the young women
to cross Westbury Avenue so as to avoid walking past the boys' building. That
boys are at the mercy of their physical passions makes them the objects of
amused pity on the part of the girls, who therefore willingly accept their responsibility to dress and behave according to tsnius. My children's tutors (a
bocher for my boys and a seminary girl for my daughter) once found themselves, because of a sudden scheduling change, crossing paths in my apart-

ment. Within an hour of the chance collision, both had spontaneously telephoned me to ask to revert to the old schedule so as not to risk embarrassing the other through a chance meeting in my stairwell again. In short, at a very early age, and without external policing, children voluntarily adhere to the separation of the sexes.

The Chassidic Rebbe

Just as the Chassidic court has no parallel institution in traditional rabbinic Judaism, the Rebbe is a distinctive Chassidic innovation. Although rabbinic Judaism created centers of learning called yeshivas that were headed by a highly respected Rosh (head of the yeshiva), a Rebbe was much more than an intellectual leader or mere rabbi. Although the rabbi or even the Rosh Yeshiva may be the closest parallel with the Rebbe, they are really incommensurate. Any determined and intelligent man can eventually achieve *smicha* (ordination), and thereby become a rabbi. He can lead a prayer service, teach, perform various ceremonies, render certain kinds of legal rulings, and give advice and comfort.

Unlike a rabbi, the Rebbe is not hired or appointed. He has no formal contract with his Chassidim. His leadership is by acclamation, though he might be appointed by his predecessor who may be a father or blood relative or, in the case of Menachem Mendel, a father-in-law. The dynastic form of succession will be broken, however, if the successor is not suitable. There are several courts that are currently without a Rebbe, including Lubavitch. No Lubavitcher whom I interviewed even entertains the possibility that a successor to Menachem Mendel Schneerson will emerge. One court, the Bratslavers, have continued for generations without a living Rebbe. They are nicknamed "the dead Chassidim," but they are very much alive. Upon the death of their Rebbe, Joel Teitelbaum, the Satmarer community divided, some remaining loyal to the widow of the deceased Rebbe, others following the newly appointed Rebbe. Loyalty between Rebbe and Chossid runs strong, passing from parent to child, and no rabbi, no matter how erudite, kind, charismatic, or able, can duplicate this relationship.

In addition to being a scholar of great accomplishment, the Rebbe is a larger-than-life figure, a father, role model, mediator, and *tzaddick* (righteous man). The Rebbe's followers attribute to him profound spiritual qualities and even special powers to call down miracles from G-d. In the case of a great tzaddick, he may even be able to reverse divine decrees. As it is written in the Talmud, "I rule man; who rules me? [It is] the righteous: for I make a decree and he [may] annul it" (Moed Katan 16b). Some Rebbes openly declare their power; others disdain miracles. Most emphasize the power of prayer and good deeds over miracles.

But whether or not a Rebbe "reveals himself" as capable of working wonders, his Chassidim often believe that his prayers are especially influential and will come to him with *kvitls*, or petitions to G-d to restore the health of a loved one or for a special blessing for success in a new venture. They watch him pray or, as in one story, find something spiritually inspiring even in the way he ties his shoe. This is because the Rebbe has achieved a higher level of *devekus* (connectedness and closeness with G-d) than can most people, which infuses his most mundane actions with G-dliness. When Chassidim gather around the Shabbat table or at a *farbrengen* (a gathering to mark a special occasion or to reinforce communal bonds), tales of miraculous healing, visionary advice, and answered prayers are recounted. Sometimes these stories are based on firsthand experience, sometimes the source is more remote, but everyone seems to know someone who was the beneficiary of some miraculous intervention by their Rebbe.

These stories link the Rebbe to those who had no personal contact with him, through those who had direct contact, creating continuity and keeping the sense of personal proximity to the Rebbe alive. Because the Lubavitcher Rebbe made himself available for *yehidos* (personal audiences) up until the final years of his life, a remarkable portion of adult members of the community managed to have met with the Rebbe. In addition, because the Rebbe reputedly answered all correspondence directed to him, many people claimed to have received his personal approval for medical treatments, marriages, choice of profession, and the like.

Though the Lubavitcher Rebbe never claimed miraculous powers, his Chassidim constantly sought his advice during his lifetime, and since his death have continued to seek his blessings and guidance by writing kvitls and leaving them at his grave (*Ohel*). Death does not sever the bond between Chossid and Rebbe. Most Lubavitchers believe that the Rebbe's spiritual presence has intensified even as his physical presence has dissipated and still find inspiration and comfort in his writings, photographs, and memories. They do not despair that his physical absence will undermine the future of the community. This sort of love and reverence is typical of, and specific to, the feelings of a Chossid for his Rebbe. The relationship with the Rebbe is an absolutely central feature of Chassidic life, and of essential importance to the Chossid. At the same time, it is one of the most controversial and disturbing aspects of Chassidism for outsiders. Because an outstanding Rebbe would at least superficially possess many of the traits that Jewish tradition associates

with the Moshiach, it is no great surprise that a beloved Rebbe would appear
to his followers to be a possible candidate for that role as well.

A Short Course in Lubavitch (ChaBaD) Chassidim

Lubavitcher Rebbes trace directly back to the Ba'al Shem Tov, who was succeeded, upon his death in 1760, by Dov Ber, the Maggid (preacher) of
Mezritch. When Dov Ber died in 1772, Schneur Zalman of Liadi became the
third Rebbe and the first Rebbe of the Lubavitcher succession, also known,
therefore, as the Alter Rebbe (Old Rebbe). In 1796, Schneur Zalman wrote
the central text of Lubavitch Chassidism, the Tanya. The Tanya is a comprehensive system of thought describing the intense human desire to attach oneself to G-d through a lifelong process of spiritual struggle, involving the
various forms of intellect and emotion. The system became known as
ChaBad, standing for *chochmah* (wisdom), *binah* (understanding), and *da'ath*
(knowledge). In keeping with the Ba'al Shem Tov's teaching, Tanya provides
a method or system or path for a Chossid to follow. Rebbe Schneur Zalman
saw that the Jewish people were in desperate need of spiritual consolation and
uplift. This justified the dissemination of the inner dimensions of Torah, in
his view. In 1799, he was afforded an opportunity to answer his critics, who
opposed revealing the inner meanings of Torah to the unlearned. He did this
by revealing a dream that he had while imprisoned in St. Petersburg by the
Russian authorities. In his dream the two previous Chassidic Rebbes, Ba'al
Shem Tov and Dov Ber, visited him to tell him that the heavenly court had
decided that he should intensify his efforts to spread Chassidus. The hallmark Lubavitcher outreach program, therefore, traces back to no less of an
authority than the Alter Rebbe and the Ba'al Shem Tov himself.

The succession of Rebbes who followed Shneur Zalman faced no fewer
challenges than he had in keeping the movement alive. Circumstances always
seemed to justify the Lubavitcher approach, right up until World War I and
the Bolshevik Revolution. Many Chassidic leaders in the Soviet Union fled
to Poland, Lithuania, or the United States. The rest were imprisoned. In
1920, the sixth, or Frierdiker, Rebbe, Yosef Yitzhok Schneersohn, who had
refused to leave Europe, continued to fight for religious freedom. He was arrested in 1927 in Leningrad, but gained release after the intervention of foreign leaders, including President Calvin Coolidge. Yosef Yitzhok then settled
in Warsaw, calling his son-in-law, Menachem Mendel, back from his engineering studies at the Sorbonne to his side to be his assistant. Shortly afterward, Yosef Yitzhok visited the United States to solicit funding and support

for what became an underground network of schools and institutions that almost miraculously managed to survive throughout the Soviet era. In September 1939, with the Nazi invasion of Poland, Yosef Yitzhok and several members of his family, including his daughter, Chaya Moussia, and son-in-law and future Rebbe, Menachem Mendel, arrived in New York. A number of his students managed to reach Shanghai as well. However, most of the Lubavitcher Chassidim were caught up in the war and perished in the concentration camps, including the immediate relatives of the Rebbe, who died in Treblinka.

Having established his headquarters in Crown Heights, Brooklyn, the sixth Rebbe gathered the remnants of his Chassidim and transformed Lubavitch into an international movement with outposts in Europe, Israel, South America, the United States, and Canada. He sent emissaries to dozens of North American cities, and established yeshivas and girls schools, summer camps, a publishing house, and a network of social services. By the time Yosef Yitzhok died in 1950, and was succeeded by his son-in-law in 1951, Lubavitch had become a thriving movement once again.

The seventh Rebbe of Lubavitch, Menachem Mendel Schneerson, was born in Nikolayev in the southern Ukraine in 1902. His father, Levi Yitzhok Schneerson, was a renowned scholar and rabbi, and his mother, Chana, was from a respected family. When he was five years old, Menachem Mendel's father was appointed chief rabbi in Dnepropetrovsk. Menachem Mendel quickly achieved a reputation as a prodigy. In 1923 he met Rabbi Yosef Yitzhok Schneerson, the Lubavitcher Rebbe at that time. In 1928, in Warsaw, Menachem Mendel was married to the second eldest daughter of the Rebbe, Chaya Moussia. The couple moved to Berlin, where Menachem Mendel studied math and science. They moved to Paris in 1933, and Menachem Mendel continued his studies at the Sorbonne. On June 23, 1941, the couple joined the Rebbe in Brooklyn, New York, where he had recently established himself. In his forty-four years as Rebbe, Menachem Mendel achieved far-reaching influence, both within and beyond the Jewish community. He brought to his leadership a distinctive practical perspective, reflecting his secular as well as his Torah education.

Lubavitch now has ChaBaD institutions in 109 countries. More than 4,000 *shluchim* (emissaries) have been dispatched worldwide. Although there is some tension between Lubavitch and other branches of Judaism over Lubavitch's proselytizing among them, not only do other Jewish groups grant Lubavitch grudging respect but several Orthodox rabbis and recently even the Conservative Jewry has begun to send emissaries out domestically and internationally in the ChaBaD style. The ambivalence of other Jews toward

Lubavitch does not keep them from being its biggest financial donors, contributing the lion's share of Lubavitch's annual operating budget, which is estimated at between $500 million and $700 million.[1]

Perhaps it is Lubavitch's reputation for combining intellectualism and mysticism, perhaps it is its equally widespread reputation for throwing a great party, but the appeal of Lubavitch has been strong. This probably reflects gratitude among Jews to Lubavitch for at least partially reversing the trend toward assimilation and for revitalizing faltering American Jewish life. With fourteen hundred institutions in six hundred U.S. cities, Lubavitch has brought Judaism into the public domain with mixed, though now increasingly positive, reactions. As one non–Lubavitch observer put it, speaking of Rebbe Menachim Mendel, "Tens of thousands around the world feel and act a little more Jewish because of him; no one else comes close to that achievement."[2]

Therefore, assessing the influence of Lubavitch cannot be based on a count of black hats and beards. According to Lubavitch sources, there are probably 150,000–200,000 Lubavitchers worldwide, but at least 250,000 more Jews have close ties to the movement. Lubavitch is not opposed to using technology to extend its reach. Occupying its place in cyberspace since 1994, the Lubavitch Web site has been listed among the top 5 percent of sites on the Internet for its innovativeness and popularity. The ChaBaD Web site receives a million hits a week. It has even earned a permanent pictorial exhibit in the Smithsonian's American History Museum.[3] Lubavitch holiday programs reach ten million Jews each year, or 75 percent of the world's Jewish population. Over one million Jewish children worldwide participate in Lubavitch-sponsored educational or recreational programs. From Anchorage to Bangkok, from Rio (my Brazilian cousin is now a Lubavitcher rabbi) to Burlington, Vermont, Lubavitch has become a familiar presence.

Menachem Mendel Schneerson has been characterized as a "field general rather than a mystic seer."[4] Although his collected lectures (*sichos*) are voluminous, he will perhaps be best known to future generations of Lubavitchers as an institution builder, innovator, and risk taker. There is no doubt that his years of secular studies attuned him to developments in science and technology and contributed to his interest in the practical side of life, including politics. His special talent was his ability to draw on aspects of modern life without being drawn in by it.

But his riskiest strategy was probably the one that has paid off the most. It involved sending young Lubavitchers out into the world to contact Jews and encourage their observance of Torah commandments. The Rebbe was not blind to the dangers inherent in encouraging his Chassidim to interact even selectively and discriminatingly with the secular world. Its attractions are abundant and obvious. The practice, for instance, of sending emissaries (shluchim) into communities far from home and supervision makes them especially vulnerable. Usually shluchim are young, newly married couples who establish ChaBaD Houses near college campuses, run children's camps, and hold classes and lectures, holiday and Sabbath meals, and religious services. While many of these centers are in large urban areas, many others have been established in small and remote towns where the shluchim minister to dwindling Jewish communities no longer served by a rabbi or by Jewish schools or institutions. Despite the hardships of mobilizing their own financial resources, putting down roots in an unfamiliar community, and even mastering a new language, young people vie for the opportunity to serve far-flung outposts in difficult settings like the former Soviet Union.

Many people have had their first encounter with Lubavitch through the young yeshiva students who stop people on the city streets. After ascertaining that they are Jews, they invite the men to put on *tefillin* (phylacteries) and the women to take home Sabbath candles. My son is thrilled to accompany the older students on these *mivtzoyim* expeditions.

Other Chassidic courts consider this policy extremely foolhardy. This is illustrated by an anecdote attributed to a Klausenberger Chossid and frequently related by Lubavitchers: "A man is out in a lake in a storm, drowning. Three Chassidim are standing on the shore: a Klausenberger, a Satmarer, and a Lubavitcher. The Satmarer runs away and saves himself. The Klausenberger gets a rope and throws it in for the victim to grab, and the Lubavitcher jumps into the water himself."[5]

The Lubavitcher response to these warnings is to reassert the Rebbe's confidence that his Chassidim go into the world with a strong anchor. If other Chassidic courts feel less secure about their foundations and therefore need to erect boundaries to protect their youth from contamination, this is seen as a sign of spiritual weakness. Other Chassidim counter that Lubavitch youth cannot shake off the spiritual degradation that mere exposure to worldly influence causes. Both positions are correct. Lubavitcher enclaves, simply by dint of being located in urban areas, are not impermeable to outside influences. The Rebbe was mindful of this when he adopted a strategy that is not unlike the one employed by Mormons. Lubavitcher youth go out to proselytize at the time of life when they would be most likely to waver. Attempting to persuade skeptical Jews in the streets or on college campuses strengthens their own commitment. Confronting the outside culture reinforces, rather than erodes, boundaries. But quashing or redirecting the rebelliousness of Lubavitcher youth was not the major objective.

The Rebbe was very much concerned about the rebelliousness of secular Jewish youth whose frustrated natural energy could find no healthy outlet and was therefore being squandered on materialistic, self-indulgent lifestyles and religious cults. Instead of keeping these disaffected Jewish youths at arm's length, he saw their spiritual potential: "The rebellion of youth must be directed against the status quo and toward the sublime, toward G-d, and toward a higher meaning."[6] The Rebbe employed quasi-military terminology and created a sense of constantly being on a battle footing. The war, in this case, has no external enemy, no hatred, and no weapons. Young people are mobilized against the *yetzer hora* (evil inclination) in each of us. Under the Rebbe, the youth group called Tzivos Hashem (the Army of G-d), with ranks equivalent to those in the U.S. Army, enrolled thousands of boys and girls. Their newsletter is full of edifying stories and games and "mitzvah challenges." Moving up the ranks is accomplished by earning points for performing mitzvot. In addition, beginning in 1974 the Rebbe launched a series of campaigns, each emphasizing a particular mitzvah, observance, or practice. These included *tzedakah* (charity), building a Jewish home library, providing a Jewish education for one's children, Sabbath candle lighting, affixing mezuzahs, keeping kosher, and the like.

These campaigns brought ChaBaD to the attention of the public. Being approached by black-hatted young men emerging from "mitzvah tanks" (the fleet of vans used to transport them) became routine on city streets. All of the campaigns were predicated upon the notion of the spiritual equality of all Jews and the principle of *ahavas Yisroel* (love of the Jewish community). In addition, the Rebbe was highlighting a much deeper theological point: the wholesale return of the Jewish people is a requirement for bringing the Moshiach.

Redemption (*geulah*) hinges on everyone's efforts. For most Chassidim, bringing the Moshiach depends primarily on the pious. For Lubavitch, every Jew's mitzvot count equally. It could just as easily be the act of a less observant Jew that tips the scale as the act of the most pious one. Lubavitch is exceptional among Chassidic groups in identifying its mission as renewing Jewish commitment among the unobservant. They cite the passage from Perkei Avot (Ethics of the Fathers) that says that "one mitzvah brings forth another" to support their strategy of encouraging the nonobservant to undertake one mitzvah at a time. This is also a practical decision, in the light of experience that requiring "all or nothing" from the newly observant is likely to yield nothing rather than all. The incremental approach to observance has had great success in winning adherents, and therefore appears to Lubavitchers to be both theologically and practically sound.

The Controversy over the Moshiach Question

The claim that we are "just a mitzvah away" from the ultimate redemption maintains a vital tension and sense of urgency in the community.[7] Redemption will be triggered by the arrival of the Moshiach. This concept is not unique to Lubavitch. All observant Jews, in the three daily services (morning, afternoon and evening, seven days a week) and in reciting grace after meals, will invoke the Moshiach. They subscribe to Maimonides' twelfth principle of faith, which states, "I believe in the coming of Moshiach, and though he may tarry, I will continue to wait." But the confidence in his imminent arrival is a distinctively Lubavitcher characteristic, or, in the eyes of their critics, idiosyncrasy. Even more controversial is the conviction among some of the Rebbe's followers that the Rebbe is the Moshiach. This claim is not unprecedented in Jewish history. Nachman of Bratslav, the Rizhiner Rebbe, and the Stoliner Rebbe have all been proclaimed as the Moshiach by their followers. Even among Lubavitchers, some were disappointed when the sixth Rebbe, Yosef Yitzhok, died in 1950 without revealing himself as the Moshiach.

Jewish thought holds that the Moshiach will be fully human and that a potential Moshiach is born in every generation. This makes extraordinary *tzaddikim* (righteous men) appear to be eligible candidates to their followers. Venerating holy men has ancient and enduring roots in Judaism. The idea that the Jewish people in each generation have a Rosh B'nei Yisroel (head of the people) as a spiritual leader derives from the adage, "He who cleaves to a [Torah] scholar cleaves to the *Shechinah*" (divine presence). In other words, the leader of a generation is the man who has attained, through Torah, a connection to G-d, and from this lofty place is in a position to provide spiritual guidance to others.[8]

According to Torah, the Moshiach will be a righteous leader descended from David (which Menachem Mendel Schneerson reportedly was, through the Maharal of Prague) who will teach and reveal Torah, rebuild the Beit Hamikdash (Holy Temple) in Jerusalem, gather in all of the Jews from *golus* (exile), and usher in an era of universal and eternal peace and justice. There will be no more poverty, war, famine, envy, or competition. Jews will devote themselves to the study of Torah and fulfill all of the mitzvot detailed therein, while non-Jews will keep the seven Noahide Laws (the laws G-d gave to Noah, that is, to all of humanity). All nations will acknowledge and serve G-d. In the final stages, the dead will be revived and nature itself will change. While all traditional Jews may share the belief in the Moshiach and even the expectation, or at least fervent hope, of his imminent appearance, throughout Jewish history ordinary Jews and rabbinical authorities alike have been divided about whether or not humans could, through their own actions, hasten his arrival. (This division is evident, for instance, between those Jews who recognize the state of Israel, and those who withhold their recognition, believing that it is blasphemous for humans to "jump the gun" and establish a state in the Holy Land before the Moshiach does so himself.)

It is unclear whether Menachem Mendel encouraged the conviction among some of his followers that he might be the Moshiach, but he was almost certainly aware of this development. The Rebbe had stated that enough mitzvot have accumulated during the years since Sinai to make the world ready for the Moshiach. In 1951, when Menachem Mendel succeeded his father-in-law as Rebbe, he announced that this would be the last generation in exile because the arrival of the Moshiach was imminent.

In the context of a culture in which both the Rebbe and the Moshiach are central characters and are fervently loved, it is no wonder that this particular Rebbe would ignite hopes and speculation of this sort. The claim in some quarters that the Rebbe was the Moshiach caused a rift among Lubavitchers and alienated and antagonized many non-Lubavitchers. Some people accuse the Rebbe of having simultaneously fueled and squelched the murmurings, of which he must have been well aware. In 1991, he declared that the end of the Persian Gulf War was the preface to the coming of the Moshiach, which led to speculation that he was referring to himself. That the Rebbe did not make an overt declaration would not necessarily quell the rumors since tradition has it that the Moshiach will keep his identity hidden, only gradually revealing himself through such hints. The most striking of these hints came as part of what is now called the Rebbe's April 11th Speech, when he announced that he had done all that he could up until now; that his efforts had come to "futility and emptiness"; and that it was now up to his followers to "do what they could."

Emboldened by such hints, many of his followers began to declare Menachem Mendel Schneerson to be the Moshiach and waited with confidence for him to reveal himself to the world. Among this group were those who wanted to openly publicize that the Rebbe was the Moshiach, and others, while firm in their conviction, who felt it would be ill-timed and counterproductive to publicize it. On the other hand, there were many Lubavitchers who, though they revered the Rebbe deeply, did not believe he was the Moshiach, or at least, if they hoped he was, they were waiting for clearer proof. They feared the public ridicule that came from many sources, especially other Chassidic courts and non-Chassidic Jews. Many otherwise sympathetic outsiders began to regard the movement as a cult. As billboards and full-page advertisements in the *New York Times* began to appear either proclaiming or hinting broadly at the Rebbe's status, the rift began to widen in the community. While the Rebbe banned the publication of several pamphlets referring to him as the Moshiach, he never denied it emphatically enough to put an end to the issue. His supporters became even more adamant, finding hidden meanings even in his denials. Deprived of speech by a stroke, the Rebbe was ultimately unable, or perhaps unwilling, to put these claims to rest before his death.

With the passing of the Rebbe, the controversy moved onto another plane. Immediately, speculations appeared in the press and other quarters that the Lubavitcher movement would not survive without the Rebbe's leadership, or that the Moshiach controversy would splinter Lubavitchers into two distinct movements. For some who had been hopeful, even confident, in the Rebbe's status as Moshiach, his death put an end to their expectations. Others, however, remained confident that the Rebbe would reveal himself as Moshiach from beyond the grave. There then began the arcane controversy over whether or not the Moshiach had to be alive at the time he revealed himself. Some found support for the position that the Moshiach could already have died in Talmudic passages. Others ridiculed this interpretation. Responding to the publicity around the Moshiach movement, many Jews sought to disassociate themselves from the spectacle. In 1996, the Orthodox Rabbinical Council of America declared that it was contrary to Judaism to believe that the Moshiach will begin his mission, only to die, be resurrected, and then complete his mission. They felt that the Lubavitch controversy was divisive and embarrassing to American Jewry.

At its peak, in the first several years after the Rebbe's death, the conflict became so heated in Brooklyn that yeshivas and seminaries split in two, opposing families would not intermarry, and two separate factions developed at the Lubavitch world headquarters, 770 (770 Eastern Avenue). Rabbi Yehudah Krinsky, the Rebbe's former secretary and right-hand man for thirty-six years, and the non-Moshiachists occupy the upstairs where they pray and conduct ChaBaD's global affairs, and the Moshiachists occupy the downstairs for prayers and business. At one point, there were two separate budgets in different banks, and it appeared that the movement, now a rudderless ship, would dissolve. This fear was well founded because Lubavitch has always had a very loose organizational structure, under which operations and fund-raising are conducted by the largely autonomous local entities. In the face of centrifugal forces, the movement is already poised for factions to break away and become independent—although this rift has been papered over, at least publicly.

In Montreal, the division was much the same, though less intense. People prayed at different shuls (synagogues), depending on their personal position on the issue. In yeshiva in Montreal, there is a group of mostly young students that proclaim "Yihiyai!" ("He lives!") after prayers. Some proclaim the Rebbe openly to be the Moshiach. Others share this view but keep it private. A certain set of code words seems to be used to reveal a person's position. For instance, reference to "King Moshiach" identifies the speaker or writer as a *heisse Moshiachist* (hot Moshiachist). Some people initially did not mark the Yahrzeit (anniversary of death) of the Rebbe, as is otherwise customary among Jews, in the desire not to acknowledge that his absence might be permanent.

It must be noted that the rift never resulted in anything like a formal division into opposing camps. Now that more than eight years have passed, a lot of the intensity has died down. People still wait for the imminent arrival of the Moshiach, and many still hope that the Rebbe is the one, but more seem quietly to have let the issue drop. There is still an active, separate Web site that publicizes the Rebbe as King Moshiach and gathers harbingers of his imminent appearance. There are several journals catering to the hot Moshiachists as well. Many booklets containing blessings used in the celebration of Shabbos, weddings, and *bris* (circumcision) are still printed with blessings for the Rebbe, King Moshiach. A favorite *nigun* (melody sung at Shabbos tables) celebrates this claim.

But whether they view him as the Moshiach or not, Lubavitchers still feel the Rebbe's spiritual presence. Every home has at least one large and ornate photograph or painting of the Rebbe, and his name is constantly spoken in homes, shuls, schools, and camps. A whole generation of children is being raised feeling a concrete attachment with and love for the Rebbe. Young couples are going out in ever-greater numbers as shluchim of the Rebbe. In short, his physical absence and his failure to reveal himself as the Moshiach have done nothing to shake the confidence and solidarity of his Chassidim, who seem committed to carrying out the Rebbe's mission, perhaps even more than when he was physically among them.

The Lubavitch publication society has been bringing out the Rebbe's writings, particularly the *Sifrei Igros Kodesh* (books of his letters), at a rapid pace. Twenty-three volumes are in print. They serve as guideposts for many Lubavitchers. They are significant for the hot Moshiachists because "the Rebbe Melech Ha Moshiach [King Moshiach] insisted before Gimmel Tammuz—the day of the Rebbe's concealment—on the publication of the *Sifrei Igros Kodesh*, as we now have a vehicle to communicate with him."[9] For those who do not believe the Rebbe is the Moshiach, or at least are not sure, the letters still provide them with comfort and guidance. Many Lubavitchers derive what they understand to be specific instructions from these writings and they feel confident that neither individual Lubavitchers nor the movement will lose its way.

As for the campaign to publicize the Rebbe as Moshiach, that has been largely set aside. Most Lubavitchers understand that non-Lubavitchers find the claim hard to swallow. There seems to be an unspoken consensus that pushing the point publicly at this time would be pointless, even detrimental. The significance of the Rebbe's confidence that the world was on the threshold of redemption, whether he or his followers believed him be the Moshiach or not, lies in the fact that it provided, and continues to provide, the impetus behind the institution building, outreach programs, and political activism of Lubavitcher Chassidim.

The Rebbe's legal role was chief executive officer of a board of directors, the Rabbinical Council. But this title cannot begin to capture the actual role of the Rebbe. It is difficult to find the language or the concepts to describe the relationship between Lubavitcher Chassidim and their Rebbe. All of the Rebbe's followers credit him personally with the accomplishments of the past forty years. No one else shares his stature. Even the Rebbe's closest lieutenants are largely unknown outside Brooklyn. While a few figures, such as Rabbi Manis Friedman, a charismatic national, if unofficial, spokesman for Lubavitch, and Yehudah Krinsky, the Rebbe's longtime personal secretary and workhorse for the movement, have some public prominence, none of them can compete in terms of leadership or influence with even the memory of the Rebbe.

The important question for our purposes has to do with the future of Lubavitch in the political realm. Will the community find sufficient guidance in the Rebbe's writings to continue to be active in politics? Without official leadership, is the community capable of generating positions on specific political issues and making itself heard at the polls and in the halls of political power? Will a new source of unified political power emerge within the community to analyze and respond to political events in a coherent and effective way? Will the community be able to take political initiative, or will it be left reacting in a piecemeal fashion to the political world around it? Most Lubavitchers expect community life, including politics, to continue pretty much unchanged, even in the absence of strong leadership and a centralized organization. Although its amorphous structure has served Lubavitch fairly well since the death of the Rebbe, it will become clear in later chapters that significant disadvantages have begun to emerge, at least in the context of the political life of the community in both the United States and Canada.

CHAPTER THREE

Lubavitch and American Politics

In both the United States and Canada Jews have earned a repu-
tation for being the most politically liberal, or consistently "left of center," of
any ethnic, religious, or racial group. Stouffer's Tolerance Test[1] reveals that
Jews consistently show the highest commitment to democratic norms. They
are living disproof of the Marxist claim that economic class determines
political views. S. M. Lipset is reported to have quipped, "Jews earn like
Episcopalians, but vote like Puerto Ricans." Analysts have attributed this tendency to the Jewish historical experience of marginality and persecution. In
addition, even before the turn of the century, a majority of American Jews
identified with Reform Judaism. Its emphasis on the ethical and prophetic
aspects of Judaism created a strong theological basis for the inclination of
American Jews to back just and humane economic and social policies. By the
middle of the twentieth century, as Jews attained a secure footing in American political, economic, and social life, they transformed their position as un-
derdogs into that of watchdogs of individual rights and became the most
reliable supporters of the Democratic Party. Having risen in U.S. and Canadian society on the strength of individual initiative and a good public education, Jews have been the strongest supporters of both.

Because the Orthodox (which include Chassidim) are a small minority of
the Jewish population of the United States, and because they are more recent
arrivals to the United States, their entrance into politics has done little to
change the image of Jews as the most consistently and disproportionately liberal of all ethnic and religious groups. The difference in political attitudes
and behavior between observant Jews (Chassidic and Orthodox) and mainstream Jews (Conservative, Reform, and Reconstructionist) stems from historical, theological, and organizational differences.

Reform and Conservative Jews are much more likely to retain the memory of the protracted battle for the full rights of citizenship. Early on in U.S. history, Jews were granted the rights of citizenship, land ownership, and the right to "exercise in all quietness their religion,"[2] but this did not translate immediately into equality. Jews were still subject to various disabilities and burdens such as blasphemy laws, Sunday "blue" laws, Christian oaths and tests, and restrictions on franchise and the right to hold public office at the state level. By 1840, Jews had won formal political equality in twenty-one out of twenty-six states, and they continued to fight for full legal equality for themselves and for other minorities as well.

But because Jews had initially received their rights along with everyone else on an individual rather than corporate basis, they could continue to fight for their rights in the language of patriotism and American citizenship rather than special group pleading. The first significant wave of Jewish immigrants arrived in the early and mid-19th century looking for political freedom and economic opportunity. Many assimilated within a few generations. Others established Reform and Conservative congregations. Most of these Jews, having come from western or central Europe, had some exposure to democratic ideals. The second, much larger wave of immigrants came between the 1880s and the early 1920s. They were seeking escape from devastation left in the wake of a series of Russian pogroms. Many of these Jews had been exposed to socialist and Zionist ideas and had no desire to reconstruct traditional Jewish life. Nor were they enamored of freewheeling capitalism.

Descendents of these immigrants, Reform and Conservative Jews, draw upon a different political history, one marked by political struggles and, ultimately, successes. Accordingly, they emphasize the political realm as the natural setting to act out Jewish principles. Reform Judaism claims that Enlightenment views are not alien but congruent with the ancient federal and contractual structure of the Jewish polity in the period of Brit Ha-Melukhah, or Federal Monarchy (1004–721 B.C.E.). The Twelve Tribes were, in this view, a *foedus* (covenant), contractually bound in mutual obligations and partnership. This federal tradition persisted as a force shaping Jewish communal life in Conservative and Reform Judaism.[3] Their adaptation of the congregational and federal form is understood by them as an expression of the traditional principle of Keter Malchut (rulership).

The redemptive and messianic streak in Judaism, which gives rise to the injunction to repair the world (*tikkun Olam*), found expression among Reform and Conservative Jews in political action, specifically the fight for civil rights and civil liberties for themselves and for other minorities. The aspiration for social justice was religiously motivated, drawing upon the ethical and universalistic prophetic tradition in Judaism while rejecting the traditional notion that human redemption awaits the arrival of the messiah. For these Jews, liberalism has become the theological essence of Judaism,[4] making democratic politics the sphere in which religious and ethical yearnings are played out.

Unlike their predecessors, Chassidim came to the United States as a handful of survivors of World War II, in which nearly 90 percent of Chassidim had perished. They came intent on reestablishing their religious communities according to the traditional pattern, intent, therefore, on maintaining their separateness. For European Chassidim, the Enlightenment promise of relief from persecution had not been fulfilled. Newton, Locke, Voltaire, the assorted rationalists and Deists, as well as their Jewish counterpart, Moses Mendelssohn, offered two sides of the same coin: emancipation and assimilation. Nor was Jewry well served by democracy or socialism. The Jewish communities of eastern Europe and Russia had continued to survive by the grace of civil authorities or the church and the experience of precariousness has left a deep imprint. Suspicion of government is the ingrained political attitude of many Chassidim. The ghettos to which they were consigned from the Middle Ages onward were perceived as repressive but also protective. Jews were forced to develop self-sufficiency. The elaborate *kehillah* or *kahal* was the Jewish response to ghettoization. Within the confines of its tightly knit structure, Jews developed the habits of self-help and self-governance.

The kehillah often achieved a fair degree of political autonomy, in keeping with the widespread European corporate political form of organization. Interaction with the state was avoided when possible, but when contact with state officials became necessary, the Jewish community traditionally relied upon an intermediary (*shtadlan*) to intercede on behalf of the community. His job was to stave off disaster or to lessen the severity of injurious decrees. This was seen as an adaptive mechanism, part of a continuous political history in which the existence of the Jewish community in exile hung always by a thread, at the mercy of rulers from Xerxes II of Persia to Stalin. This habit of relying on personal contact is hard to break, as is distrust of government.

The theological and organizational principles of Orthodox and Chassidic Judaism are, in many respects, incongruent with liberalism's premises. Because the organizational structure of Chassidic life is based on a communal model, the court, where religious authority is concentrated in the Rebbe, Chassidim are more comfortable with the corporate political model than the individualistic one. They do not share other American Jews' allergy to hierarchy and centralization. Although they acknowledge that the good of the community, as well as its final redemption, depends on the actions of each individual member, they do not emphasize, as Reform and Conservative Jews do, the absolute authority of the individual conscience. The notion of individual moral autonomy and sovereignty is regarded by Chassidim as an import from Protestant Christianity.

Although acclimating well to American political life, Lubavitchers' attitude toward government still shares some of the defensiveness and wariness of other Chassidic Jews, although they recognize that government is a hedge against the imperfections of human character. Ancient wisdom probably best captures their contemporary attitudes, as in the prophet Jeremiah's injunction, "Seek the welfare of the city and pray to G-d for it, for in its peace you shall have peace" (Jeremiah 29:7). Rabbi Chanina, a deputy high priest and revered sage, said, "Pray for the welfare of the government, for were it not for the fear of it, men would swallow one another alive" (Pirkei Avot 3:2). Yet, while government might rescue humans from a worse catastrophe, it is no great boon either. Political power breeds its own special kind of corruption. Rabbi Gamliel warned, "Be wary of those in power, for they befriend a person only for their own benefit" (Pirkei Avot 2:3). Rabbi Shemaya counseled, "abhor taking high office, and do not seek intimacy with the ruling power" (Pirkei Avot 1:10). Just rule belongs to G-d. Human political wisdom is the instrumental art of making the best of life in a degraded world.

Lubavitch, like other Chassidim, arrived on the political scene too late to share the early political struggles and victories of American Jews. Chassidim, untempered by the experience of using politics to demand and then successfully gain full rights of citizenship in their countries of origin, and with their only political memories being of fascism and Bolshevism, did not "hit the ground running" when it came to American politics. The first significant political issue to affect them after they settled in the United States was education. The public schools had long been a flash point in the debate over religion in the public realm. For Jewish immigrants to this country in the nineteenth century and the first half of the twentieth century, the public schools represented, in addition to entrée into American economic life, the highest in American ideals of tolerance, civility, and nondiscrimination. It was out of devotion to these ideals (rather than fear of exposing their children to Christianity) that mainstream Jews became early and staunch supporters of strict separationism, opposing even nondiscriminatory or impartially distributed state aid to parochial schools.

The Jewish experience with the system of public education was far different from the Catholic one. Catholics, having exhausted all political attempts to remove the heavily Protestant influence from the schools, established their own network of private schools. They then adopted the strategy of attempting to qualify their private school system for limited public funding. The battle for impartial public funding for private religious schools was not one the Jewish community initially intended to join. By the late 1920s most Jewish schools had ceased to operate, making state support for parochial schools a far less salient issue for the Jewish community.

Yet, as described by Sarna and Dalin, there had always been a small minority of Orthodox (including Chassidic) rabbis and Jewish educators who believed that the future of Judaism in America was tied to the survival of Jewish schools. They supported "released time" religious instruction outside of public school premises as well as federal funding for parochial schools. They also favored nonsectarian religious instruction in the public schools. For Orthodox Jews, the threat of an amoral culture, disorder, and lawlessness loomed larger than the threat of the de facto establishment of Christianity.

A consortium of Orthodox rabbis under Agudath Israel and the league of Orthodox day schools, Torah Umesorah, supported federal aid to all private and parochial schools as being good for Jews and for America. By the 1960s and '70s more Jews were backing the Catholic demand for public funding for bus transportation, textbooks, remedial education, and school lunches. In addition, the number of Jewish day schools, many of them non-Orthodox, reached 604 by 1990. This caused even some Conservative and Reform rabbis to reassess their opposition to government aid.

In recognition of the need for a more formal and unified voice, the National Jewish Committee on Law and Public Affairs (COLPA) was created as a troubleshooter for the Orthodox community. Since 1967, COLPA has appeared as amicus curiae in numerous court cases on an array of public issues of concern to the Orthodox community. Even though they were not always successful, Orthodox Jews had begun to develop the habit of engaging in political activity on their own behalf. Although the vast majority of American Jews made their stand on the establishment clause, an increasingly visible minority of Orthodox Jews made their stand on the free exercise clause.

When the Lubavitcher Rebbe launched his campaign in the 1970s to display menorahs publicly, the Jewish community became openly polarized. Conservative and Reform Jewish organizations took the anti-establishment-clause position, fearing the door would be opened to the Christianization of public life. Throughout the next two decades, they would see many of the Rebbe's activities as unacceptable breaches in the "wall of separation." This signaled both the entrance of Lubavitch into conspicuous, national politics, and the collapse of the stereotype of all Jews as political liberals.

Lubavitch in Politics: A Tentative Political Debut

Lubavitch never shared the political fatalism of other Chassidic courts. Luba-vitchers cut their political teeth in a courageous cat-and-mouse game with the Russian and then the Soviet government. Not only did the sixth Rebbe, Yosef Yitzhok, openly engage the Soviet government in legal action to preserve religious freedom but when those overt actions failed he and his followers continued to pray and teach Judaism in an elaborate underground network.

Lubavitch has been conducting negotiations with the Russian government to regain possession of synagogues and collections of Chassidic books. Politics is an acknowledged part of the Lubavitch strategy to renew and expand as well as to defend and protect the Jewish community. In a bold move, Lubavitch succeeded in June 2000 in having Russia's interior ministry grant official recognition to the Lubavitch-dominated Federation of Jewish Communities, which elevated the federation to the same status as the "establishment" organization, the Russian Jewish Congress. This move positioned Lubavitch to become a major actor in both the religious and political life of contemporary Russia. The revival of Judaism and the reentry of Lubavitch into the politics of the country in which it originated and suffered tyranny and persecution holds tremendous symbolic significance for its members.

The Rebbe Menachem Mendel credited the years he spent in the Soviet Union as a young man, interceding on behalf of the Jewish community with scornful Russian officials, with providing him with public relations and political negotiation skills.[5] If Lubavitch could navigate the dangerous waters of Soviet and post-Soviet politics, there was no reason not to become engaged in America's far more hospitable political arena. The Rebbe fully understood the value of political activism, particularly in a democracy, though he rarely spoke directly of politics or political issues. His entrance into the public realm was prompted by his "universalistic love of humanity."[6] His characteristic outreach style was a natural outgrowth of his dynamic personality and his perception of Americans as a "good people" on the brink of fulfilling their role in the perfection of the world. The Moshiach, according to the Rebbe's view, would arrive when the entire world, not just Jews, had achieved the requisite level of readiness. He believed that Americans had reached this level.

It is critical to understand that Lubavitcher political activity, like that of other American Jews, has deep theological roots. It draws on different sources, primarily the conviction the world is ready for the timeless message of G-d. This makes sense, for instance, of Public Law 102–14, 105 Stat. 44 (1991), which was promoted by Lubavitch. This statute states that the seven Noahide Laws have been the bedrock principles of society from the dawn of civilization. The role of non–Jews in readying the world for redemption is to follow these seven laws: belief in G–d, respect for G–d, respect for human life, respect for the family, respect for others' rights and property, creation of a judicial system, and respect for animals and all creatures. In Lubavitcher thought, all of humanity is bound by the laws given by G–d to Noah, which predate the giving of the Ten Commandments to the Jews at Sinai. The Rebbe's view that Lubavitch has a responsibility to foster these universal ethical principles among non–Jews was something that the more isolated and reticent Chassidim found rather shocking.

The Rebbe never directly endorsed political candidates; neither did he speak to journalists. His political references were most often oblique. The Rebbe only rarely left his headquarters at 770 Eastern Avenue. Political hopefuls occasionally visited him there. The Rebbe's Chassidim contend that politics was merely an instrument for promoting his real interest, the well-being of his individual followers, whom he daily provided with practical advice on everything from upbringing and marriages of children to new business ventures. He devoted hours in private meetings (*yehidos*) with individual Lubavitchers, often well into the night, receiving *kvitls* (petitions) for blessings for the ill or the childless.

Though his heavy daily responsibility to his Chassidim did not leave him much time for political forays, it is fairly clear that he had an impact on elections in New York (for instance, the mayoral elections of 1989) and Israel (his endorsement of the Agudat Israel Party helped the party win five seats in the 1988 Knesset election). This most overt foray into international affairs proved to be somewhat of a disaster from a public relations point of view. Many Israelis expressed resentment that a man who had never set foot in Israel would attempt to influence Israeli voters from afar. But when the party he supported championed a move to change the Israeli Law of Return so that the only converts to Judaism eligible for automatic Israeli citizenship would have been Orthodox converts, a hue and cry went up from the non–Orthodox American Jewish community. They realized that the damaging and divisive question of "Who is a Jew?" was about to be reopened. The Rebbe, while not openly reversing himself, made a tactical retreat, withdrawing personally from the fray.

Henceforth, he left this particular initiative to his supporters in Israel and the United States. This debacle probably reinforced the understanding that it is better not to create the appearance of overt interference in politics at the local, national, or international level. Thereafter, Lubavitch showed a preference for broader, more symbolic political and moral statements rather than for specific policy initiatives.

The Rebbe Menachem Mendel Schneerson can best be characterized as a friendly critic of American democracy. He continually expressed his appreciation for the religious freedom that American life afforded. As long as Jews remain in *golus* (exile), the United States and Canada are considered among the best and most just regimes. But he did not believe that the secularization of American culture had been a boon to the Jews or any other Americans, and stated his view that "religious beliefs are the secret of America's endurance."[7]

In his view, the principle of separation had been misconstrued. He did not believe that a commitment to justice could be sustained in the absence of religion. The role of government, he stated, "is to balance communal and individual good."[8] This is only possible in a society governed by principles of morality, justice, law, and order. Self-interest always threatens to subvert justice, and must be checked: "Any government built solely on human judgment is bound to be subject to prejudice, subjectivity, and arbitrariness—but G-d, who created all people equal, also gave them a system of absolute morality and justice."[9]

That America provides Jews with the opportunity to practice their religion freely is a valuable thing, but in an environment devoid of religious values and belief in G-d, these freedoms may not be relied upon. According to the Rebbe, democracy is fragile and must be supported by morality. Morality has no legs of its own to stand on, but must be grounded in religion. In his view, government should ensure the spiritual and moral welfare of the community through education. This education must teach citizens not only how to find rational solutions to complex problems but how to live. Divine laws, according to the Rebbe, should be included as part of the public school curriculum. As early as 1962, the Lubavitcher Rebbe dissented from the majority Jewish position by submitting an amicus brief in support of retaining the New York Regents' nonsectarian school prayer in the case of *Engel v. Vitale*.[10] Throughout his life, the Rebbe continued to press for school prayer or a moment of silence in the belief that Jews were better off in a society that respects G-d, even if that respect finds expression in Christian terms in the public realm.

It has been noted that the Rebbe found himself on the same side of several issues as the Christian right, including: school prayer, a moment of silence, school funding, character education, and objections to sex education and Darwinian theories of evolution. While analysts, especially critics of Orthodox Judaism's conservative political leanings, want to make much of what they perceive as an alliance between right-wing or fundamentalist Christians and Orthodox Jewish organizations, the alliance, such as it is, is superficial and based on opportunism by both sides. Orthodox Jews are not so politically unsophisticated as to be unable to grasp that a shared political position does not indicate a shared long-term agenda or permanent meeting of minds. They understand fully that the tendency to line up on the same side of some issues does not change either side's theological commitments. Jews recognize that their role in right-wing Christian eschatology is temporary and limited, and therefore so is the political alliance. Moreover, the Rebbe broke ranks consistently with the Christian right by criticizing market capitalism and excessive economic inequality and by supporting women's rights and social welfare spending.

The Rebbe embodied a "unique blend of spirituality and practicality."[11] His innovation was to bring to Lubavitch a form of political activism reflecting a more nuanced and sophisticated understanding of the world. Because he believed that humanity was on the cusp of redemption, he broke with other Chassidic courts by reaching out to secular Jews and Christians as well. But he did not have in mind some form of ecumenicism or interfaith dialogue. He made his perspective on the relationship between Jews and Christians clear:

> The brotherhood of man is a positive concept only when it is confined to such areas as commerce, philanthropy, and various civil and economic aspects of society, wherein peoples of various faiths and minority groups must live together in harmony, mutual respect, and dignity. Far from clarifying matters, interfaith activities have, at best, added to the confusion, and at worst, have been used with missionary zeal by those religions committed to proselytizing members of other faiths.[12]

When the Rebbe spoke about religious matters with non-Jews, it was to promote a healthy spiritual climate for all Americans. To the extent that he voiced his opinions on school prayer and economic welfare, it was with the intent of promoting an atmosphere of justice and spirituality, thus hastening redemption. The sincere ring to his political statements prompted Newt Gingrich to comment that Lubavitch "doesn't want anything. All they want is for us to be good."[13]

If characterizing the political stance of the Rebbe is complicated, it is because the Rebbe did not strategize the way public figures usually do; he did not care whether his position won or lost or was popular or unpopular. Public opinion figured not at all in his reasoning. He wanted Lubavitch to be the conscience of American politics. While he voiced tremendous respect for the Constitution and demanded that his followers be scrupulously law abiding, he proposed openly that if the Constitution prohibits school prayer, then the Constitution ought to be changed.

The key to understanding the Rebbe's political positions is to understand his application of Torah to contemporary issues. It was his strong conviction that the Torah could not be at odds with the public good, and therefore, that advocating the Halakhic or Jewish law position on any given policy issue could only benefit all Americans. Because of this, Lubavitch, which might otherwise be described in terms of interest group politics, falls through the cracks of this model, at least at the national level. Here, Lubavitcher initiatives are always intended to promote the common good and often have no particular, concrete relevance to the Lubavitcher community at all.

Lubavitch rarely lobbies for specific legislation. When Lubavitch initiates or backs legislation, it is usually a symbolic and educative law such as PL 102–14, 105 Stat. 44 (1991), which simply recites the seven eternal ethical principles that apply to all of humanity. Another example of a symbolic act was having President Ronald Reagan sign a into law a resolution declaring April 13, 1984 as Education Day, U.S.A. "in honor of Menachem Mendel Schneerson's role in strengthening education and returning moral values to our society."

The Rebbe's political positions are coherent only when viewed in the context of Torah. Against the standard measure of political coherence employed by Americans, that is, left and right or liberal and conservative, Lubavitch political positions could easily appear inconsistent or contradictory. As the Lubavitcher *shliach* (emissary) in Washington, D.C. put it, Lubavitch is sometimes to the left of the Democrats and sometimes to the right of the Republicans.[14] For instance, while all of the Lubavitchers I surveyed found abortion personally distasteful, because there is no hard and fast Torah prohibition against it, they, like the Rebbe, would keep abortion "safe, legal and rare" and up to the individual woman.[15] Here, Lubavitchers offer even fewer restrictions than many Democrats do. On the other hand, Lubavitchers who I surveyed follow the Rebbe's position on school prayer, supporting either a moment of silence or a generic prayer in the schools. Here, they are to the right of some Republicans. They are to the left of many Democrats in terms of their strong support for social welfare programs, education, and employment, but they are equally strong supporters of school vouchers and military spending. They are opposed to the official recognition of homosexual unions, but they favor criminalizing "hate speech" and strongly oppose discrimination against any minorities.

Lubavitch is officially bipartisan, and Lubavitchers can be found voting for candidates of either party. The Rebbe was careful to cultivate a bipartisan image, which is one reason he never endorsed the candidacy of individuals. His contributions to American life have been officially recognized by every administration, whether Democratic or Republican, since Richard Nixon's.

In short, any attempt to capture the Lubavitcher political worldview according to the traditional standards used by political scientists will inevitably miss the mark. Lubavitch possesses a coherent worldview, but its coherence is derived from Torah. Its precepts are certainly not alien to American political and legal culture.

Lubavitch and National Politics

The Rebbe had a simple agenda with respect to national politics: to infuse American life with greater decency and morality, which in his view requires a return to the eternal moral values set out by G-d. Lubavitchers see this as fully consonant with America's political and constitutional heritage, which they read as being "shamelessly religious." The major tactic of Lubavitch under the Rebbe was to educate and publicize, usually through broad symbolic gestures.

Lubavitch continues to follow the approach established by the Rebbe. Lubavitch wants to educate Americans about Judaism, and thus make them more sympathetic to Jews, but, in addition, Lubavitch feels that if Christians become stronger practitioners of their own religion, it will improve the social climate for everyone, Jews included. Lubavitch did not throw its weight behind the Religious Freedom Restoration Act of 1993, which was an unsuccessful attempt by Congress to restore the "compelling-interest test" used in earlier Supreme Court decisions but reversed in a 1990 ruling. Nor does it lobby, as do other Jewish organizations, for religious school funding and other concrete benefits for the Jewish community. In short, Lubavitch sees itself as generating goodwill, educating the American public about Jewish traditions, inculcating pride among Jews, and generally promoting spiritual values. It does not aspire to be functionally or operationally effective in generating legislation and policy. This it leaves to other Jewish lobbying groups.[16]

Courts as a Political Forum

In our litigious society, a good deal of our political activity and policy making occurs in the courtroom. Lubavitch may not actively seek out confrontations that land it in court, but it does not shy away from them. It also has offered amicus briefs in many cases in which it was not a litigant. According to Jerome Mintz,[17] Chassidim feel on more familiar ground in the courtroom than most other immigrant groups because of their close study of Talmud, or Jewish law. But Chassidim have their own legal code and court of adjudication, known as the Beit Din, and when the parties to a legal controversy are Jews, they strongly prefer not to resort to the civil courts if they can avoid it. This habit goes back to Europe where controversies in the community that ended up in civil courts were often exploited by civil authorities, in several cases with disastrous results.

In rare cases, internal struggles have ended up in U.S. civil courts, among them the 1985 dispute about whether the library of the fifth Lubavitcher Rebbe was personal property, and thus the possession of his heirs, or whether it had been held in trust for the Lubavitch community. Chassidim have welcomed taking on constitutional issues, and three cases involving Chassidim have ended up before the Supreme Court, among them the much-publicized "menorah cases," which are still ongoing. The Lubavitcher Rebbe came to national political attention with his attempts to place menorahs on public ground beginning in the 1970s. This was one of a succession of campaigns intended to increase Jewish pride and awareness. It involved the placement of Chanukah candelabra or menorahs on public grounds, which ignited a huge controversy in the Jewish community, pitting Lubavitch against other Chassidic courts and most Reform and Conservative Jews. The seemingly endless litigation at the state level to this day has not been interrupted by the 1989 Supreme Court judgment that public displays of the menorah are constitutional. The decision was ambiguous. The central constitutional question remains: Should the public square be devoid of any religious symbols, or should it be open to all religious symbols? Liberal Jews tend to support the first option; Orthodox, the second.

Chanukah, which is celebrated annually for eight days beginning on the twenty-fifth of the Hebrew month of Kislev, marks the victory of a small band of Jewish soldiers over the Syrian Greeks in 165 B.C.E. In addition to the political and military victory, Chanukah marks a spiritual victory in which a miracle occurred as the Jewish soldiers rekindled the holy eternal light in the Temple that had been desecrated by the Greeks. The single flask of pure oil that was found was only sufficient for one day, but it continued to burn for eight. It was declared that each year the miracle would be commemorated by each family lighting a menorah and placing it prominently in a window so as to be visible to all. It was a longstanding law and custom to publicize the miracle, and the Rebbe sought to extend the display into the public realm in order to bring nonobservant Jews back to Torah.

For Lubavitchers, erecting giant menorahs on public ground, which was already crowded with Christmas displays, could not be construed as an affront to anyone. Nor was it a violation of the First Amendment's establishment clause, which had permitted Christians to station symbols of Christmas on public land, argued COLPA lawyers who represented Lubavitch. The strong opposition voiced by other Chassidim did not relate to constitutional issues. Their concerns arose from the fear of antagonizing non-Jews and from their belief in the futility of using such displays to attract nonobservant Jews. To them, such visible and public exhibitions of sacred objects only degraded their spiritual significance and opened Jews to ridicule.

By contrast, most other American Jews lined up against the Lubavitch menorah policy on legal and constitutional grounds. Liberal Jewish organizations, such as the American Jewish Congress and the Reform movement's Central Conference of American Rabbis, argued that displays of religious symbols, be they Christian or Jewish, violate the principle of separation of church and state. As Rabbi Allan Nadler, director of the YIVO Institute for Jewish Research, expressed it, "The kindling of huge menorahs in public places across America opens a dangerous constitutional can of worms."[18]

Critics felt that if Lubavitch's policy went uncontested, it would weaken the hand of Jews when they attempt to "protest the intrusion of Christian doctrine into the public life of American citizens."[19] These concerns could not be assuaged by the promise of "equal time" for Jewish violations of the Constitution. Liberal Jews who had been raised believing that civility demanded that they be Jews in private but otherwise indistinguishable from other Americans in public were somewhat embarrassed by the controversy. Many had also been raised to believe that assimilation was the cure for anti-Semitism, and therefore any lingering anti-Semitism in American society must be the fault of those Jews who refuse to assimilate. Some felt that the "ultra-Orthodox extremists" would give all Jews a bad name and undo the gains of the hard-fought battle of Jews to be accepted as full Americans.

The Rebbe felt that the real sentiment behind the strict separationist position was the belief that only Jewish invisibility would keep anti-Semitism at bay. It was also commonly asserted that Judaism's fragile hold on its members could not survive in the face of state-sanctioned Christian culture, the power of which would be even more overt if it were permitted access to the public realm. But Menachem Mendel argued that anti-Semitism and assimilation increase when Jews attempt to hide or compartmentalize their religious lives. Abandoning one's heritage only aroused suspicion, not admiration. He regarded the menorah campaign as a step toward reviving Jewish identity and pride and toward reducing anti-Semitism.

In 1986, Lubavitch of Vermont placed a large menorah in City Hall Park in Burlington.[20] The Reform rabbi, a Unitarian minister, and a lawyer for the ACLU brought suit two years later. The federal district court in Vermont granted permission for the menorah to be placed on public ground. The case went to the U.S. Court of Appeals for the Second Circuit in New York. Meanwhile, a similar challenge had been brought against Lubavitch for placing a menorah in front of Pittsburgh City Hall, next to a 45-foot Christmas tree. Inside the Pittsburgh County Courthouse, a nativity scene had been erected. A local chapter of the ACLU brought suit against the presence of religious symbols on public ground in December 1986. This suit moved ahead of the Vermont case and in 1989, the Supreme Court heard it, ruling that the Pittsburgh menorah, because it stood in the company of a Christmas tree, was permissible (whereas the isolated menorah in Burlington, Vermont, violated the First Amendment). Justice O'Connor argued that while the nativity scene and tree were clearly Christian symbols, the menorah stood for "a recognition of cultural diversity"[21] and therefore counted, as far as the Supreme Court was concerned, as a secular, political symbol.

Lubavitch was not unhappy with this reading of the menorah's significance because the Rebbe had emphasized the political as well as spiritual symbolism behind it. Once the menorah is determined to be a political symbol when in the company of a Christmas tree, however, it is not clear why it should not be so regarded when it stands alone. In fact, the menorah display is still banned in Burlington. (The ban is not enforced. The menorah is erected on public ground without the companionship of a Christmas tree, though no longer in City Hall Park.) Similar litigation is underway in several other American cities. Nathan Lewin, the lawyer for COLPA who has represented Lubavitch and other Orthodox Jewish groups in court, takes the position that banning religious speech while permitting all forms of secular speech in public places discriminates against religious speech. If this strategy is successful, these suits will certainly stimulate attempts by Christian activists to reintroduce religious symbols into the public square. Lubavitch recognizes this, but does not regard it as more threatening than the already well-established, unofficial cultural hegemony of Christianity.

Lubavitch in Washington

In 1993, the Rebbe decided that there should be a permanent Lubavitch presence in Washington, D.C., and sent Rabbi Avraham Shemtov (the father of the current envoy) as his emissary. Rabbi Shemtov founded the American Friends of Lubavitch initially to serve the Washington Jewish community and to bring "Yiddishkeit [Jewish life and practice] to the Hill," rather than to engage in political activity. Rabbi Shemtov quickly became a go-between between the Rebbe and the federal government. Shemtov coordinated communications between members of Congress and the various shluchim (emissaries) nationally and internationally. Because there is no established hierarchy of command, and each shliach, or emissary, is effectively autonomous, the Washington office has interacted directly with these emissaries in the field without any consultation with or intervention from Brooklyn. There has never been an official legislative committee in Lubavitch to send down explicit directives from Brooklyn. This is as true today, under the informal leadership of Rabbi Yehudah Krinsky, as it was when the Rebbe was alive.

The tone and direction of day-to-day Lubavitcher operations in Washington is therefore determined almost completely by the young Rabbi Levi Shemtov, son of the founder of American Friends of Lubavitch.[22] He characterizes his personal political style as "high level, low profile." He views the ease with which he negotiates the corridors of power as reflecting his generation's complete comfort as Americans, as opposed to the more deferential immigrant attitudes of his father's generation. He prides himself on his understanding of the norms of the Hill, his enormous network of contacts, the increasing visibility he has achieved for Lubavitch in Washington, and its influence on the Hill. He measures Lubavitch's influence by the number of phone calls he receives from congressional staffers asking Lubavitch's position on an array of bills and issues, on the number of Jewish congressional staffers that attend his shul and religious events (the Capital Jewish Forum that Shemtov founded has about five hundred Jewish congressional staffers), and, more than anything, by the enormous success of his fund-raising activities. He measures influence by his ability to block the National Park Service's attempt to ban the placement of the menorah on the Ellipse simply by mentioning the possibility of the adverse publicity for the Park Service that would be generated. He measures influence by the fact that in 1993, on the occasion of President Clinton's hundredth day in office, the president met with eight Lubavitcher rabbis in the Oval Office.

Rabbi Shemtov measures influence by Lubavitch's ninetieth-birthday testimonial celebration in honor of the Rebbe, which was attended by dozens of Congressmen, Senators, public officials, and ambassadors. Lubavitcher Rabbi Shmuel Butman opened the U.S. House of Representatives with a prayer in honor of the Rebbe's birthday. He measures influence by the fact that the Rebbe was awarded the Congressional Gold Medal in 1994 from among twenty-three nominees. Shemtov attributes this award to the political skills of Lubavitch in assembling a huge number of both Democratic and Republican sponsors, more than two hundred and sixty in all, including such politically disparate figures as John Lewis and Newt Gingrich. Finally, Rabbi Shemtov measures influence by name recognition. Lubavitch is pretty close to a household word on the Hill, and Shemtov feels that he is an increasingly familiar face, well received wherever he goes in Washington political circles, reflecting recognition of Lubavitch's moral authority, if not its ability to command votes or contribute to campaigns.

Rabbi Shemtov is poised to take advantage of the Bush administration's welcoming attitude toward religion in public life. But the White House's receptivity will probably not tempt Lubavitch to change its symbolic and indirect approach to politics. For instance, while supportive in principle of President George W. Bush's White House Office of Faith-Based and Community Initiatives, Lubavitch was careful not to become visibly entangled in what developed into a partisan battle on Capitol Hill. An overt or partisan strategy risks contravening Lubavitch's primarily spiritual mission, squandering its credibility and political capital, and alienating segments of the American Jewish population.[23]

Lubavitch will probably maintain its characteristic symbolic approach, as was demonstrated once again by Rabbi Avraham Shemtov at the Chanukah party hosted by President Bush at the White House on December 17, 2001. Rabbi Shemtov intoned blessings upon the president and promised that the community would "pray on your behalf, on behalf of our government, on behalf of our Armed Forces, and on behalf of the entire world."[24] In his address to the president, Rabbi Shemtov restated the willingness of the Lubavitch community to do "our patriotic duty" to support the government in its antiterrorist mission, and took the opportunity to link U.S. interests with the fulfillment of G-d's will, not only regarding the United States but "G-d's assignment of the Holy Land to the Jewish People forever." This is the sort of gentle, indirect lobbying that Lubavitch perceives as most effective. That the president warmly embraced Rabbi Shemtov afterward is regarded as confirmation of its approach by the community.

Local-Level Politics: Lubavitch in Brooklyn

The political activities of Lubavitch in its home community of Brooklyn, New York, have been described by the press either with admiration or derision, depending on the perspective of the reporter. Lubavitchers cannot help but arouse mixed emotions because they are seen as "anti-individualistic and radically exclusive," despite being acknowledged as "fundamentally law-abiding."[25] One reporter characterized Lubavitch as "the world's most ambitious, aggressive, and, at times, detested Jewish movement."[26] Another quoted a local police officer as saying that the Chassidim are "pretty basically un-American."[27] One reporter characterized the Chassidim as "a model of modern machine politics. U.S. senators, cabinet officers, mayors, and Washington bureaucrats pay regular homage, courting its bloc vote. Hasidic lobbyists draw millions of federal dollars here."[28] Yet another noted that "their spirituality and their isolationism have not, however, prevented the Hasidim from becoming a formidable thorn in Mayor Dinkins' side."[29] While they may disagree on the motives and tactics of Lubavitch, the one point of agreement is that Chassidim, despite their insularity and separation from the secular world, have an "appetite for politics."[30] While not all reporters can keep their Chassidim straight and often treat them as an undifferentiated monolith, Lubavitchers, more than other Chassidim, are often in the news because they are perceived as being "on the front lines of urban and world affairs."[31]

Because of their small numbers, Lubavitchers could not affect the outcome of national elections even if they wanted to do so. But their concentrated residential pattern allows them to have an impact on local races, particularly in the Crown Heights section of Brooklyn. They are often aggressively involved in local politics, especially when their interests are directly at stake. Many of those issues arise as part of a common American phenomenon of neighborhood transition, whereby one ethnic or racial group replaces another geographically. Sometimes it makes race or ethnicity appear to be the central issue, when most often it is not. Crown Heights is an interesting case because the racial and ethnic balance of the neighborhood has been relatively stable; despite tensions, it is one of the few remaining racially integrated neighborhoods in New York. The community is vital and renovation and new construction is ongoing, defying the more common trend toward urban atrophy and decay. The media is less likely to rush to the scene to document the many examples of neighborhood cooperation and self-help that cross racial and ethnic lines than it is to bring the occasional conflicts and catastrophes to the attention of the public.

Chassidim constitute 20 to 30 percent of the population of Crown Heights, but their high voter turnout makes them a stronger force politically than their numbers would suggest. The Lubavitch community makes full use of this advantage. Assessing a community's political clout is difficult. Whether myth or reality, the impression was created during the Rebbe's lifetime that he was a political touchstone who had the power, through a well-placed word, to sway an election. Candidates in local and even statewide races did pay the Rebbe a visit, no doubt in the belief that his backing was important. That the

Rebbe met twice with David Dinkins during the 1989 mayoral race is often cited as having contributed to Dinkins's victory over Rudy Giuliani. It has been claimed that the Rebbe's merely saying "good luck with your venture" or "your venture is going to be successful" was enough to signal the Lubavitch voting community.[32] Because of the lack of exit polls, it is very difficult to know whether Lubavitchers vote as an organized bloc. Even if it could be determined that they do, it could not be known whether that is simply a reflection of their shared interests and worldview or some more direct guidance from the Rebbe or the current leadership at 770.

Recognition of the Chassidim's political skills and small successes often evokes intense resentment, which is often tinged with admiration. In a cramped world where low-income families are often pitted against each other for limited public resources, political life resembles a zero-sum game. Despite the undeniable minority status of Jews in America and the low income of New York Chassidim, they are not regarded as disadvantaged by other minority groups in their neighborhoods. After ten years of political struggle by Chassidim, their certification in 1984 as a "disadvantaged minority" by Commerce Secretary Malcolm Baldrige was perceived as favoritism by other minorities, even though they were eligible for similar programs. Chassidim now had access to minority business funds and special grants and contracts, along with blacks, Hispanics, and Asians. The fact that the per capita income of Chassidim is low enough to qualify them and that they have historically faced social and economic discrimination was dismissed in some quarters as an election-year attempt at a rapprochement with the Chassidim by President Reagan and the Republican Party.[33]

When unfortunate incidents of racial tension occur they are depicted as ongoing trench warfare between Chassidim and other minorities. The situation is no worse than in the rest of New York, where life is rife with inter-ethnic and interracial tensions pitting Italians against blacks, Haitians against Koreans, West Indians against American blacks, and blacks against Hispanics. Crown Heights and Borough Park, the Brooklyn neighborhoods with the highest concentration of Lubavitchers, are among the few integrated neighborhoods in New York. Here, Chassidim, blacks, and Hispanics occupy the same apartment buildings and streets. This is because Chassidim resisted the panic-plying tactics of real estate agents and did not run from racial integration. In the late 1960s, when a mass exodus of white people to the suburbs was occurring, with real estate agents fueling the panic, the Lubavitcher Rebbe halted the flight by announcing in his Passover speech of 1969 that Lubavitch would stay put. Ironically, the decision to stay in Crown Heights has put Lubavitchers in a predicament. The neighborhood is populated by minorities, which have all experienced both discrimination and economic hardships.

Lubavitch's political edge is a product of its unity. "The Lubavitchers are practicing ethnic power in a form that black power advocates would be happy to achieve."[34] But their success is also the cause of resentment among their neighbors. What the Lubavitchers regard as looking out for their legitimate interests often evokes hostility. Combine the rapid expansion of the Lubavitch population with their capacity to organize and bring their needs to the attention of local politicians, and it is understandable why Chassidim seem to Hispanics and blacks to be getting more than their fair share of units in new housing projects as well as other goods and services.

In addition, Lubavitch often pools its resources to acquire real estate and convert it into schools and hotels for their expanding community. Some black politicians have declared these attempts to rehabilitate housing as a threat to racial proportions. At one point, some African Americans likened the racial situation in Crown Heights to South African apartheid. But Lubavitchers see their territorial expansion as the inevitable outcome of demographics. In the American, and particularly New York, tradition of neighborhood succession, there is nothing new about one group supplanting another, and whichever group is perceived as the interloper is attacked by the existing residents. In Crown Heights, Chassidim are the longtime residents. It is the simultaneous expansion of the Chassidic population and the influx of immigrants that has made the housing crunch so acute. It would be as desirable as it is rare in the United States if the neighborhood could be stabilized so as to maintain diversity.

Not everything is bleak in neighborhood relations. A positive, though fairly short-lived, show of cooperation occurred in 1980 when Lubavitchers joined forces with blacks in South Crown Heights to create the Rainbow Coalition. For several years, black and Lubavitch politicians ran together and served together. Even when more militant adversaries defeated the Rainbow Coalition, it continued to be influential in community affairs.[35]

The mayoral race of 1989 also demonstrated the ability of the community to rise above racial tensions. The vast majority of Lubavitchers voted for David Dinkins, a black man, rather than incumbent Mayor Edward Koch, a Jew, in the Democratic primary. Their reasoning was purely pragmatic. Dinkins, who beat Koch in the primary and later defeated Rudy Giuliani in the general election, was judged to be more concerned with the neighborhood and more likely to respond to its nitty-gritty needs. This typifies the local-level political behavior of both American and Canadian Lubavitchers.

But the honeymoon with Mayor Dinkins came abruptly to an end because of a tragic incident that would trigger the worst crisis ever between African Americans and Jews in Crown Heights, one that would be felt nationwide, and from which, despite the uneasy current tranquility, the community has not fully recovered. The city's delayed response to the riots that followed contributed to Dinkins's defeat by Giuliani in the 1993 election.

On August 19, 1991, a vehicle that was part of the Rebbe's motorcade spun out of control, killing Gavin Cato, a seven-year-old black child, and injuring his cousin. While the Chassidic driver, Yosef Lifsh, tried to assist the child, he was robbed and beaten by an angry mob, which, in its attack on Lifsh, ignored the injured children. When the Hatzolah ambulance arrived, the driver took the injured Chossid instead of the child. A group of African Americans marched on Lubavitch headquarters, stoning Jewish homes, painting swastikas, smashing cars, shouting "Kill the Jews" and "Heil Hitler," and attacking Jews on the street.

A young rabbinical student from Australia, Yankel Rosenbaum, was surrounded by a mob chanting anti-Semitic slogans and stabbed four times. He died shortly thereafter. Police Commissioner Lee Brown met with African American and Lubavitch community leaders to try to restore peace, but rioters continued through the next several days to loot stores and burn cars. Black leaders from outside the neighborhood, Al Sharpton and Sonny Carson, threatened to have Lifsh "taken out" if he was not arrested. (Ironically, several years before this incident, Lifsh had rushed into a burning building to save two children who happened to be African American.) On the third night of rioting a thousand police were sent into the neighborhood, but they remained to the side and did not intervene. Mayor Dinkins finally ordered Brown to take stronger measures. On the fourth night of rioting, two thousand police moved in and made sixty-two arrests, bringing the riots to an end.

On August 23, moderate black leaders called a press conference to denounce anti-Semitic acts. There was virtually no press coverage. On September 5 the grand jury cleared Lifsh. Several days later, Mayor Dinkins referred to the murder of Rosenbaum as a "lynching." Meanwhile, Lemrick Nelson Jr., the young man who was charged with the murder of Rosenbaum, and Charles Price, the man accused of inciting the mob, were being held for trial. On October 29, 1992, they were acquitted by a jury, despite the fact that the police found Nelson in possession of the murder weapon covered with Rosenbaum's blood, and even though witnesses, including the victim before he died, identified Lemrick Nelson as the killer. This case has widely been perceived as an example of jury nullification, fueling not only anger that justice was not done but fears in the Lubavitch community that the legal system would neither prevent nor punish any such future crimes against their members.

Mayor Dinkins commented after the Nelson acquittal that he did not find any reason to doubt that the justice system had operated fairly. Nonetheless, in the aftermath of the four days of rioting, Governor Mario Cuomo ordered a state inquiry into both the Nelson trial and the police handling of the riots. On November 19, Police Commissioner Raymond Kelly admitted that the police in Crown Heights had adopted a "holding approach," but he insisted that it was not on the mayor's orders. On November 25, Mayor Dinkins appeared on television to ask for "reconciliation and redemption."

During the next five years, the Rosenbaum family pressed for filing of federal charges, adopting a tactic that had been pioneered in the American South in the 1960s to pursue racially motivated killers who had been acquitted by local juries. In 1997, Lemrick Nelson Jr. and Charles Price were indicted on federal charges of violating Yankel Rosenbaum's civil rights in having targeted him for murder because of his religion. Both men were convicted in federal court, but the verdict was voided by the U.S. Court of Appeals for the Second Circuit on January 7, 2002. It determined that the trial judge had violated jury selection rules in an attempt to achieve a racially balanced jury and thereby avoid the problem of jury bias that had clearly been at play in the original trial.

Although a good deal of outrage among the Lubavitch community greeted the decision, no one predicts a replay of the 1991 rioting. Leaders of the Lubavitch, African American, and Caribbean communities joined in a press conference on the day of the decision, vowing that the "'new Crown Heights' is diverse enough to accept the overturned convictions and the prospect of a new trial." The executive director of the Crown Heights Jewish Community Council stated that the mixed population of Crown Heights has proven several times that it is not the same neighborhood that it was in 1991.[36]

As this sad chronology of events reveals, underlying racial tensions in the community ran deep a decade ago. Still, many residents, both African American and Lubavitch, testified that the rioters were primarily outsiders and opportunists. Many neighborhood residents offered assistance to Jews, but this was largely ignored by the press, just as the pleas of the community's real leaders for restraint had been ignored by the press. Today, some of the tension has dissipated, though the peace of Crown Heights is likely to be interrupted periodically as inevitably happens among neighbors who live in close proximity but too often remain strangers. In the absence of real warmth, mutual respect and civility may be the most that can be achieved. While not a model of heavenly peace, Crown Height's interethnic relations are cordial for the most part, testimony to the basic decency and good citizenship of the area's residents, of all races and religions. Chassidim will not abandon the neighborhood in which their Rebbe made his home and headquarters. They trust that mounting demographic and related economic pressures and racial tensions are not insurmountable.

Through the skillful and pragmatic use of politics, Lubavitchers have secured their future in Crown Heights and America. They are politically involved and politically astute, sharing many of the same loyalties, concerns, and interests of other Americans. Although they do not always share liberal values, they clearly share democratic ones. They value their rights and respect those of others, they seek to improve their lives through the political realm, and they do not begrudge others the same opportunity.

CHAPTER FOUR

Lubavitch and Canadian Politics

Despite the fact that they are both liberal democracies, Canada and the United States are different in ways that bear on the political outlook and behavior of their Jewish citizens, including Chassidim. In Canada, according to Daniel Elazar, one of the foremost scholars of the American and Canadian Jewish communities, Jews are an ethnocultural minority in an ethnically diverse society that values cultural pluralism.[1]

Jews are a multicultural community, par excellence, combining a high degree of cultural retention with mainstream economic success.[2] Though they are categorized as European, rather than as nonwhite, non-European "visible minorities," Canadian Jews share the political perspective of the underdog, just as in the United States. Canadian Jews, like their American counterparts, consistently vote liberal and are strong defenders of civil liberties, both their own and those of other minorities.

Nathan Glazer, in contrasting American and Canadian Jews, emphasizes that Canada, because it was based on two distinct national groups at its founding, gave more opportunity for incoming minority groups "to select group maintenance as a possibility. Thus, it appears there is somewhat less integration, somewhat greater commitment to group maintenance among Slavic groups and Jews who went to Canada, compared with groups of the same origins that went to the United States."[3] The ideal in the United States was one of unitary culture and shared American identity. Whereas the United States was established as a federation of states defined politically and territorially, Canada was established as a federation of peoples organized into different provinces.[4] For this reason, Canada is more receptive to the concept of group rights. Its political system is also more responsive to organized political activity by groups.

Canadian Jews have an ambivalent status in the Canadian polity. They are counted in the official Canadian census as both a religious and an ethnic group. Jews are the only group that the Canadian census, Statistics Canada, permits to fall into two categories. Canada has considered "Jewish" to be both a religion and an ethnicity for a century. Censuses in years ending with one have asked about religion and ethnic background since 1901. (Mini-censuses in years ending with six ask about ethnicity only.) The 1991 census found 318,000 respondents who claimed to be Jewish by religion and 368,000 who listed themselves as Jewish according to ethnicity.

Academics contest the meaning of the numbers, with some arguing that the higher the percentage of Jews identifying themselves by ethnicity, rather than religion, the higher the rate of assimilation. Whatever the significance of the breakdown itself, it is clear that the Canadian political system, and Canadian Jews, view Jews as both a religion and an ethnic group, whereas in the U.S. census, Jews as a group are invisible. There is no category that would identify Jews by either religion or ethnicity.

Whether or not Canada's policy of recognizing Jews as both a religion and ethnic group affects how Jews are regarded and responded to in the political process is unclear. There is no indication that Jews in Canada have, as a result of their official categorization, enjoyed more political clout than their counterparts in the United States. Since both countries' electoral systems register only individual votes, Jews in both countries are, at least as a group, at an obvious disadvantage, numerically speaking. Only in local elections, where there is a large enough concentration of Jews in a given district, can Jews wield any kind of group power at the ballot box. Accordingly, Jews in both Canada and the United States have developed other political strategies to make their collective voice heard on those issues in which there may exist something like a shared Jewish interest. Despite feeling at home in Canada, Jews are acutely aware of their minority status. Like American Jewry, they retain a certain sense of political insecurity, despite the fact that by all measures they have done well for themselves in both countries. As the old joke goes, "Jews just can't take 'yes' for an answer."

On October 8, 1971, Prime Minister Pierre Elliot Trudeau declared that Canada "has no official culture," making it the first nation to formally endorse multiculturalism with legal authority, declaring it a positive attribute of Canadian society worthy of official and financial support. The Charter of Rights and Freedoms of 1985 and the Multiculturalism Act of 1988 reinforced the status of the "third force" (recent immigrants), First Nations (native peoples), and the Quebecois. Multiculturalism is intended to preserve cultures without hampering access to equality of opportunity in the economic and political realms.[5] This makes Canada the world's first society to have transcended the idea of a unified national culture to which all ethnic groups ideally must assimilate.

The fact that Canada has been more inclined than the United States to recognize multiculturalism is part of the legacy of a society that from its earliest history was divided along ethnic, religious, and linguistic lines. The First Nations have operated under a different legal status than have the native peoples of the United States. Juxtaposed upon these original inhabitants, the British and French colonizers constitute two additional permanent political entities. By the 1970s, what became known as the "third force," or recent immigrants, increasingly from Third World countries, began to vocalize their desire that minority cultural groups be granted more political recognition, commensurate with their new prominence.

Unlike the United States, which had a Bill of Rights attached to its Constitution before it went to the separate states for ratification, the Canadians had no specific protections for individuals. Rights were granted to groups. For instance, Jews received their rights as Jews, not as individuals, by a special act called the "Jew Bill" of 1832. It was a law "to declare persons professing the Jewish religion entitled to all the rights and privileges of the other subjects of his majesty in this Province." Without a bill of rights, the Canadians managed to solve the problem of state-backed religious discrimination. The Canadian government did not have to contend with the complications of federalism, in which individual states could impose laws in contradiction to the federal constitution. In Canada, the provinces could not impose legislation in contradiction to Ottawa without it being voided by the Canadian courts.[6]

In more recent times, the Canadian Constitution, and more specifically the Charter of Rights and Freedoms, have provided more detailed and concrete guarantees. Section 2 of the 1982 Constitution Act affirms freedom of religious worship, providing the legal basis for freedom of association for Jews and other religions. Section 15 prohibits discrimination, and Section 15.2 legalizes affirmative action. Section 27 enunciates the principle of multiculturalism. Therefore, the government can legislate affirmatively on religious matters, and can demand remedy for private discrimination. Apart from the Constitution, the Criminal Code of Canada now contains sections 281.1 and 281.2 against hate literature. This legislation was passed with the support of the Canadian Jewish Congress, which, while sharing its American counterpart's strong commitment to civil liberties, did not share its angst over this sort of limitation on free expression.

Quebec Province has the largest concentration of Chassidim, almost all of whom live in or immediately outside of Montreal. The British North America Act of 1867 gave Quebec powers in the area of civil law and education, which the Quebec government has sought to use to promote French cultural and linguistic dominance. Quebecois were initially hostile to the Canadian version of the Multiculturalism Act because they suspected that the concept of multiculturalism might be a cover for an attempt to reduce the political power and status of the French-speaking population, by treating it as simply one among a multitude of coequal minorities.

To prevent the French character of Quebec from being diluted, the Quebec version of the Multiculturalism Act, passed in 1988, employs the term "interculturalism." This formulation of minority cultural rights envisions the various minority cultures as existing against the backdrop of French culture, recognized but subsidiary. This continues to be problematic for non-Francophones because the logic of Quebec's own position as a minority province within Anglophone Canada requires that it be supportive of minorities within the minority. It has certainly sought to project that image. Its two stated policy objectives with regard to ethnic groups—equal opportunity without discrimination, and the preservation of culture—are vague enough to permit almost anything in reality.

It has already become a cliché to describe Canada as a mosaic and the United States as a melting pot, but despite the Canadian and Quebec provincial governments' official policies of multiculturalism, assimilation and acculturation of minority groups has proceeded apace just as in the United States. For a variety of reasons, some internal and some external to the community, Jews remain the most resistant of all Canadian ethnic groups to assimilation. They are able to preserve high levels of identification and community involvement and lower levels of intermarriage, in contrast to other Canadian minorities and to their American counterparts.

The Jews of Canada

The differences between the Canadian and American Jewish communities are often attributed to the historical differences in immigration patterns as well as to the differences in the political cultures of the two countries. Jewish immigrants' countries of origin and the sequence and timing of immigration have been different from those who immigrated to the United States. Jewish immigration to Canada did not begin in earnest until about fifty years later than that to the United States, meaning that Jews did not find an entrenched, partially assimilated, largely Reform and Conservative community when they arrived. The wave of immigrants to Canada came primarily from eastern Europe and Russia. Their communities had not been heavily influenced by the Enlightenment, so these Jews were largely Orthodox. To this day, the Reform and Conservative movements have made few inroads in Canada, especially in Quebec. In addition, after 1957, large numbers of Jews began to arrive in Canada from North Africa. These Sephardim, who are primarily Orthodox, though with their own distinctive language, customs, music, food, and traditions, now constitute close to 25 percent of the Jewish population of Quebec. More recently, Israeli, Soviet, and Ethiopian Jews have added to the distinctive Canadian Jewish cultural mix.

Finally, a higher percentage of Canadian than American Jews are foreign born, and a higher percentage of Canadian Jews are survivors of the Holocaust, which has had an impact on the political attitudes of the community. Canadian Jews, then, are religiously more homogeneous and more Orthodox than American Jews. Undoubtedly, the timing and pattern of Jewish immigration to Canada and the United States has had an influence on the development of the two communities, though sociologists like Morton Weinfeld do not rate these factors as decisive. A more significant variable is the political structure and climate in which the two communities found themselves.

In the United States, a larger role in framing political issues and divides has been played by race than by religion. Moreover, the founding of the United States was intimately connected to religious dissenters, which is reflected in the vigilance with which Americans protect the separation of church and state. Race and class have been the most salient and divisive political issues for Americans. In Canada, the backdrop against which political life has been played out has been language, ethnicity, and national origin. Canadian Jews entered a political stage on which the major actors were two nationalities and their respective religions, British Protestants and French Catholics, along with the sizable indigenous population. While Section 2 of the Constitution guarantees religious freedom, it does not strictly prohibit church-state entanglement. Canada has not, therefore, experienced the ongoing legal and legislative disputes over nativity scenes, crucifixes, or menorahs on public property that have seemed to engage, if not monopolize, Jewish political energies during much of America's history.

The Chassidic groups of Montreal tend to be understudied by analysts of the Canadian Jewish community and underrated as a political force. Just as in the United States, it is surprising how many Canadian studies of the Jewish community neglect to even mention the presence of Chassidim in their midst. This is partly explained by their tendency to shy away from involvement in institutionalized Jewish life. There are several reasons for this, including the fact that, as more recent immigrants, the Chassidim arrived to find a well-organized Jewish establishment already in place. Chassidim did not want to be associated with the political positions or theological orientation of these organizations. Chassidim in both New York and Montreal share a political predisposition that has ancient roots in Europe. They still feel most comfortable in the political realm when they can cultivate personal relationships with government officials. In Quebec politics, in particular, it is still clear that some things can best be accomplished by special pleading through the agency of a modern-day equivalent of the *shtadlan* (intermediary), who since medieval times has spoken on behalf of Jewish communities throughout Europe.

Jews in Quebec

Because the largest Chassidic, including Lubavitch, community makes its home in Quebec, it is important to focus specifically on this province. The cultural and political setting is obviously heavily influenced by the majority Francophone population. The issues of nationalism and separatism are never far in the background, creating some insecurity and inconveniences for many non-Francophone citizens. On the other hand, Canadian provincial governments, having near complete discretion over education and social services, have made Quebec a most congenial setting for Canadian Jews because of Quebec's willingness to fund private religious educational institutions.

Jewish response to life in Quebec is a paradox.[7] Here they enjoy religious freedom and public support for Jewish schools and institutions. They are the most bilingual of all of the Anglophone Quebec ethnic groups. Jews have attained a high standard of education and economic well-being. On the other hand, they maintain limited social and cultural contacts with the Quebecois community and express high anxiety about their future in the province. This may be a cause or an effect of the fact that Jews have remained aloof from, and are very underrepresented in, government.

Yet, the evolution of Jewish life in Montreal is intimately connected to Quebec politics. The exclusion of Jews from educational and social life in Quebec has had the unintended effect of stimulating an enormously vital, wide-reaching, and autonomous Jewish institutional and communal life. In Quebec, Jews are a minority within a minority. According to Weinfeld, the Quebec motto, "je me souviens" ("I Remember"), could just as easily apply to the Jews and the Holocaust as to the Quebecois and the battle of the Plains of Abraham.[8] Both minorities, he contends, are obsessed with their history of persecution, their cultural distinctiveness, their demographic indicators, their survival in the face of assimilatory pressures, and their defense of collective rights. Like the Quebecois, the Jews "behave like a majority, but think like a minority."[9]

Although the logic of Quebec's own minority status and struggle for survival might suggest that it would be especially hospitable to other minorities in its midst, and despite its public relations attempts to convey cultural sensitivity, pessimism about the future runs high among the Montreal Jewish community. Concerns about nationalism and etatism have fueled the flight of both capital and people, including many Jews, from the province. Against the backdrop of the historical results of German nationalism, which a significant portion of Montreal Jews barely survived or lost close relatives to, and the domestic version of anti-Semitism most manifest in the Duplessis era of the 1920s and '30s, the words *un vrai Quebecois* ("a true Quebecois") have an ominous ring. Jews, even the large Francophone Sephardic community, tend to be strong supporters of federalism as opposed to separation.

Although the Parti Quebecois has made repeated overtures to the Jews of Quebec, especially to the French-speaking Sephardim and to the Chassidim, it has made only minor inroads, mostly among the isolated rural community of Tash Chassidim. The vast majority of Jews, including Lubavitch, continue to vote for the Liberal Party. Even though Jews have done well economically, they express a sense of communal precariousness, which the Parti Quebecois has been unable to dispel. A survey conducted by the Federation CJA (Combined Jewish Appeal) in 1996 revealed that two-thirds of Jews felt "somewhat or very uncomfortable with the long-term social and economic outlook" in Quebec, while 80 percent found the political outlook either very or somewhat unfavorable.[10] Many Jews, particularly among the younger generation, are leaving or expressing the intention to do so. Given that the percentage of Jews with university educations is over 41 percent, as compared to the general Canadian population, in which 7 percent are university educated, Quebec could experience a serious brain drain, at the same time that the Montreal Jewish community will suffer outmigration if this pessimism is not reversed.

Even though recent surveys reveal a decline in support for separation among the French-speaking community, Jews do not feel greatly reassured. The opening of a massive new Jewish Community Center, consisting of a library, museum, athletic facilities, theater, and social service bureaus, funded in part by the government of Quebec, is a more positive development and is intended to show optimism about a continuing Jewish presence in Montreal. It was taken as a good omen that Premier Lucien Bouchard addressed the plenary session of the Canadian Jewish Congress-Quebec in September 2000.

On the other hand, it set teeth on edge when Deputy Premier Bernard Landry told an organization of Jewish businesspeople that Quebec is a nation like Israel, France, or Greece and that the Jewish community should accept that and participate in the consensus shared by Lucien Bouchard, Jean Charest and other local Quebecois political figures, or risk being marginalized politically.[11] This is the sort of talk that keeps the Jewish community off balance and wary.

Nor do demographic trends bode particularly well for mainstream Quebec Jews. In addition to the flight of young people, the birth rate is extremely low, just as in the United States, and the population is aging rapidly. Toronto has surpassed Montreal in Jewish population. At its high point in 1971, Montreal had about 125,000 Jews. Now the population is estimated at between 95,000 and 100,000. Twenty-five percent of Jews in Montreal are over 65. The only Jews for whom the demographic news is good are the Chassidim. If the demographic news is good, the economic news isn't, because large families struggle financially. They are largely indifferent to this, however, because each child is considered a blessing. While the Chassidim are by and large opposed to separation of Quebec from Canada, they have made their peace with the Quebec government and are determined to stay on. For them, Montreal offers the highest quality of Jewish life in North America. The benefits of living in a cohesive community where the government is at least benign, and in fact supports private Jewish education in ways that most other provinces do not, outweigh the nuisances associated with the threat of separation, the French language laws, and the like. For all the pessimism about their economic future, other aspects of communal life are much more promising for the entire Jewish community than is commonly acknowledged.

Montreal retains its Jewish residential patterns, which developed many decades ago. One-third of the Jewish community, including most Lubavitch, live in Snowdon and Cotes de Neiges. Eighteen percent live in Cotes St. Luc and Hampstead, the rest in Dollard, Chomedy, Laval, Notre Dame de Grace, Westmount, the town of Mount Royal, and Outrement, where the non-Lubavitcher Chassidim such as Satmar, Belz, and Vishnitzer are concentrated. These heavily Jewish neighborhoods provide safe seats for Liberals (in a late 1990s election in the riding of Mount Royal, Liberal candidate Irwin Cotler won with the largest majority ever garnered in a Montreal election).

Whereas in the United States more than 33 percent of Jews identify themselves as Reform, here only 4.5 percent identify themselves as Reform. In contrast to American Jews, Canadian Jews are much more highly affiliated with synagogues; much more observant at home; much more likely to retain Hebrew, Yiddish, and Judeo-Arabic; much more likely to live in Jewish neigh-

borhoods and to associate with Jewish friends; and much more likely to provide their children with a Jewish education. They are also more likely to make
use of the various institutions of Jewish communal life.

In Montreal alone, there are dozens of kosher bakeries, restaurants, groceries, butchers, caterers, and bookstores. There are six cemeteries and several funeral homes to meet the needs of the community. There are fifteen
Orthodox synagogues, five Conservative synagogues, one Reconstructionist
temple, one Reform temple, and twenty-two Sephardic synagogues. There
are twenty-seven Jewish day schools and academies, seven supplementary
schools, seventeen daycare centers and preschools, three CEGEPs (the rough
equivalent of junior or two-year colleges), and eight rabbinical colleges. In
addition, there are at least fourteen Lubavitcher shuls. The weekly *Canadian
Jewish News* reaches over 80,000 Jews and reportedly has the largest readership of any single newspaper in Quebec. In addition, there are many journals
and directories published in several languages distributed around the city.
This is a rather impressive array of institutions for a population of 95,000
Jews.

Beyond the informal institutions of Jewish life, there are official organizations serving Canadian Jewry. Canadian Jews are more efficiently governed
by their national and provincial organizations than the Jews of the United
States. There are two dominant structures serving the community. The political organization is called the Canadian Jewish Congress (CJC), founded in
1919, the national branch of which is headquartered in Ottawa. The CJC is
known as the "Parliament of Canadian Jewry."[12] The government understands the CJC in much the same way, seeking out its leadership's reading of
the Jewish community's response to its policy initiatives.

The other major organization serving the Jews of Canada and Quebec is
the Federation CJA (Combined Jewish Appeal), formerly Allied Jewish Community Services. Federation CJA is a philanthropic umbrella organization
comprised of more than a hundred allied agencies in the areas of health, welfare, social, cultural, educational, and recreational activities that target youth,
the elderly, the sick and disabled, the poor, and the recent immigrant. The
Federation CJA was formed over eighty years ago at a time when most philanthropic organizations were private. Because most of the existing services in
Quebec were administered by either Protestants or Catholics, it was natural
for Jews to revive and build upon their own long tradition of self-help by creating an extensive parallel set of institutions.

On the one hand, Jewish agencies, particularly hospitals, have fought to
maintain maximum authority over their operations. On the other hand, they
have become somewhat addicted to government financial support, some of it

direct and some indirect (for example, budgetary and tax policies that promote private charitable giving). In education, the major role of Federation CJA's affiliate, the Association of Jewish Day Schools, is to represent the interests of Jewish day schools before the Quebec Ministry of Education, helping them qualify for student subsidies. Quebec politics makes corporate-style organizations extremely adaptive. It is responsive to expressions of communal interests and receptive to corporate entities. This encourages minorities in addition to those officially designated as "visible minorities" to present their needs collectively. Even if Jews and other minorities were not otherwise inclined to or capable of generating group cohesion and initiative, Quebec politics arguably works to perpetuate and even elicit communal identity and solidarity. Quebec government "helps those who help themselves."

The evolution of Jewish educational institutions is a good example. Education has historically been a central political concern for Canadian Jews as much as it has for American Jews. An immediately apparent and highly distinctive feature of the Montreal Jewish community is that it has the highest percentage of Jewish children receiving a Jewish education in all of North America. About 65 percent of Jewish children attend Jewish day schools, while another 15 percent attend after-school programs.[13] This is a case in which strong communal Jewish identity may have been the product rather than the source of political activism.

Education is one of the areas that come under provincial governance in Canada. The educational system of Quebec was traditionally bi-confessional. There was the Catholic School Board (now called the French School Board) and the Protestant School Board (now the English School Board). Jews, who were a small minority at the beginning of the century, were not granted their own school board, even when their population expanded enough to warrant it. A 1903 provincial law directed Jews to the Protestant schools, though they could be expelled at any time without notice, and nearly were in the 1920s. The Catholics would not accept them. Since Jews were too few to support Jewish day schools, several generations of Jewish children were educated in the Protestant schools, where they were simultaneously anglicized. It is no surprise that most Montreal Jews developed a closer affinity for English language and culture as well as British political values. As soon as the community was large enough, Jews responded to the Christian domination of the educational system, much as they had to their domination of cultural and social service institutions. They created their own network of Jewish private schools.

The "Quiet Revolution" initiated under Quebec Premier Jean Lesage in 1960 changed the nature of education in the province. In the 1960s and 1970s, the centralizing tendencies of the government became apparent with the public takeover of many private social, educational, and health institutions and the emergence of a new Francophone middle class, which adopted a statist strategy to compensate itself for perceived previous injustices. Provincial administration flowered into a full-blown state apparatus, expanding further into sensitive areas of education and health.[14] School funding became a controversial issue. At first, Jews were not much affected by government intervention because their own institutions were so well developed. The Private Education Act of 1973 left Jews with no option but to apply directly to the Department of Education for funding. Previously, they had negotiated privately for funds with Jewish agencies, but now Jews were forced to lobby the provincial government in Quebec City, which was far from the Jewish population concentrated in Montreal. Bending to the new reality of the centralizing efforts of the Quebec government meant developing a new and more formal approach to politics.

A major turning point for Quebec Jews was 1974's Bill 22 followed by the Parti Quebecois' victory in the November 1976 election. Until then, Jews had been able to rely upon their comfortable relationship with the Liberal Party. Bill 22 was replaced by the sweeping Charter de la Langue Francaise in 1977. While not opposed to the flourishing of French culture, Jews were opposed to what they regarded as coercion. The Jews remained in political purgatory until the Liberal Party returned to power in Quebec in 1985. Resentment increased among Anglophones, including Jews, with the imposition of Bill 101 in 1988, which accelerated the transition to French language in the economy. Another law, Bill 178, made French language on signs a requirement. Jews and other Anglophones regarded this law as an infringement on human rights as guaranteed by the Canadian Constitution.

In 1989, the CJC denounced the law as a violation of individual rights. Its position was that the protection of individual rights supersedes all other political objectives. In their meeting with Quebec Premier Bourassa, representatives of the CJC stressed that communication needed to be improved between the Quebec government and its minorities. Measures needed to be taken to prevent the erosion of Jewish collective life, in the framework of a truly pluralist Quebec, respectful of individual rights and tolerant of the beliefs of other cultural communities.[15]

With the election of Lucien Bouchard, the leader of the Parti Quebecois, as premier in 1998, the attempt to define and clarify the status of Quebec has continued, though surveys reveal declining support for sovereignty (hovering around 40 percent), which will probably delay any future referendum on the subject. The CJC realizes that it must tread lightly with respect to these issues, as is evidenced by its recent decision to remain silent on the Clarity

Law, which says that any vote on secession in Quebec requires both a "clear question" and a "clear majority." On the other hand, the CJC Quebec has not been silent when the rights of Jews are in jeopardy. In the spring of 2000, Quebec announced that it planned to invoke an extremely controversial clause in order to override the Canadian and provincial human rights charters. The clause will be used to preserve the historic privileges of Catholics and Protestants in the public school system, as part of Bill 118, introduced by Education Minister Francois Legault in May 2000. The bill will maintain these denominations' exclusive right to engage in religious instruction, "notwithstanding" the fact that Quebec schools have been designated according to linguistic rather than religious categories since July 1998. The CJC-Quebec deplored the use of this clause as a violation of legally protected human rights, namely, the guarantees of equality and freedom of religion.[16]

Lubavitch in Quebec

While Chassidim seem to play a bit part as actors on Quebec's political stage, their impact is far from negligible. For instance, in Outrement, the Satmar Chassidim, in the words of one fairly sophisticated Satmar community leader, exercise the "swing vote." Their extremely high voter turnout compensates for their numerical marginality.[17] In addition, Chassidim go out of their way to create a network of personal ties with government officials. Their agenda is "the same as everyone else's: employment, economic well-being, education, and immigration."[18] Although Chassidim are acutely aware that government money comes with strings attached, they are confident they can get their share without becoming entangled in a way that would compromise their stringent lifestyle.

Montreal City Councilor Sidney Pfeiffer, a lawyer and vice president of the Association of Jewish Day Schools, has represented a ward containing many Chassidim for nearly twelve years. He estimates Chassidic voter turnout at over 80 percent. He finds that Chassidim prefer to contact him personally, thinking of him as an ally, or at least a reliably sympathetic listener. Most of the issues that concern them are quite local. They need parking variances for Sabbath, holidays, parlour (political) meetings, *sheva brachas* (seven nights of celebrations in honor of newly married couples), and *shivas* (seven days of mourning). They need crossing guards, garbage removal, and fallen trees hauled away. In short, they focus on the same sorts of local issues as do other citizens.

Sidney Pfeiffer counts his three reelections so far as a sign that he does a fairly good job of representing his constituents' interests. He regards the fact that he, though an observant Jew, is not Chassidic as a political asset. Pfeiffer believes that if he were a member of one Chassidic court, his candidacy would likely fall prey to rivalry among courts. This phenomenon also accounts, in Pfeiffer's estimation, for why Chassidim rarely run for political office even in Chassidic neighborhood strongholds.[19]

On the provincial level, Chassidim represent a smaller portion of total voters, but because of their concentration in certain regions, such as St. Therese north of Montreal and Outrement and Snowdon within Montreal, they have the potential to become politically significant. Their significance derives less from their power at the polls than from the fact that Quebec politicians, particularly members of the Parti Quebecois (PQ), are anxious, almost desperate, to demonstrate their receptivity toward minorities in their midst. It is considered a political boon when the PQ can show that it has garnered the support of non-Francophone minorities, and Chassidim have learned to play this to the hilt.

I have heard politicians of both the Liberal and PQ parties express confidence that they have won over the Chassidim as allies, only to have that claim rejected by Chassidim. They react with amusement to claims by any politician to know the mind of the community, preferring to think of themselves as possessing too much inscrutable political savvy to be understood by any outsider. The PQ overrates its support among Chassidim, but the Liberals also take too much for granted.

Michel Archambault, who was the assistant for cultural affairs for Gerald Tremblay, the Liberal deputy for Outrement on the provincial level, understands that Chassidim have no unshakeable commitment to the Liberal Party in principle.[20] PQ officials seemed less perceptive about the fact that Chassidim are pragmatic political actors. While several PQ officials believed that they had the loyalty of their Chassidic constituents, several Chassidim told me that no matter what the PQ thinks, Chassidim do not vote for the PQ on the provincial level but only on the municipal level where they can hope for concrete benefits. In short, "grudges, interests, and preferences rule the political choices of Chassidim."[21]

An example of this type of political interaction involves Robert Kieffer, a member of the Assemblee Nationale. His district includes St. Therese and Boisbriand, with its large community of Tasher Chassidim. He considers himself an expert on what he affectionately calls "his Chassidim" because even before he represented the Tash community of St. Therese, he represented an area of Montreal also heavily populated by Satmar and Belz Chassidim. He is also a major proponent of independence for Quebec, and is politically canny enough to realize that the logic of this position entails that the Quebecois must be willing to commit to group rights for internal minorities as well.[22] The view of the Tash of Quebec is that as long as they are in exile, it doesn't really matter in which political entity they reside. As long as they are well treated, that is, left alone, they are truly politically impartial. That the PQ chooses to interpret this as support (they were able to enlist Tashers in a photo opportunity involving Quebec flag waving) is probably a sign of wishful thinking. The Tash, for their part, are well aware that their physical isolation in Boisbriand, complete with their own polling center, makes how they vote rather apparent.

The relationship that has evolved between the Tash and Mr. Keiffer is an interesting one. Neither side understands the other as well as it thinks, but both sides clearly are satisfied with the relationship. For his part, Keiffer feels confident that he is serving the Tash well by providing them with city services and educational subsidies despite the isolation and near autonomy of the community. He occasionally winks at their transgressions, which usually involve failure to comply with immigration regulations, tax codes, or provincial curricular requirements on a minor scale. Otherwise, he characterizes Chassidim as ideal constituents—a representative's dream. They have a zero violent crime rate, are committed to staying in Quebec even under PQ rule, and have given assurances that they will not flee even if Quebec separates. This is an enormous publicity boon for the PQ in the face of measurable flight from the province by other Jews in recent years. Not only will the Chassidim stay put, but they will never publicly attack a government in place. They recognize that they need the protection of the state, ironically, in order to maintain their semblance of autonomy.

Mr. Keiffer is comfortable with the fact that "his Chassidim" will turn out to vote in exchange for being left alone to live their lives. He prefers the Chassidim to nonobservant Jews, Sephardim, or non-Orthodox Jews because the Chassidim, in his view, are basically apolitical. He has stepped in to defend the community when their non-Jewish neighbors originally expressed some animosity toward the Tashers' unusual dress, isolationism, and habits, particularly early marriages. (Tash women commonly marry at eighteen or nineteen, but seventeen is not unheard of. The legal age for marriage in Quebec is sixteen, so there is no violation of the law.) The Tash won over their neighbors when their ambulances were the first to assist wounded bikers in the infamous St. Therese biker gang shootout. The sight of the black-garbed Chassidim hovering over leather-jacketed and tattooed motorcycle gang members is etched in the collective memory of the community.

Not everyone approves of the relationship of the Tash Chassidim to their political environment. It is an example of what Jack Jedwab, director of the Canadian Studies Association at the University of Quebec in Montreal, claims to have experienced in his interaction with the Chassidim of Quebec when he served as the executive director for intercultural relations with the Canadian Jewish Congress. His perspective is shared by many members of Canada's largest Jewish institutional body. He criticizes the tendency of Chassidim to remain aloof from the CJC, meanwhile cultivating what the CJC sees as opportunistic and self-serving direct relationships with municipal and provincial political officials. This "end-running" tactic rankles the organization, which prides itself on representing the community as a whole. Jedwab explains the political visibility and success of the Chassidim as a product of their willingness to become the Quebec government's "pet Jews." They offer no competition and no threat because they won't run for political office and won't criticize the government openly as long as they can maintain one good relationship with one sympathetic politician, and thus ensure their access to social benefits.[23] This is an unfriendly but not completely inaccurate characterization of many Chassidim, though it applies less well to Lubavitch, which occupies the middle ground. On the one hand, Lubavitchers have developed their own extensive network of charitable and educational agencies, as well as their own contacts with government officials, which allows them the independence to control the nature and extent of interaction with the mainstream Jewish organizations. On the other hand, money is extremely tight in the Lubavitch community. They have chosen to accept representation before the Quebec government by the Association of Jewish Day Schools, which is affiliated with the CJA. Detractors among both mainstream Jews and the more hard-nosed Chassidic courts see this as unprincipled opportunism because Lubavitcher schools have had to modify aspects of the curriculum in order to qualify for funds. Primarily, this has meant adding secular subjects, as opposed to subtracting Jewish subjects, an accommodation that is viewed by Lubavitch as acceptable.

The government subsidizes the secular part of the student's program, and the parents and the Association of Jewish Day Schools subsidize the religious portion of the student's program. There is a good deal of anecdotal evidence to support the claim that the Association of Jewish Day Schools and the Quebec Ministry of Education are fully aware that many of the Chassidic schools that receive government funding do not meet all of the provincial curricular requirements, either with respect to French language instruction or secular subjects. Quebec education officials have an informal policy of warning the Chassidic schools when inspections are coming up, and then turning a blind eye to certain curricular infractions.

Lubavitchers cooperate with both the association and the provincial government, particularly with respect to the girls' school, Beth Rivka. The boys' school is more problematic. Students are offered two programs. One consists only of "holy" subjects, while the other has an additional secular program added to the end of the school day. Only a small number of families opt for the secular program even though it reduces their tuition bill because it is subsidized by the government. Parents cite the academic deficiencies of the instructors (who come from outside the community and are not very well paid) as a reason for avoiding the secular program. Because so few students avail themselves of these courses, it is irrational for the administration to expend scare resources on them, thereby perpetuating the problem. Although the Lubavitch schools are officially French sector schools, most Lubavitcher boys can complete their education without much exposure to formal French or even secular instruction.

The dilemma for Lubavitch has been how to maintain religious integrity, autonomy, and also solvency. Jewish education represents a case in which the Lubavitcher community learned to work within both the Jewish institutional structure and the Quebec political system using a mixture of negotiating tactics and accommodation. Lubavitchers have opted not to place members directly into CJC or CJA positions for fear of creating the appearance of support for all of their public political positions. They are much more comfortable with indirect representation, as long as their interests are addressed. The principal of the Lubavitch yeshiva is satisfied with the way the association is meeting the needs of Lubavitcher students.[24] Meanwhile, the mainstream Jewish infrastructure has apparently recognized the importance of responding to its numerically increasing Chassidic constituency.

Although Felix Melloul, who heads the association, would probably prefer that all Jewish schools adhere strictly to secular curricular standards, he recognizes that the Chassidic Jewish schools will do so in a very limited way, if at all. He also recognizes that the non-Chassidic day school population is dwindling because of low birth rates, while the Chassidic school-aged population is rapidly expanding. To continue to come before the Quebec government as a representative of the Jewish community, the Association of Jewish Day Schools will have to represent the Chassidic population.

The Lubavitch community is enjoying the fruits of its positive interaction with the public realm. When the Orthodox confront the modern city, they discover that an urban setting can actually promote survival of the alien enclaves in its midst.[25] Lubavitchers, like other Chassidim, have created a territorial base within the city in the form of predominantly Lubavitch neighborhoods. While they do not possess the physical boundaries of a ghetto, and are not exclusively Lubavitch, or even Jewish, the concentration of many Lubavitch families in a few distinct neighborhoods allows them a fairly independent religious and cultural life. This residential pattern further enhances the community's political clout. Conducting their lives in the midst of the city generates a sort of "force field" that is more cultural than physical. As William Shaffir notes in his 1974 study of the Montreal Lubavitch community, "Insulation does not necessarily refer to spatial or ecological separation, but also to a lack of social and cultural contact with individuals and ideas foreign to the group."[26]

Lubavitchers have it better than other Chassidic groups in Montreal because they inhabit a multinational neighborhood called Snowdon, where tolerance for diversity is much higher than in other neighborhoods. For instance, in the more homogenous French Catholic neighborhood of Outrement, Céline Forget won municipal office in the last election on a single-issue platform of cracking down on alleged Chassidic violations of city zoning, parking, and other ordinances. Tensions between Chassidim and their neighbors run high, resulting in numerous incidents of petty harassment and lawsuits in her district.

By contrast, in Snowdon, the recent influx of immigrants, largely from the Third World, has contributed to good relations between Lubavitchers and their neighbors—a definite improvement over the less than warm welcome that Lubavitchers received when they first settled in this neighborhood in the 1940s. Because many of the neighbors are not only recent immigrants but religious, whether Moslems, Hindus, or Christians, they are unfazed by unfamiliar religious customs. And because they speak imperfect or accented French or English, they do not have contempt for Jews with accents. Because they maintain close extended families, they are not irritated by large Jewish families. And because they often adhere to a distinctive code of dress and behavior, Jews in black garb, hats, and beards do not seem odd. In fact, it was a consortium of Jews and Moslems who, with the help of the local representative, persuaded the municipal swimming pool to establish separate swimming hours for women and men.

The Montreal community traces its origins to the arrival of the sixth Rebbe, Yakov Yitzhok Schneersohn, in Brooklyn, New York, in 1940. Having immediately established the central yeshiva, or rabbinical college, in New York, the next year he established a similar institution, Tomche T'mimim ("Supporters of the Righteous"), in Montreal. He then arranged for the rescue of some of his students, nine of whom arrived as refugees from a yeshiva near Warsaw. Thirty-nine additional students from Vilna managed to cross the Soviet Union to Japan and then to Canada shortly thereafter. The resident Jewish community of Montreal favored the creation of a single large yeshiva, but the Rebbe prevailed in forming a separate Lubavitch yeshiva.

Very quickly, the small community of Lubavitch established a newspaper, children's classes and clubs, and a summer camp. The goal was to influence Montreal Jewry to revive their lapsed observance of key Orthodox rituals, such as the Sabbath, family purity laws, and kashrut. In 1943, twenty-five Lubavitchers arrived and the expanded community acquired what would be its quarters until 1962, on Park Avenue. The after-school program that they established quickly grew to two hundred students. In 1952, the girls' school, Beth Rivka, was established. While the community continued to expand through births, another influx of Lubavitchers arrived in 1947 from Shanghai and Paris. Between 1950 and 1953, seventy individuals joined their ranks. In 1962, the yeshiva moved west to its current location on Westbury Avenue in Snowdon. In 1967, Beth Rivka moved a few blocks to Vezina Street off of Westbury Avenue. The current enrollment of the schools now tops twelve hundred students. Families followed their children's schools to Snowdon. Although there was a petition drive in opposition to the settlement of Lubavitch in the neighborhood, it did not deter the establishment of the community.

In 1974, when Shaffir studied the community, it numbered about one hundred families. Today, there are more than three hundred families. It is difficult to determine the actual population because the Canadian Census does not break down the Jewish community by affiliation. Moreover, the basic unit for Chassidim is the family, not the individual. Accordingly, when asked about the size of the community, the answer will always be expressed as the number of families. Given that the average number of children per family is between eight and ten, it can be estimated that there are between two and three thousand Lubavitchers in Montreal.

The population of eligible voters, of course, is much smaller because a large percentage of the community consists of minor children. In addition, a significant number of adults are ineligible to vote because they are not Canadian citizens. There is a large community of Americans; in fact, marriage partners are often sought in the United States because the Lubavitch population is so much larger. Constant contact is maintained with New York. A weekly private, direct bus connects the two communities. Montrealers and New Yorkers are bound by family, business, and cultural ties. Since Shaffir wrote his study over twenty-five years ago, English has supplanted Yiddish as the language of daily life, both in the streets and in the home, except among the very old. There are increasing numbers of Lubavitchers from North Africa, South America, Europe, the former Soviet Union, Australia, Britain, and Israel. The multinational character of the population has an impact on the political behaviors and attitudes of the community, with Americans probably exerting the most profound politico-cultural influence.

Lubavitch, despite its small, residentially concentrated population, has carved out a visible presence in the city. It has built support among the non-Lubavitch community through its outreach programs because its members are perceived as sincere, hospitable, and kind. While some Jews find them an annoying or embarrassing presence, many more regard them with affection based on nostalgia and admiration for the fact that Lubavitch has undertaken to keep Judaism alive. The summer camps, after-school educational programs, and even day schools are used by non-Lubavitchers to provide their children with a good grounding in Torah, which the parents may regret that they do not possess. The various celebrations and activities centered around the Sabbath and the cycle of holidays draw large crowds, including many non-Lubavitchers, because of their reputation for a lively, joyous, kid-friendly atmosphere where all Jews, even the most nonobservant, are made to feel welcome and valued.

The community needs a good deal of financial support from outsiders to operate these many programs. Because their own members receive only a modest secular education, their economic mobility is extremely limited. A number of Lubavitchers have become near-professional fund-raisers who try to forge partnerships within the non-Lubavitcher business community. The success of their fund-raising efforts was demonstrated when a Montreal businessman, himself not Lubavitch, contributed the lion's share of the funds to build the Bais Chaya Mushka Seminary, the women's teachers college that opened in 1999. These sorts of donations, large and small, have become essential to the community.

Because not all of the necessary economic support can come from private sources, Lubavitch has learned to engage in the political equivalent of fund-raising. They have learned to seek out sources of public support not only for their schools but also child subsidies offered by the Quebec government to large families, services for youth and the elderly, educational and career training, student loans, zoning allowances, employment services, health benefits, and the like. This represents a change from the political behavior of the community nearly three decades ago when William Shaffir found that political involvement "begins and ends with the casting of their vote during municipal, provincial, and federal elections."[27]

Being able to "think outside the box" has made it possible to access many sources of public funding. If this meant, as in the case of the schools, switching to French or adhering to provincial admission policies, building codes, and tax and zoning requirements, this did not impose any substantial hardship or compromise with religious practice. In turn, the provincial and municipal government will, for various reasons, initiate the contact, which requires being able to identify a Lubavitcher in a leadership position. Lack of leadership, either elected or appointed, is a significant political disadvantage. Any Lubavitcher who speaks to the press or government officials understands that he has no formal backing, and in reality speaks only for himself.

There are several members of the community whose opinions carry a fair amount of weight within the community, though they may or may not be known to those outside it. For instance, in matters pertaining to Jewish law, Rabbi Hendel, the head of the Va'ad Ha'ir, has nearly universal respect. (Although even his authority is now questionable, as he is quite elderly and there is dissension brewing over which of two candidates will replace him.) No individual or group within the community is regarded as authoritative in all areas pertaining to Lubavitch concerns. Individuals may be sought out by other individuals when their specific expertise is required, but no person has been imbued by the community as a whole with any special, all-encompassing authority to speak or act for it. This is best illustrated by the fact that virtually all political successes and failures are traceable to the style, leadership, and political acumen of the individual who undertook the project in question, rather than to the organizational skills of Lubavitch as a group. In this sense, Lubavitch is very far from operating as a true interest group. A few examples drawn from recent political engagements serve to illustrate this point.

Five Cases of Political Entrepreneurship

The Elected Official

An exception to the general rule that Chassidim rely on intermediaries and ad hoc political contacts to carry their interests to benevolent public officials is the example of a Lubavitcher who ran for, and won, political office. Sauli Zajdel has been a city councilor from the Riding of Victoria since 1986, and is now a member of the Montreal City Council. He is a consummate local politician. He is proud that 90 percent of Lubavitchers in his riding turned out for his nomination, but his election would not have been possible had he been unable to win the allegiance of other residents in this predominantly non-Lubavitcher area. Zajdel is very much aware that of the 25,000 voters that he represents, only 30 percent are Jewish, and of those, only 10 percent

are Lubavitchers. His constituents include many ethnic minorities and Zajdel knows what it takes to get into and to stay in office.

His contributions to the community include a new sports center with separate swimming hours for men and women (in deference to his Moslem and
Jewish constituents); Quebec family allowances to assist large families; housing grants awarded after the Snowdon area was designated for revitalization;
a Wal-Mart; and a host of small zoning and parking tolerances, stop signs,
and the like. While the Lubavitch community refers to him affectionately, in
most cases, as "their city councilor," Zajdel, whatever his personal loyalties,
refers to himself as an ordinary politician.[28]

Zajdel prides himself on his service not only to the Lubavitcher and Jewish communities but to his other constituents, the largest percentage of which
are Filipino. To the extent that he has been able to deliver goods to the Lubavitcher community it has been because these goods are desirable from the
perspective of the rest of the community as well. The CDN Sports Center,
the Wal-Mart, and the neighborhood rehabilitation funds benefit the community as a whole. His agenda, coalitions, and distribution of favors and attention all reflect political realities.

Moreover, he understands the need to meet the informal code of dress and
behavior in City Hall, and has cultivated a manner and style of dress that is
consistent with that of any seasoned politician. Only his adherence to Jewish
laws and holidays, and the inconspicuous kippa on his head, announce his differences from his mainstream colleagues. Political success, he understands,
requires that Lubavitch package both its political demands and its political
representatives in a way that is consistent with local political norms and
styles. The goal is political adaptation without co-optation.

The city councilor's comfort in secular political settings is respected by
members of the Lubavitcher community, who view his adaptations to public
life as a sacrifice that they are glad someone is willing to make, since no one
else in the community expressed any willingness to take on the unappealing
job. People recognize the benefits of having constant political representation,
but for the most part political involvement remains an ad hoc affair, an individual's response to political crises as they arise. Some people acknowledge
that it might be beneficial to have a proactive, coherent, long-term political
agenda for the community, but no one is willing to design it or push it forward.

The consensus among Lubavitchers is that Sauli Zajdel is doing an adequate job, and nothing more is really required. No one has thought past his
tenure in office and no one, apparently, has expressed a desire to replace him
when he retires. Therefore, although Zajdel has wide support in the com-

munity as "our man" in city government, it is not at all clear that Lubavitch will attempt to make sure that one of their own stands for election when Zajdel steps down. Because there is no designated or recognized central leadership in the community, there is no way to see that a replacement is groomed. Nor is there an agreed-upon political agenda. With no board, committee, or council to set the agenda, political action is likely to remain ad hoc. Having a permanent presence in city government will continue to rely on the personal ambition of an individual. Zajdel could be both the first and the last Lubavitcher elected official.

The Mediator

Another visible Lubavitch figure in public life is Rabbi Zushi Silberstein, who, because of his lively personality and his rare grasp of French (he was born and raised in Belgium), is often in the political limelight. He contends that he neither seeks out nor avoids political involvement. He believes that his involvement is guided by the principles of the Rebbe's outreach program, specifically his understanding that the Jewish and non-Jewish world is ready for redemption, which practically propels Lubavitch into political life. In Silberstein's view, even when Lubavitch pursues what appears to be its local self-interest, it is in fact benefiting the whole community. As Rabbi Silberstein understands it, his forays into the political realm have promoted the common good.[29]

In one case, he helped mediate a dispute between the Chassidic community of Outrement (non-Lubavitchers) and their Catholic neighbors. In another case, he came to the attention of the public by mediating a conflict over an autopsy. Quebec law demanded that an autopsy be performed on an Orthodox murder victim, because a conviction could not be achieved absent autopsy evidence confirming that a murder had been committed. Jewish law, however, prohibits autopsies. Rabbi Silberstein demonstrated the skillful compromise that Lubavitch is known for, without sacrificing either Jewish or secular legal codes. In a Solomonic compromise, Silberstein was allowed to be present at the autopsy to ensure that the body was reassembled in its entirety. This episode illustrated the strong desire of both the government and Lubavitch to work things out without rancor. Silberstein sees his success as a victory for all ethnic and religious minorities because it has further sensitized the Quebec government to the cultural differences of its citizens. But more than anything, it testifies to Silberstein's personal powers of persuasion and his ability to make the Lubavitch position on autopsy comprehensible to public officials.

Because of his visibility, Silberstein is regarded by Montreal public officials as an official spokesman for Lubavitch. He is characterized by David Sultan, a highly placed CJA official, as Lubavitch's "official crisis manager."[30] As he himself acknowledges, though, Silberstein speaks in his own words, reflecting his own (he hopes accurate) understanding of the Rebbe's principles. Although Silberstein may be seen as the point man for Lubavitch by the Quebec government, CJA, and the press, Lubavitch has no official role for him as liaison, public relations officer, or the like.

The Benefactor

Another example of individual political entrepreneurship on behalf of the community was the establishment of a Jewish paramedic squad called Hatzolah. The squad was created through the initiative of one man, Zevi Neuwirth,[31] based on the American model in which he had served. Neuwirth arranged for the training of a contingent of Montreal Lubavitchers and other Chassidim as paramedics equipped to serve the special religious requirements of the Orthodox community. These requirements include specific instructions for handling the dead and respect for the modesty of women. In addition, knowledge of Yiddish is essential because many older members of the community do not speak sufficient French to communicate with the city's emergency services personnel. Convincing the city government of the need for this service was a big problem because private ambulance services are prohibited. A temporary compromise has been worked out that allows Hatzolah members to respond to the scene, but they in turn must call on the city emergency service for backup and transport to the hospital. This defeats the purpose of the organization, precisely because Hatzolah has an incredibly rapid response time and its Quebec counterpart is notoriously slow to arrive on the scene. The founder of Hatzolah understands that someone must continue his battle for legal recognition up the ladder of the Quebec bureaucracy. But he is exhausted and wants to turn his attention to his job and family. He expresses reluctance to trade on personal connections with Quebec officials for fear that if he pushes too hard, too fast, city union members will put him out of business permanently through a legislative initiative. At this time, no one has stepped forward to take up where Neuwirth has left off. Everyone supports Hatzolah in principle and its members are dedicated and trusted (this is one of the few organizations that unites all Chassidim citywide) because of their skills and rapid response time. But while the future of Hatzolah is pretty much assured, the expansion of its activities, which will require a concerted political effort, is very much in doubt as long as no new leadership emerges.

The Builder

Another instance in which the political initiative of one individual failed for lack of timely and appropriate community political support involved the attempt to find a permanent location for a new ChaBaD center. On the surface, the case has all the markings of a battle about neighborhood transition, pitting neighbor against neighbor in the overwhelmingly Jewish, though non-Orthodox, area of Montreal called Cotes St. Luc. Less observant Jews reacted with hostility to what they saw as an invasion of more Orthodox Jews and the destruction of the traditional character of the neighborhood. (The fact that this particular ChaBaD center was being constructed with the Sephardic community in mind may have been an additional irritant.) The attempt by Rabbi Mendel Raskin to construct a large community center provided an opportunity and a political forum for the inevitable conflict that was brewing between the two communities.

The proposed location required the vote of the Cotes St. Luc Council. The project became embroiled in controversy when the council, in a split vote that required the mayor to break the tie, decided to grant permission to Lubavitch to build on their proposed location. The council was required to rezone the site to accommodate the structure. In addition, the city agreed to drop the 25 percent that it customarily adds to the valuation of the property it sells, which would have been a significant financial bonus for Lubavitch.

Over the next several months, local opposition mounted over issues like crowding, traffic, noise, decreased sunlight for a local gardeners' club, and the appearance that a special deal had been cut with respect to zoning and taxes. Rabbi Mendel Raskin did not assume a position of political helplessness. He had already garnered the support of the Quebec government, which, citing the benefit to the Francophone Jews, promised to give $820,000 to the project. He enlisted supporters from ChaBaD centers, and letters flowed in from Russia, the United States, South America, and Australia as well as from local Lubavitchers. The letter-writing campaign was received badly by opposing councilors, who read it as an attempt at pressure politics. After all, these letters, though quite numerous, merely demonstrated the ability of Lubavitch to enlist its far-flung membership in a crusade. They could safely be ignored because they did not come from local constituents or even Canadian citizens. The letter-writing campaign hardened the resolve of the opponents of the ChaBaD center by confirming, in their minds, their worst suspicions about the allegedly conspiratorial nature of Lubavitch and its alleged readiness to circumvent democratic procedures in order to get its way. Despite the demonstrated benefits of the ChaBaD center to a large portion of the community and its many local supporters, the personal appeals of Rabbi Raskin and some influential non-Lubavitcher supporters neither succeeded in quelling the opposition nor building sufficient support. In the final analysis, Lubavitch did not come close to getting the numbers they needed.

The opponents' petition drive to initiate a referendum on the proposed center netted over nine hundred signatures, far in excess of the five hundred required. The referendum was not held, however, because Rabbi Raskin decided to give up on the proposed site and seek another that would elicit less community ire. In August 2000, yet a fourth site was rejected by the Cotes St. Luc City Council, which suggests that the rancor directed toward either Lubavitch as a movement or the tactics it employed had not dissipated. Although a compromise site was later agreed on, this foray into local politics was not a triumph for Lubavitch.

Looking for Friends in the Wrong Places

Another recent case of political failure involved two Lubavitcher professors of math and computer science. On their own initiative, in order to create Montreal's only postsecondary educational opportunity for Chassidim, in September 1999 they pushed for a joint educational venture between TAV (Torah and Vocational Institute) and UQAM (Université du Quebec a Montreal). A partnership between a French language university with known nationalist leanings and an Orthodox Jewish college, the objective of which is to teach Orthodox men and women a profession, was certainly a novelty. The largely technical program accepted students from all backgrounds, but accommodated the special needs of the Orthodox men and women to be taught separately.

But political activism in this case, just as in the Cotes St. Luc case, did not end happily for the community. Perhaps this was because the initiative was undertaken by only one or two individuals without organized, widespread backing, or perhaps for other reasons. Early in the year 2000, the TAV-UQAM joint program came under attack by the professors union at the Université du Quebec. They charged that classes segregated by sex violated the mission of the university, and, according to Louis Gill, head of the union, that this segregation is a form of discrimination that keeps Jewish women in "half-servility." Allegations of insufficient French language teaching were also raised, but the main complaint had to do with accommodating the religious requirement to segregate the sexes.[32]

Defenders of the program within UQAM pointed out that it had fulfilled the university's mission statement respecting the inclusion of diverse populations that would otherwise not have access to higher education. They also showed that the Chassidim, particularly the women, were excelling in the program. Nevertheless, UQAM decided to break its contract and abruptly cancel the program. In an uncharacteristically politically savvy and assertive response, Torah and Vocational Institute filed a request for a permanent injunction in Quebec Superior Court in early May. This request was denied. TAV is continuing to press its case in the courts, contending that UQAM terminated the program in violation of its contract and on the basis of "pure discrimination and intolerance."[33] In an interview with Eli Meroz, dean of TAV, he indicated a willingness to pursue the matter, but he understood that TAV, while run by Lubavitchers, could not count on the community to back it before the government or the courts. To date, no community protest has been launched. The entire project, still waiting for resolution in the courts, rests on two individuals.[34]

Four Challenges

If the Lubavitch community wants to enhance its likelihood of political success, it will face at least four challenges. First, it will have to develop some institutional or organizational coherence, including some formal leadership. Second, it will have to develop some sort of political agenda based on an assessment of the community's long-term needs. Third, it will have to learn to package its interests and concerns so that they appear to be congruent with those of the general public. (The more alien the agenda item, the more difficult it will be to sell.) Fourth, in addition to getting out the vote (which it does very well), it will need to master other ways of achieving political clout. In short, it will have to behave more like an interest group or lobby.

As political entrepreneurs Rabbi Silberstein, Zevi Neuwirth, and City Councilor Zajdel, the deans of TAV, and Rabbi Raskin have demonstrated, at least some individual Lubavitchers have adopted the strategies, judgment, and skills of secular politicians. But in four of the five cases, the political entrepreneur relied heavily, if unconsciously, on the old shtadlan model of personal leadership and personal contacts. Special pleading by individuals is as likely to fail as to succeed, just as it has done throughout Jewish history.

Many members of the community do not perceive its political inefficacy. They trust that a combination of the Rebbe's legacy of spiritual and practical guidance and ad hoc political engagement will be sufficient in the future. Most members admit that the community is in a state of congenial, harmonious anarchy, and cannot think of any urgent reasons to change this. Others think that the movement suffers from "too much democracy."[35] But it does not appear that any individual plans to come forward and shoulder the responsibilities of leadership. Were someone to do so, it is not clear that he would have any support.

Lacking political leadership in setting or pursuing an agenda may not threaten the survival of the community, but it will keep it from operating as a bona fide interest group. It will keep it dependent on the shtadlan or the good will of a benevolent government official, the CJC, and other outside institutions. This is unlikely to be a winning combination in the long run. But the status quo is not without some advantages. On one level, the loose and ill-defined structure of the community has worked for it. Like a blowfish that creates the illusion of size and ferocity when under attack, the Lubavitch community is seen as a political force by local politicians. Every official I interviewed miscalculated the size of the community, estimating its voting population at ten to fifty times its actual size. Despite their organizational deficiencies, Lubavitchers were uniformly credited with political strength.

A CJA official remarked that "Lubavitch is a model of marketing and communication, able to get to the well-positioned people."[36] A Satmar leader found Lubavitch to be an intimidating political force because of its members' polish, education, connections, and political sophistication.[37] Gerald Tremblay's assistant marveled at "their ability to make their projects acceptable in order to get money without the Liberals delving too deeply into the details of the project." He also appreciated their willingness to play tit for tat, for instance, Zevi Neuwirth's willingness to use Hatzolah's fleet of ambulances to ferry elderly (and heavily Liberal) voters to the polls. According to the same Liberal Party official, Lubavitchers' chief political skills are that they are strategically located, bipartisan, more astute than most groups, nonideological, tremendously persistent in getting to key people, and highly visible. In addition, they are "amusing, interesting little rabbis, and we respond to them positively."[38]

Despite or perhaps because of Lubavitch's general lack of identifiable leadership, organization, and coherent agenda, it somehow creates the illusion of multiple sources of power and massive size and weight, rather than fragmentation. This illusion works to the advantage of the community in obvious ways. Some symbolic gestures by the Canadian government suggest that Lubavitch has established itself as a visible force in Canadian life. For instance, Prime Minister Jean Chretien declared the first week of July, corresponding to the sixth anniversary of the Rebbe's death, as Lubavitch Week in Canada.[39]

But the real needs of the community arise, and must be met, at the local level. Lubavitch has been most successful in getting the government to respond to the ordinary, local, and mundane needs of the community, when those needs are shared by non-Lubavitcher residents of the neighborhood and can be justified in purely secular terms.

But the political downside of Lubavitch's organizational laxity becomes obvious in cases like those of the TAV program, the ChaBaD center zoning variance, or the ambulance service. When the community makes a request that requires understanding and accommodation of its distinctive cultural and religious differences, it is more likely to generate opposition. When it is unable to square its values and interests with those of the majority culture, Lubavitch's initiatives most often fail. This is particularly true when its opponents can claim that they are against the Lubavitcher community's request because it is incongruent with liberal values. Here, the community's failure to master interest group tactics has made it harder to push its case in the political arena. It must rely on the ability of a concerned member of the community to use his personal influence with some government official. This may work with individual public officials, but it rarely wins over public opinion. The more alien the value or practice at issue appears, the more likely Lubavitch is to encounter blank incomprehension and even hostility. It is to this confrontation between Chassidic values and liberal values that we now turn in the next several chapters.

CHAPTER FIVE

Liberalism: Reason, Autonomy, and Sources of Self

Chassidim are more interested in fulfilling their contract with G-d than persuading us of the correctness of their vision of the good.

Martha Minow, *The Constitution and the Subgroup Question*

For believers there are no questions, for non-believers there are no answers.

The Chofetz Chaim

For the most part, Chassidim live according to the norms and rhythms of their lives without drawing the attention of outsiders to anything other than their quaint clothing. But when they collide with the liberal, secular world, these collisions are often attributed to the unwillingness of Chassidim to respect the laws of the land. In fact, the conflict represents a much deeper collision between what John Rawls called "comprehensive conceptions of the good," what Alasdair McIntyre called "incommensurable" moral codes, or what Stephen Macedo called the "clash of ultimates."[1] There are several features of liberalism that are simply irreconcilable with Chassidic theology. The existence of Chassidim in liberal societies tests the extent to which liberals are willing to honor one of liberalism's foundational attributes, namely, toleration. It is much easier to withhold toleration when a group's rejection of liberal values is misconstrued as a rejection of democratic citizenship. This chapter will look at several of the problem areas in the relationship between liberalism and Lubavitcher Chassidism. Rather than different views of the meaning of democratic citizenship, these problem areas consist primarily of conflicting understandings of the individual, reason, autonomy, tolerance, the nature of the good, and sources of identity and preferences.

The preeminent philosophers of liberalism, John Locke, J. S. Mill, and John Rawls, emphasized individual freedom, the rule of law, limited government, consent of the ruled, the public justification of the exercise of power, respect for rights, and a set of institutional arrangements that would allow the citizenry to periodically express its will through its elected representatives. In addition, though less explicitly stated, there is a moral core to liberalism.

The reticence about expressing it explicitly comes from the fact that liberal governments are supposed to maintain a neutral stance toward the various conceptions of the good life held by their citizens.

Still, most theorists hold that there are ideals and practices without which liberal societies and democratic polities could not function. The list of dispositions or habits that are highly salutary, if not necessary, to liberal democracies might include tolerance (related to equal respect for others as autonomous individuals), personal responsibility, honesty, social solidarity, interest in and willingness to contribute to the public welfare, capacity to exercise responsible political judgment, civility (or exercising "public reasonableness"), and law-abidingness. But what about the distinctly liberal values of individuality, autonomy, and critical rationality? Are these qualities required in order to meet the standard of democratic citizenship? Does a democratic government have a legitimate interest in the values and preferences held by its citizens? If there are virtues that must be possessed by citizens of democracies if those democracies are going to thrive, are these virtues identical to those associated with the liberal personality?

The classical liberal view, which developed in the seventeenth and eighteenth centuries in tandem with the theory of market capitalism, held that no special civic virtues were required of the citizen. Analogous to the market's ability to achieve the greatest good for the greatest number by pitting commercial and acquisitive passion against passion, the liberal democratic polity had the ability to achieve relative harmony by pitting interest against interest and faction against faction. The artful arrangement of institutions could compensate for the "defect of better motives," allowing individuals to define and pursue their own life plans without being harnessed to a higher common purpose. A good constitution was all that was necessary to rule even a band of devils. Self-interest was no longer considered detrimental to social harmony; on the contrary, it was transformed in liberal and capitalist theory into the lubricant that kept the twin automatons of market and society running.

Individual freedom was not understood merely in political or economic terms as the pursuit of self-interest. The liberalism of Immanuel Kant and J. S. Mill made human dignity the point of individual freedom. The free individual is an autonomous agent who is free to choose his ends. Since individuals will choose different ends, if all individuals are to be accorded equal respect and dignity, their ends must, in principle, be accorded equal respect. This in turn implies that government must remain neutral toward its citizens' law-abiding pursuits, refraining from throwing its weight behind one conception of the good over another.

Some contemporary liberal theorists, including John Rawls, Bruce Ackerman, Ronald Dworkin, Thomas Nagel, and Charles Larmore, have continued to build on this line of reasoning. Governments in liberal democratic societies should maintain neutrality with respect to their citizens' choices about the good life as long as the pursuit of their life plans meets some minimal, usually procedural standard of justice such as "fair social cooperation," civility, tolerance, and reasonableness. Theorists such as Rawls are confident that almost any individual or group in a liberal society can participate in this "overlapping consensus" or "shared political conception" without sacrificing or jeopardizing their "comprehensive conception" of the good.

State neutrality toward citizen's conceptions of the good was intended by the framers of the Constitution to prevent the establishment of an official religion, and thereby to protect individual conscience. Now, according to some, the neutrality that was intended to prevent the establishment of a state religion has been used to create a positive secular order. Thus, neutrality comes under fire from two positions: those who think the state should openly eschew neutrality and actively promote a positive, secular liberal state, and those who want the state to refrain from promoting the "religion" of secular liberalism.

Theorists such as William Galston, Michael Sandel, Alasdair McIntyre, and Charles Taylor contend that the liberal state cannot avoid tipping the scale in favor of some lifestyles. They acknowledge that what the liberal majority experience as neutral is likely to be experienced as hostile by some minorities. As Galston expressed it, liberalism "embraces a view of human good that favors certain ways of life and tilts against others."[2] For instance, the so-called neutralist ideal tilts the scales in favor of the liberal definition of "reasonableness," thus excluding the religious point of view, contend Stephen Carter, Michael McConnell, Kent Greenawalt, Sanford Levinson, Richard Neuhaus, David Smolin, Stanley Fish, Patrick Neal, and Ronald Thiemann.

While the first set of critics intend to expose liberalism's putative neutrality as fraudulent, claiming that it puts an unfair burden on many minority cultures and religions, another category of critics of neutrality includes those, such as Stephen Macedo, Amy Gutmann, Jeff Spinner, Ira Lupu, Christopher Eisgruber, and Ronald Beiner, who argue that there are traits and virtues without which liberalism can neither be justified nor perpetuate itself. With varying degrees of militancy, these "comprehensive liberals" or "liberal perfectionists" argue that core liberal virtues need to be acknowledged. Many of these theorists want to take the discourse on liberal virtues into the area of education and character formation. Because they tend to see personal virtues as closely linked to political virtues, and liberal virtues as closely connected to democratic virtues, they are acutely interested in the process of value formation and transmission. Public education, as the primary vehicle for inculcating civic virtues and their supporting liberal personality traits, has become a particularly contentious issue, raising the sensitive question of when the state has the right to compete with and even override parental authority. Some see it as the business of the state to rescue children from the narrow confines of parental values.

The core virtues commonly identified as intrinsic to democratic citizenship by the liberal perfectionists are actually components of the liberal personality. These include individual autonomy, toleration, and critical rationality. Herein lies the problem for Lubavitchers and other cultural and religious minorities: in failing to meet the liberal standard of individual autonomy and a particular style of reasoning called critical rationality, they are deemed by militant liberals to have failed to meet the standard of democratic citizenship. This being the case, the right of free exercise "ends at a point where it conflicts with the right of the state to prepare citizens."[3] This sort of claim would strike Lubavitchers as a groundless liberal conceit that the liberal personality possesses a monopoly on reason.

If liberals can lay claim to a monopoly on reason, they can feel justified in forcing minorities to conform by simply raising the accusation of "bad citizenship," to use Jeff Spinner's words. Arguably, any society would be justified in revoking its tolerance when faced with bad citizens. John Rawls provides a good framework with which to analyze this dilemma. He was concerned that moral pluralism might threaten social unity in a liberal society, prompting his search for what he called common or neutral ground. The search for a conception of justice to which all citizens could assent led him to distinguish between a political (procedural) conception of justice and a comprehensive (substantive) conception of justice. Political life, he recognized, is only a portion of our complete life; therefore, the political conception of justice should not presuppose the acceptance of any specific comprehensive religious, philosophical, or moral view. Rawls expressed this political conception as "justice as fairness," in which ideas of the good must respect the political supremacy of rights, procedures, and rules.

Justice as fairness is not purely procedural but includes certain substantive political virtues such as civility, tolerance, reasonableness, adding up to a sense of fair social cooperation.[4] His political conception does not, in his view, constitute a comprehensive doctrine of the good, and therefore does not compete with comprehensive moral or religious views. The basic list of rules, virtues, and values that constitute the public political culture merely obligates citizens to respect each others' freedom and equality, and therefore can be affirmed by all without endangering anyone's comprehensive conception of justice. The state should take only those measures necessary to strengthen fair social cooperation between its citizens, without advancing a particular comprehensive doctrine.[5] Liberal society, Rawls admits, may prove inhospitable or uncongenial to certain comprehensive doctrines and ways of life, but no society can promote every way of life equally. As long as there is no unjust bias against certain comprehensive conceptions, such that, for instance, only individualistic ones could endure, then the neutrality and fairness of the political conception is upheld. If Chassidic communities and other communities and cultures that are not individualistic at base were forced to conform to the requirement of critical rationality or autonomous individualism, their survival would surely be threatened. This ought to qualify under Rawls's definition as an "unjust bias."

Rawls's political liberalism conceives of social unity in a diverse society as possible on the basis of an overlapping consensus about the political conception of justice as a system of fair social cooperation,[6] which would not challenge anyone's convictions about transcendent good. He believes that the cause of conflict over fundamental religious, moral, and philosophical values can therefore be removed, at least from the political realm.

Rawls has a fairly undemanding view of what is required of a citizen in a liberal democracy. As long as all citizens affirm and live up to the political conception of justice, they are free to maintain any comprehensive conception they choose, even if it is at odds with those of other citizens. While the liberalism of Kant and Mill advances the values of autonomy and individuality, Rawls's political liberalism requires far less. Accordingly, the state's interest in the formation of its citizens' character or process of reasoning is considerably reduced. As far as Rawls is concerned, the state need only concern itself with educating its future citizens in the political conception of justice. Students should be taught to understand their constitutional rights, to cooperate with others, to be self-supporting, in short, to honor the terms of social cooperation.

Where religious enclaves are concerned, Rawls states that "justice as fairness" honors, as far as it can, the claims of those who wish to withdraw for religious reasons, "provided only that they acknowledge the principles of the political conception of justice."[7] Otherwise, Rawls gives very little attention in his writings to the role of groups, either as political actors or as incubators of individual values and preferences. Nor does he discuss the claims that substate groups may make upon an individual's loyalty and conscience. Therefore, he does not provide a context in which Lubavitch can be understood.

According to the more militant breed of liberal political theorist, Rawls's standard of good citizenship is not exacting enough. For them, the ideals and practices of democratic citizenship are intertwined with liberal values and perspectives. One's private and public values must be congruent. A person cannot realistically be expected to hold nonliberal values in private and liberal democratic values in public. In this respect, they take individual's competing loyalties and commitments more seriously than Rawls does. Since a citizen cannot operate with a split personality, and must either reconcile the liberal to the nonliberal or the nonliberal to the liberal, it is the responsibility of the state to ensure that liberal values prevail.

In this view, while the state's methods must stay within constitutional boundaries, it is justified in attempting to inculcate liberal values in its future citizens. Since all citizens benefit from living in a liberal democracy, they have an interest, whether they understand it or not, in preserving it. The moral core of liberalism ought to be attractive and unobjectionable to all citizens. This moral core, according to Stephen Macedo, Richard Arneson, Ian Shapiro, and Amy Gutmann, consists of certain irreducible values in addition to those most critical to Rawls. In addition to the rules of fair play that make up Rawls's political conception of justice, the militant liberals would require that citizens share the values of individualism, critical rationality, and autonomy. To them, these three are core values and are therefore as nonnegotiable as the procedural ones that Rawls promotes.

They criticize Rawls for failing to appreciate that people will try to avoid direct conflict between their personal and political values. Rawls both misunderstands the extent to which liberalism constitutes a comprehensive conception and underestimates the ability of people to resist opposing comprehensive ideals without feeling the need to revise their preexisting comprehensive ideals. Either one or the other comprehensive conception must prevail. Liberalism, then, is more demanding than a mere set of rules for interacting with one's fellow citizens. According to Macedo, "Liberalism requires, therefore, not merely an overlapping consensus but a consensus that practically overrides all competing values."[8] Liberal values "occupy much the same space as personal comprehensive ideals, religious and otherwise."[9] When liberalism is acknowledged to be a comprehensive conception of justice, it becomes clear why conflict must arise. Liberalism cannot brook competition from nonliberal comprehensive conceptions of justice because two foundational belief systems cannot coexist as equals.

"The liberal virtues are at once political and personal, civic and private."[10] Personal shades into political, meaning that the success and stability of liberal politics demands that citizens' private beliefs and commitments become liberalized, that is, "deeply rooted as personality traits."[11] Liberal political autonomy is understood to be nearly synonymous with personal autonomy, thus making it acceptable for government to promote personal autonomy as a liberal political virtue.

Of course, its means are limited. "People have the right to lead lazy, narrow-minded lives."[12] However, society need not passively acquiesce to this choice, even when it is freely made. Liberalism is justified in endorsing and promoting not just a set of superficial political ideals but a comprehensive personality type. "The autonomous character is capable of affirming, rather than bemoaning liberal modernity, with its many possible ways of life, the openness of all choices, and its protean ideal."[13] Quiet obedience, deference, unquestioned devotion, and humility could not be counted among the liberal virtues, whereas self-criticism, introspection, perhaps also a degree of self-absorption or even narcissism are fully consistent with liberal virtues and personalities. If this is true, the Lubavitcher Chossid shares few of the attributes of the ideal liberal personality.

It is not entirely clear how the liberal personality produces responsible political deliberation in its citizens, or why the liberal virtues are seen as both civic and personal, public and private. The virtues of self-control, compromise, and accommodation, broad sympathy for others, and appreciation of inherited social ideals would no doubt be beneficial in any setting. Although the other liberal civic and personal virtues that are named—critical reflectiveness, willingness to experiment, and active, autonomous self-development—may glorify and protect individualism and perhaps even make for a more interesting life, they are hardly essential for political deliberation. The connection seems to be that these traits foster an appreciation of the many possible lives that might be ours. Liberalism, it is stated, encourages people to "regard their own ways as open to criticism and choice." The experience of inner value conflict encourages tentativeness in our commitments. "The liberal personality does not thrive on a harmonious inner life."[14]

The sensation of inner conflict or confusion is a characteristic of the liberal personality, preparing an individual for responsible citizenship by fostering the ability to make choices in a complex moral and political world. This implies that the ability to sift through complex information about the world around us is found only in those who have no strong foundational commitments. There are two opposed personality types, the liberal one, which is open-minded, and the nonliberal one, which is bigoted and xenophobic.[15] Phrased this way, there is no reason to mourn the extinction of the latter.

The quasi-Darwinian process of selection would undoubtedly mean the extinction of those cultures that cannot maintain their market share. As Stephen Macedo maintains: "Certain things of value may be lost in, or absent from, the forms of the good life that flourish in open, diverse, critical, experiential, uncertain, and ever-changing liberal societies. Stronger forms of community, deeper, unquestioning, untroubled forms of allegiance that might embody genuine forms of the good life are lost to societies that flourish in a liberal way."[16]

Clearly some choices preclude others. Once exposed to liberal society, "one can not choose to be simple or unworldly."[17] Liberal society would likely produce more uniformity or homogeneity by crowding out traditional communities. It is liberalism, not diversity, that is valued here: "Liberalism holds out the promise, or the threat, of making all the world like California. Liberalism creates a community in which it is possible to decide that next week I might quit my career in banking, leave my wife and children, and join a Buddhist cult. Life in a pluralistic liberal society is a smorgasbord confronting us with an exciting array of possibilities."[18]

This openness is not attractive to everyone. It is not obvious to everyone that moral relativism, which is often the product of the liberal personality, produces either individual or social good. Moral relativism can just as easily permit fascism as democracy. In fact, the growth of traditional religious movements whose ranks are swelled by refugees from liberal lifestyles refutes the contention that nonliberal values cannot compete with the overwhelmingly attractive liberal lifestyle. But, even if liberal theorists concede that one can autonomously choose a nonliberal lifestyle, they do not necessarily concede that this autonomous choice is therefore worthy of respect, as other autonomous choices might be. It has been asked, "Why respect a life that is servile, vile, conformist, even if autonomously chosen?"[19] If the culture of choice is clearly superior to any other culture, then the good life may require that we never develop a permanent allegiance to any specific conception of the good life. As political theorist Charles Larmore puts it: "We should always maintain only a contingent and never a constitutive allegiance to any substantial view of a good life, that is, to any concrete way of life involving a specific structure of purposes, significances, and activities . . . or to a particular religion. . . . The source of value, and so the supreme value, is what is expressed in this posture of choice."[20]

For some theorists, there is a clear connection between the individual as autonomous chooser and the democratic citizen. Since the ability and inclination to choose freely requires the ability to evaluate available choices, this skill becomes a valid public concern. The state must teach future citizens the art of "rational deliberation" in addition to the less demanding, more Rawlsian notion of "mutual respect." Freedom is simply not compatible with a life of unswerving faith. Rawls, according to this view, is too lenient about the political demands of democratic citizenship. Rawls contends that we can teach only the skills and virtues necessary to liberal democracy, without aspiring to teach autonomy and individualism. Those who disagree believe that the skills of democratic citizenship include the skills and virtues of autonomy and individualism and the ability and willingness to reflect upon many complex issues and lifestyles, including one's own. If these skills and virtues conflict with the religious convictions of the parents, so be it. "The skills of political reflection cannot be neatly differentiated from the skills of evaluating one's own life."[21]

That democratic education will interfere with the ability of some parents to transmit their values to their children does not constitute an injustice. When the state adopts a policy of civic education, it is not regarded as overbearing, though interfering with parental authority, yet "parents who would teach their children how to live their life" are condemned as "morally pretentious."[22] The government's attempts to transmit values do not elicit a similar condemnation. Is it because the government should be granted greater authority than the family, or is it because the government is transmitting substantively superior values? Apparently it is a bit of both. The government, through public education, is understood, in this view, to increase children's capacity for exercising freedom of choice, whereas parents, by attempting to raise their children with a specific set of values, restrict their children's capacity for exercising free choice.

It might be claimed that no single source of values, whether parents or schools, should be allowed a monopoly. Children should be exposed to many possible lifestyle choices without being indoctrinated with a single set of ideals. While the schools should recognize that "no single method of child rearing provides the unique path to liberal citizenship," and society should recognize a child's need for cultural coherence, parents, for their part, must come up with "a neutral justification for moral vocabulary and perceptions."[23] Here, authority over children is not justified by adult pretensions to moral superiority: the ultimate choice of a way of life is not up to teachers or parents but to children.[24] The role of liberal education is to provide cultural materials to allow for the elaboration of choices. The outcome of the educational process will be good citizens who refrain from imposing their perspectives on others out of a commitment to equal respect and moral equality. This allows a citizen to focus on justice in the political realm while avoiding the temptation of trying to impose a particular conception of the good. Although it is claimed that the principle of "neutral justification" for moral claims imposes the same burden on all parents and teachers, no Chossid could possibly come up with a neutral justification for his or her moral vocabulary and perceptions.

Perhaps there must be congruence between private and public values, meaning that we will put our system at risk if we fail to attend to the connection between the moral and political cultures. But the extent of overlap between democratic and liberal virtues is often overstated. In particular, critical rationality and autonomy are not demonstrably necessary components of democratic citizenship. I side with Rawls on this point. Critical rationality is as capable of producing incapacitating relativism as political commitment.

Autonomy and Reason

Liberalism has a particularly difficult time making sense of forms of reasoning that deviate from the Enlightenment model of individual rationality. Critical rationality is an offspring of the Enlightenment and its attitude toward other forms of reason smacks of sibling rivalry. Liberals claim that critical rationality is integrally linked to autonomy, and that both are essential to democracy. Other ways of knowing the world, particularly through faith, are denigrated. In fact, turning the investigative and rational powers of the human mind on nature has yielded remarkable improvements in human life, so much so that it is understandable why critical rationality has nearly eclipsed epistemic diversity and become an object of veneration itself. But how did it become part of the schools' civic as well as intellectual mission, enforceable even over some parents' objections? Why are religious beliefs, even when they do not in any way subvert the Constitution, assumed by many liberals to be antithetical to rational inquiry?

One can understand why civic peace, as liberals long ago discovered, is best maintained when the state prevents the public clash of fundamental and opposing beliefs. But assuming that opposing religious groups agree to comport themselves peacefully in the public realm, on what other grounds should we link the way in which they process information about the world to their civic competence?

Recent literature that pits critical rationality against religion does so on the assumption that received truths, in addition to probably not being true, are intellectually stultifying simply because of the way they are acquired. Trusting authority renders an individual incapable of distinguishing between fact and superstition. It would be better, in some views, to recognize the multiplicity of "truths," the subjectivity of "truths," and the relativity of "truths," even the nonexistence of "truth," rather than to accept any claim as true without personally dragging it over the coals of "critical thinking." Demonstrating the capacity for critical reason requires uncoerced, even unpersuaded, choice among options. But this doesn't require that the substance of the choice meet any standards of rationality or goodness. The process becomes more important than the content of the choice itself. This presupposes that a life in which autonomous choice is constantly exercised is, ceteris paribus, better than a life in which autonomous choices are not constantly exercised, without ever scrutinizing the choices according to some standard of worthiness.[25]

This conclusion would not strike everyone as reasonable. It presupposes that there is a moral reason to prefer the process of political deliberation over the outcome of such deliberation because autonomy only makes sense as a priority if we do so. The connections among autonomy, reason, and good citizenship are actually more tenuous than many liberals acknowledge. While the ability to deliberate about public policy and to critically evaluate candidates and elected officials is clearly a requirement of political judgment and civic competence, it is not clear that this form of rationality is incompatible with holding some values or accepted truths on faith. One must be careful not to confuse critical rationality with radical skepticism.[26] The state can fulfill its objective of preparing competent future citizens without casting doubt on their received moral and religious views.

A useful distinction between two forms of reasoning, which does not invalidate or derogate either, has been proposed by Robert Lipkin. Rejecting the overused dichotomy between communities of "faith" versus "reason," he says liberal societies may play host to two different kinds of communities, each possessing its distinctive form of reasoning and conception of the good. The first fits comfortably with liberalism. He calls this community "deliberative." People in this community are socialized in the use of critical rationality and encouraged to challenge and revise that society's norms and truths. They value change over continuity, novelty over tradition. The second type of community Lipkin calls "dedicated." People in dedicated communities employ a form of reasoning that emphasizes stability and continuity. They adhere to unchanging conceptions of truth, good, and the purpose of life. They see no reason to criticize or tamper with a perfected standard.

A liberal society need only require the employment of the deliberative attitude in the context of political reasoning and justification.[27] Otherwise, the dedicated attitude toward the world is not a liability to a democratic polity. But liberal theorists have a hard time finding dedicated cultures and their nondeliberative form of reasoning intelligible. This leads many liberals to doubt that members of these dedicated communities are capable of adopting the deliberative mode of reasoning when faced with political decisions. But an individual is capable of exercising both modes of reasoning, perhaps main-

taining a dedicated attitude with respect to her religious life and a deliberative stance with respect to her professional life. Whether Lubavitchers compartmentalize their religious and political lives and modes of reasoning will
be explored in the next chapter, but they clearly fit Lipkin's model of a dedicated community living in the midst of a deliberative one.

Diversity as a Good

As Isaiah Berlin poignantly notes, "There is no social world without loss."
But those worlds that are lost are not necessarily worse than those that flourish; they are simply unable to survive the corrosive forces of liberal freedom.[28] It is not clear that the loss of worlds is the price we must pay for social
unity. And if it is, the value consensus that emerges must be superior to the
normative diversity it replaces. Specifically, it must be more conducive to
democracy than what it replaces.

William Galston presents two models of free association, one based on the
principle of diversity and the other on autonomy. The autonomy model
would prohibit a group's nonliberal internal practices (leading to cultural homogeneity), and the diversity model would permit groups their illiberal internal practices as long as they permitted their members to exit freely. The
diversity model would preserve, in his view, elements of both diversity and
autonomy.

If we adopt something like the diversity model, would it become impossible to reach a social consensus on a core list of what constitutes "civic competence"? Galston believes that citizens only need to share the willingness to
coexist and exercise "minimal conditions of reasonable public judgment. . . .
Neither of these civic requirements entails a need for public authority to take
an interest in how children think about different ways of life." Civic virtues
are compatible with personal commitments of many sorts. The state over-
steps its authority when it attempts to "foster in children skeptical reflection
on ways of life inherited from parents or local communities."[29]

Emphasizing what might properly be called personality traits rather than
essential citizenship competencies violates the stipulation that "the government cannot throw its weight behind a conception of the human good unrelated to the functional needs of its sociopolitical institutions and at odds with
the deep beliefs of many of its loyal citizens."[30] Unless the state can show a
compelling interest, free exercise of religion, including the right to pass on
religious beliefs to one's children, ought to prevail. Galston shares the concern expressed by Rawls, Gutmann, Macedo, and other liberal theorists that

a line must be drawn between "reasonable" and "unreasonable" forms of diversity. But he feels that they have drawn the line in too restrictive a way. It should be drawn, in his view, "between those that do or don't reject the essentials of democratic regimes,"[31] rather than between those that do or don't possess liberal personality traits.

Lubavitcher parents, teachers, and school principals that I interviewed were divided on the need to introduce civic education into the curriculum. Some thought it might be useful. Others, who disapproved, did so not on grounds that good citizenship is a trivial concern but out of confidence that these skills can be acquired without any special tutoring, simply by dint of living in one's country. Many expressed the view that teaching a child to be a Torah-respecting Jew is tantamount to teaching him or her to be a good citizen.

As for the putative need to teach children to reason critically, Lubavitchers, to a person, were quite confident that their children were being taught to reason carefully. The curriculum of the boys' yeshiva is divided into two tracks: holy and general. Only a tiny fraction of the parents (myself included) put their boys into the program that includes a secular component. That means that the vast majority of Lubavitcher boys will have virtually no contact with secular subjects after they become Bar Mitzvah, but it does not mean that the students do not learn how to think precisely and carefully, if not "critically."

My fourteen-year-old son spends many hours a day memorizing a handful of lines of Gemara, the part of the Talmud that contains commentaries on *mishnahs,* or laws. These laws are decidedly arcane. The various commentaries are exceedingly difficult to penetrate and class discussion can go on for hours over minutiae, the very definition of hairsplitting. Most philosophy and law professors I know would have to struggle with the passages that comprise the daily study of these boys. Many liberal educators, focusing on the hours of memorization and close analysis of the material that comprise Lubavitcher education, would proclaim it to be slavish, intellectually stultifying, and the very antithesis of the training needed to think creatively, freely, and critically.

In fact, this sort of study produces a style of reasoning that, while cautious, humble, and hesitant, is keen, acute, and very clear. One could easily call it critical rationality, as long as this term is not understood to mean radical skepticism. Although it would be considered arrogant for a young student to indulge in flights of interpretive fantasy or treat the text as a vehicle for developing his own personal opinions in the face of two thousand years of scholarly exegesis, being able to raise an insightful question and eventually offer an incisive interpretation are the eventual goals for most students. The "uprooter of mountains" is a rare scholar indeed. The sages emphasize that there are four types of students: one like a sponge, who absorbs everything uncritically; one like a funnel, through whom everything passes; one like a strainer, who allows the wine to flow through while retaining the sediment; and one like a sifter, who keeps the fine flour while losing the chaff.[32] The last student is clearly the ideal. In any case, it is understood that being able to receive precedes being able to criticize, challenge, or contribute to the body of knowledge.

The complexity of Jewish texts and laws has meant that the scholarly tradition has been replete with conflicting interpretations and even paradoxes through the ages. There has been no attempt to force consensus when disagreements over interpretation have arisen. The very structure of a page of Talmud suggests this: at the center of each page is a portion of mishnah surrounded by several, often contradictory, commentaries. A distinction is drawn between "controversies which are for the sake of heaven" (as in the disagreements between the great sages, Hillel and Shamai, who are both declared to be correct) and "controversies which are not for the sake of heaven" and therefore, like sophistry, will have no "abiding result" (*Perkei Avot* 5:17). The constant tension involved in the struggle to rise above one's natural, physical, moral, and intellectual constraints in order to live in accordance with G-d's demands belies the stereotype of religious people as relying on a handful of simplistic accepted truths or blind faith. Against the intellectual intricacies of Torah, Talmud, Kaballah, and Tanya, most political issues must appear relatively straightforward. There is no reason to believe that the nature of reason exercised by Chassidim, despite its departure from the Enlightenment model, incapacitates the Lubavitchers as democratic citizens when they wade into the complex world of politics.

In short, determining the proper scope and content of civic education relies on answering the question of what belongs on the list of essential citizenship virtues. The state may properly foster certain salutary political habits and skills, but beyond that it should refrain from interfering with family life, as long as parents do not "impede the acquisition of basic civic education to function competently in civic affairs."[33] A few basic skills are required for political deliberation, and critical rationality and autonomous reflection on one's received values are not among them.

The Liberal Personality: Autonomy and the Open Life

Does democracy entail a commitment to individual autonomy? Many liberals hold that autonomy is the basis of both freedom and democracy. The con-

ception of the individual as an autonomous agent that freely selects and revises his or her life plans and values is a cornerstone of liberal theory. This is
hardly a neutral conception of human nature, but supposing that it could be
demonstrated that autonomy is a desirable human trait or goal, can it therefore be demonstrated that autonomy is a necessary trait of good citizenship?
Does democracy entail skepticism about one's conception of the good? Does
the lack of skepticism about one's conception of the good render one incapable of the sort of political deliberation that is required in a democracy?

The liberal concept of autonomy derives from the Enlightenment conviction that the individual is the source of his or her own values and preferences.
He or she need not rely on external, preexisting authorities, traditions, customs, or faith, which had historically guided human actions. Reason and
autonomy are conjoined because reason confirms and is confirmed by the evidences of the senses. Unshackled reason can prevail over superstition and
ignorance, with unfettered progress the result. Some religions (such as
Protestant Christianity or Reform Judaism) conform to the Enlightenment
principle that "free religious exercise can only be entered into by an act of
autonomous will," but other religions do not and are thus condemned as
"mindless, cultish behavior."[34]

As William Galston points out, "autonomy-based arguments will marginalize those who do not share the Enlightenment project."[35] For him, the hallmark of the liberal state is tolerance of diversity, which means the refusal of
the state to use its power to impose one way of life by altering the practices
of groups that do not accept it. "Liberalism is about the protection of diversity, not the valorization of choice."[36] Autonomy, then, is not one of the
"shared liberal purposes" because it is not essential to good citizenship or the
functioning of the democratic state.

However, other theorists treat autonomous critical thinking as a requirement of good citizenship. For them, it is autonomy even more than critical
rationality that creates the imperative behind the state's educational program.
A child possesses a "right to an open future." The ability to evaluate political candidates is only a part of this right. As for parental claims, "The rights
of parents are positive rights granted by the state, and can be rescinded by
the state."[37] In commenting on *Yoder v. Wisconsin* (1972) Richard Arneson
and Ian Shapiro contend that the Supreme Court underrated the connection
between autonomy, critical reflection, and democracy. Yoder should have lost
on grounds that the Amish deny their children critical, rational autonomy,
whatever the other virtues of the Amish way of life.[38]

Making individual autonomy the cornerstone not only of the liberal personality but of the democratic one licenses the state to interfere with parental authority. But there may be a "disconnect" between autonomy as a value and autonomy as a democratic skill. While the modern arguments for limited government, toleration, and political freedom are all intertwined with the liberal conception of humans as individuals, the elevation of the private individual and his pursuit of self-interest is not essential to the normative argument for democracy. In fact, as has been noted, excessive individualism and self-absorption can be detrimental to democratic citizenship. What is at stake is the demotion of the ideal of public life and the pursuit of a common good. Ironically, many political theorists recognize the need to reinstate public life but are at a loss about how this can be accomplished without jeopardizing individual autonomy.

That the state and public life would become the handmaidens of individuals is an inevitable consequence of the liberalism of J. S. Mill, Emerson, Thoreau, and Whitman, who all contributed to the sanctification of individualism and the idea that society should not only respect but create the preconditions for the full flowering of individuality. "Human flourishing" is equated with the cultivation of one's individuality. Society becomes the backdrop against which the individual, like some modern-day Odysseus, undertakes his journey of self-creation. "The autonomous individual [turns] his participation in social practices into performances expressive of his individuality."[39] There is an ambivalent note here. On the one hand, the state may indoctrinate students in a set of skills designed to serve the common life of the polity; on the other hand, the state is understood to be the stage on which the individual plays out his personal pursuits. The reconciliation of private and public ends seems to be found in the claim that the skills and values of liberalism simultaneously cause both the state and the individual to flourish. What gets left out of the picture is the array of attachments and loyalties to subnational units possessed by most individuals. The state is neither the sole protector of an individual's rights nor the sole source of coercion.

Both political freedom and personal freedom are the means by which people escape the rule of force, and the means whereby they exercise self-creation, self-critical evaluation, and the revision of values and plans. In this view, freedom requires throwing off the yoke of all noncontractual, nonvoluntary obligations, values, and duties imposed by tribe, clan, family, religion, nation, tradition, custom, sentiment, and the like, but not the underlying obligation and loyalty to the state. Freedom is attained when one breaks free from external authority and from particular or local attachments, but not from the external authority of the state. The liberal personality "has the capacity to welcome rather than fear or find unsettling the availability of a wide range of choices,"[40] but it nonetheless presumably autonomously chooses to be subject to the state. Political freedom and individual autonomy become congruent, even synonymous. But what is missing is associational life, which creates the buffer that protects both individual freedom (from encroachments by the state) and the democratic institutions of the state (from the retreat of the individual into private life). Groups serve the interests of both states and citizens, yet they are not integral to liberal theory.

Sources of Identity, Values, and Preferences

If there are a variety of valid forms of reason, there are a variety of sources of the self. How we come by our identities, values, and preferences is of particular interest to communitarian critics of liberalism. Michael Sandel views the neutrality doctrine of liberalism as useful because it provides a matrix for individual choice, but he criticizes the liberal understanding of the choosing individual in isolation from his or her social or cultural milieu. The liberal individual is described by Rawls as a "self-originating source of valid claims," unencumbered by any purposes, plans, objectives, or commitments that he or she has not freely chosen. The self is therefore prior to its ends. This being the case, by implication "rights" must be prior to the "good," and government, in order to respect individual choosers as equals, must remain neutral with respect to the various conceptions of the good that these individuals select. Sandel calls Rawls's priority of right over good liberalism's foundational flaw. He questions not only the plausibility of this conception but its impact on community. By adopting the Kantian principle that all obligations must be voluntarily and contractually undertaken by individuals, liberals have a hard time respecting notions of community ties, duties, and commitments that do not appear to have been consciously chosen by the individual who is bound by them. Sandel criticizes liberal theory not simply because it pretends to be neutral when it actually affirms individualistic values, but because it fails to adequately account for the source of our identity and our preferences. "The vaunted independence of the deontological subject is a liberal illusion."[41]

The liberal conception of the individual is particularly manifest in its characteristic voluntarist position on religion. The core ideals of autonomy and neutrality require that religious beliefs worthy of respect are autonomously and voluntarily chosen by a chooser who is unencumbered by any convictions prior to the choice. Freedom of conscience is defined as the right to choose one's beliefs. This perspective both misunderstands and invalidates the commitment of many religious people, Lubavitchers included, who understand themselves as claimed or chosen by their religious convictions. The goal of their religion is not to serve a broader mission of protecting individual autonomy or to advance individual self-fulfillment.[42] They cannot make sense of the liberal ideal self as free from customs, loyalties, faith, tradition, law, duties, community, and responsibility. To Lubavitchers, the "right" to voluntarily choose one's religious beliefs may be consonant with the Protestant understanding, but it is not the Jewish one.

It is not that Lubavitchers fail to respect freedom, it is that they hold a different view of it: Freedom is achieved in the fulfillment of one's responsibilities to G-d and the community. Freedom is defined by the sages as a life lived according to Torah. One may freely choose to cleave to Torah or reject it, but a life contrary to Torah, although the product of choice, cannot itself be free. In addition, the valid source of self-originating claims is outside of humans. G-d's Torah, in this view, is not an instrument through which Jews are enabled to "find themselves" or even to live a good or happy life.

A Jew is a Jew, in their view, because of their relationship to Torah. He or she can be a good person, a happy person, or even a spiritual person without observing the commandments. The justification for living according to Torah is not that a Torah life is better, more individually fulfilling, or happier. The purpose of following G-d's commandments in the Chassidic view is because that is what G-d wants. A Torah life draws one beyond the self. Although this sort of religious conviction may not emphasize individual autonomy, it does not erode the civic virtue required by citizens of a democratic state. If anything, Chassidim are uniquely prepared for the idea of obligation to something beyond the self, which gives them a leg up on more individualistic citizens.

Will Kymlicka defends liberalism against what he believes is Sandel's overstatement of liberalism's deontological bent and disregard for its teleological bent. Social roles and relationships are important in the individual's process of preference formation. Like Sandel, Kymlicka understands that choices are developed and exercised in a social context and that humans are social beings. The more contexts, presumably, the more values and identities from which to choose. This leads to Kymlicka's characteristic concern for the preservation of minority cultures. But he still can't or won't make the case for preserving any specific culture as opposed to another. He would not be likely to validate the claim that Lubavitchers would suffer irreparable loss of freedom and identity if deprived of Chassidic culture, as long as alternative cultures were available to them.

While many liberals like Rawls hold that we have a highest-order interest in our capacity to form and revise our rational life plans, for Kymlicka we have an interest in deliberating about and pursuing not just any life but as good a life as possible.[43] For Kymlicka, the question is whether liberal society provides us with the means to do this. His two preconditions for fulfilling this interest in leading a good life are, first, "That we lead our life from the inside, in accordance with our beliefs about what gives value to life"; and, second, "That we be free to question these beliefs, to examine them in light of whatever information and examples and arguments our culture can provide."[44] He concludes that liberal societies provide sufficient resources to allow individuals to explore possible lives and values.

Liberalism is not indifferent to how we come by our preferences, projects, and values, or how we decide which are worthy. While Sandel doubts that humans can detach themselves from "authoritative horizons," which are provided by our communal and cultural practices, and "shared constitutive ends," Kymlicka believes that liberals and communitarians are not really that far apart on the issue of our ability to detach ourselves from our ends and scrutinize them.

Kymlicka attempts to reconcile strands of liberal and communitarian theories of the self, drawing upon Sandel and Rawls. For Rawls, the self is prior to its ends and its boundaries are fixed. The individual is not bound to or identical with his ends, but can freely revise them. For Sandel, the individual is constituted by his ends and his boundaries are fluid. For Rawls, the individual chooses his ends; for Sandel, the individual discovers his ends. But they both agree that the person exists in essence independent of his chosen ends. For Kymlicka, the issue of whether we perceive ourselves as prior to our ends or see ourselves as embedded in a culture and encumbered with ends that we discover, rather than choose, is not as divisive as many liberals and communitarians contend.

Kymlicka finds common ground in the fact that both liberals and their communitarian critics agree that "no end or goal is exempt from possible reexamination."[45] "We have lost the naïve faith necessary to consciously let the community set goals for us,"[46] presumably whether that community is religious, liberal, Marxist, and so forth. Any individual is capable of imagining himself with a different set of ends and values than those he now possesses. We may be shaped by our cultural context, but we maintain sufficient detachment and objectivity at the same time. The boundaries of the self are permeable, no matter how carefully reinforced they are by culture. Maintaining a traditional stance has become a self-conscious choice.

Once they acknowledge that even the most encumbered individual retains the capacity to reexamine his or her constitutive ends, communitarians fail to prove that individuals should not be given the conditions necessary for this reexamination. But by implication, once it is established that the individual, no matter how encumbered by prior values and commitments, always retains a degree of distance and objectivity, there is no excuse to deny that in essence all individuals, Lubavitchers included, retain a degree of autonomy. Communitarians may have failed to justify any major revision of liberal political principles, yet liberals have failed to justify their claim that autonomy is either a specifically liberal trait or that it comes in a package deal with critical rationality. Even if autonomy is a condition of democratic citizenship, by this account we all possess it. In short, autonomy, the open life, and critical rationality may all be ingredients of the liberal life, but they are not essential to the functioning of the democratic citizen.

A Note on the Concept of Tolerance

Why does liberalism have such a hard time tolerating nonliberal ways of life? Toleration is supposed to be a central liberal virtue, and the one most likely to support diversity on normative grounds. As long as the concept of toleration is derived from the principle of equal respect, it can support diversity. But most arguments in favor of toleration seem to be harnessed to a higher goal. Rarely is toleration regarded as a good in its own right.

John Locke was perhaps the first to articulate the practical relationship between tolerance and peaceful coexistence among citizens of different faiths. His approval of toleration as a political virtue was guarded and prudential. J. S. Mill is often characterized as the strongest voice in favor of toleration, yet he also understood tolerance in instrumental terms, as a remedy for slavish intellectual conformity that stood in the way of individual creativity, and hence of social progress. Toleration was intended to allow alternative views to contend in order that the truth might be revealed. Neither Locke nor Mill made a case for normative toleration as mutual respect.

To this day, the two most common forms of toleration proceed out of forbearance and intellectual humility. The first variant has us put up with others' substantive choices that we find personally obnoxious and even abhorrent. We feel compelled to permit these choices so long as the law does. An alternative variant derives from intellectual humility. Because we are not certain that truth is knowable or even exists, we tolerate other versions in the hope that ours will be tolerated. If all human reason is fallible, then toleration is the only justifiable, or at least prudent, stance. Both forms of toleration can be seen as democratic virtues in that they permit civil harmony.

Lubavitchers find both forms of toleration to be potentially pernicious, despite the ironic fact that they are often its beneficiaries. It is precisely because they acknowledge the fallibility of human knowledge that they rely on the absolute, eternal, and comprehensive truth of the Torah. While they are quite happy to tolerate others under the principle of "live and let live," they are fully aware of the potential danger of this seemingly benevolent attitude.

Tolerance as a product of human fallibility and intellectual humility promotes, in addition to the virtue of forbearance, two ugly possibilities. The first is moral relativism in which the actor, either the individual or the society, flounders in moral uncertainty and is unable to exercise moral judgment. Although this form of tolerance may not commit evil, it will certainly not intervene to prevent it. The other ugly possibility is that tolerance will transform itself into its opposite, and ironically, become something of a sacred cow. Originally the by-product of intellectual humility, it now becomes an absolute dogma. Toleration can then be exercised as a lever against nonliberal cultures, demanding that they reciprocate by practicing the liberal virtues in the name of toleration.

Then liberal society can justifiably withhold toleration from the intolerant, meaning the nonliberal communities in its midst. Tolerance as reciprocity can be found at the heart of ecumenical religious services. While Lubavitchers might be quite welcoming to Christians who want to visit their shuls, they cannot reciprocate by attending church services. There are theological reasons why it is impossible for them to do so. It would be difficult to explain these reasons to a Christian friend, but the reasons outweigh even the desire not to hurt a friend's feelings. It is not a manifestation of intolerance. It only appears to be when one confuses respect and reciprocity. Chassidim respect Christians who attend church, and prefer in principle Christians who do so. Here, tolerance means respect not reciprocity.

Similarly, I am quite happy to have my Christian friends to my house for a meal, but I cannot reciprocate. It may appear intolerant that I am unwilling to accept their hospitality when they accept mine, or experiment with their customs and cuisine when they experiment with mine, but they make no religious sacrifices to eat my food, whereas, for purely religious reasons, it is out of the question for me to reciprocate by eating theirs.

Therefore, although Lubavitchers' refusal to participate in cross-cultural exchanges may be vilified as intolerant, this misses the point. Lubavitchers are respectful of other peoples' practices. They are so respectful, in fact, that they take the religious content of these practices more seriously than some Christians do. Christmas, from the viewpoint of Lubavitchers, is really a religious holiday, even when it is passed off as neutral or as a secular "winter festival." Accusations that they are being intolerant do not move them.

Groups that are often condemned for their refusal to tolerate (meaning, to embrace) antithetical values are most often the ones that have to exercise de facto tolerance anyway. They have no choice because they are in the minority.

The minority is less threatening to the majority than the other way around since it is unable to impose its values outside the narrow confines of its community. Regardless of how distasteful it may find the culture or habits of the majority, it has no choice but to exercise tolerance. Yet, all that is required of the majority toward the "diverse" elements of society is a bit of forbearance, as long as the behavior of these groups remains within the boundaries of the law. Requiring that the minority serve liberal purposes is an excessive show of liberal muscle flexing when minorities are hardly in a position to undermine liberal society. Minorities, unlike majorities, cannot rely on passive absorption to pass their traditions on to their offspring, but must make a concerted effort to do so. Finally, it is disingenuous to argue that the majority is justified in withholding toleration from minority groups that do not fully reciprocate. Toleration may take the form of respect, rather than reciprocity.

With a foundation in autonomy, liberalism can do no more than accept the toleration of non-autonomy-valuing subgroups as a necessary evil, not as a genuine good. As Susan Mendus argues, "Indeed, arguments from autonomy tend to construe toleration as the right of the tolerated, not merely as a virtue in the tolerator. Therefore, toleration is something which may be claimed as an entitlement, since it is this alone which displays due and proper respect for persons in all their diversity."[47] Liberalism will find a more solid position from which to exercise toleration if it can find an intrinsic reason to value diverse groups unrelated to their ability to serve liberal purposes.

How are we to understand Lubavitchers and other nonindividualist cultures in the context of the debate over the source of our sense of identity and our ends and preferences? Certainly, these are people who conform more closely to the communitarian model because they understand themselves to have been born to fulfill a set of constitutive ends. They would not deny that their values and ends were established by ancient authority long before they received them. Yet, they understand their acceptance of them as voluntary. Voluntary acceptance of this charge from G-d and community is the central aspect of the milestone of Bar and Bat Mitzvah, when boys and girls willingly take upon themselves the fulfillment of the *mitzvot*, or commands of G-d.

Asked if they have chosen their ends in the liberal sense, most Lubavitchers would say no. Asked if they freely accept these ends, all would say yes.

Asked if these ends are reasonable, all would say yes again. Although aware of other values and ends that exist in society, they see themselves as having reasonably rejected them in favor of the good life. Their capacity to reason, according to Lubavitchers, is fully operational. They do not suspend it in order to be able to maintain their world of meaning.

CHAPTER SIX

Lubavitch Reason: Intellect,
Faith, and Obligation

And the intelligent will understand. . . . The devout will perceive.
                              Likutei Amarim, vol. 2, chap. 35

Faith is not the absence of reason, it is a skill in its own right, which, when
cultivated, allows us to experience the ultimate.
        Menachem Mendel Schneerson, "Toward a Meaningful Life"

When collisions occur between Lubavitchers and liberal soci-
ety, the parties often find each other unintelligible. From its position of dominance, liberals can claim a monopoly on political reasoning and cast doubt
on the political competence of their Chassidic neighbors. Lubavitchers, for
their part, see political reasoning as indistinguishable from common sense,
requiring nothing special in the way of discernment or profundity.

   Is there anything inherent in the concept of rationality that justifies making a distinction between those who possess reason and those who do not, or
at least not in the sense that secular liberalism understands? Can a citizen exercise political judgment without adhering to the liberal conception of autonomy and rationality?

   Lubavitchers exercise their reason differently from the general, or at least
secular, public in many respects. They believe some things that outsiders
would find strange, incomprehensible, even downright crazy. For instance,
people accept that the earth is 5,763 years old. No one believes in evolution.
Everyone believes in the power of prayer. Everyone believes in *hashgacha protis* (divine intentionality) in everything that happens in the world. Everyone
believes that *tzaddikim* (righteous men) achieve special closeness to G-d and
may also possess miraculous powers in the tradition of the *ba'al mofsim* (master of miracles).

   Consonant with this belief, many Lubavitchers sought out the advice and
blessings of their Rebbe, Menachem Mendel Schneerson, when he was alive,
and continue to do so now that he is dead. Lubavitchers come from all over
the world to pay visits to the Rebbe's grave (*Ohel*) in Brooklyn. Many leave

written requests on the grave, confident that they will be fulfilled. Many people e-mail or fax the Ohel from their personal computer.

The principal of the Montreal yeshiva, a respected scholar and sensible
man, described to me how his father was forced to put aside his skepticism
about the Rebbe's powers because he could no longer dismiss the sensory evidence that supported them. Lubavitchers will tell you that they, just as you,
are unable to believe in something that is not supported by their reason and
senses. I will leave it to psychologists and sociologists to attempt to explain
how otherwise sane and practical people can believe things that leave secular
minds incredulous. I suppose one could simply label all Lubavitchers irrational, or one could find them partially rational, with respect to their mundane activities, and partially irrational, with respect to their religious life.

Lubavitchers do not regard themselves as possessing split personalities or
dualistic worldviews. They will tell you that they do not live in two worlds,
but one unified world, with a few levels. They will tell you that their thought
processes are both reasonable and rational, and that what they believe about
the world is both sensible and true. They will tell you, like all good empiri-
cists, that their senses compel them to believe what they believe.

Although it is not for outsiders to assess the truth claims of the Lubavitch,
by presenting the core of what Lubavitchers believe from within their world
of meaning, I hope their form of reason will not seem so alien, even though
it diverges to a degree from the form of rationality that gained epistemic
dominance, if not monopoly, after the Enlightenment. It is not my purpose
to try to "unseat the monologue of reason" or to reveal it as a historically contingent view of reality that is rooted in power relations. That can be left to
Michel Foucault and his followers. Rather, I will discuss the predicament of
religious citizens who may find themselves labeled as "irrational" by liberal
society because of the way they deliberate about politics and the language
they use to justify their political choices. They may be so labeled even though
the outcome of their process of deliberation, in terms of voting and other political behavior, may be indistinguishable from the majority's. But even if they
still retain that aura of irrationality in the eyes of outsiders, the only relevant
question for the rest of society is whether the particular form of reason possessed by Lubavitchers—and other deeply religious individuals—incapacitates them from exercising their citizenship responsibly.

Arguably, in a liberal democracy we need not concern ourselves with our
fellow citizens' thought processes, for, to paraphrase Thomas Jefferson, as
long as our neighbor neither breaks our leg nor picks our pocket, what harm
can there be if he believes things that we find eccentric? Whether our neighbors seem to us to be rational is not a political issue, but how they express

their views in the public square might be. Of course, we have little evidence, other than self-reporting, about how individuals deliberate on a policy issue or candidate. The raw data contained in a vote is not very revealing. Two people can vote the same way for very different and perhaps equally irrational reasons. Yet if an individual reports that his vote was based on self-interest, this fits the liberal model of rational behavior. If an individual reports that he put aside his self-interest in order to cast his vote in favor of a common good, he is regarded as noble, if somewhat quixotic. But if an individual reports that he voted based on religious dictates, he is regarded as irrational.

When the motivation behind political action is revealed in political speech, there are legal and political theorists who demand that the reasoning process conform to certain standards of rationality, which, not surprisingly, serve liberal purposes. Some insist that whatever their process of deliberation, citizens in a liberal society have an obligation to purge their thought processes of nonsecular motives or justifications. Others, slightly more realistically, ask only that individuals refrain from voicing justifications that are not secular or else find a way of couching their motives in justificatory language that is secular by the time it reaches the public square.

In his book *The Culture of Disbelief*,[1] Steven Carter made the argument that religious citizens are sidelined in the political process because of the silence imposed on them by the requirement that they keep their form of reasoning out of the public realm. This claim sparked a great deal of interesting debate across a wide spectrum. A significant portion of the scholarly discussion has focused on the First Amendment, the framers' "real" intentions, or the various possible interpretations that can be attributed to the ambiguous language of the establishment and free exercise clauses contained within it. For the purposes of this discussion, the relevant concept is "public reason."

Various views about what sorts of arguments, reasoning, and justifications ought to be recognized in the public square have been expressed. The neutralist position demands that political choices not be made that cannot be defended without relying on religious beliefs. The neutralists include John Rawls, whose achievement of an "overlapping consensus" relies on each citizen exercising self-restraint by not importing their comprehensive moral or religious conceptions into the public realm. The appropriate posture for citizens might be one of "epistemic abstinence."[2]

Political speech may be religious not because of what is said but because it is justified by scripture or revelation rather than by neutral, universally accessible reason. We must accept the notion of public (secular) reason because only secular arguments can persuade rational beings. Since laws are coercive, we have the right to impose legal restrictions on others only if we can offer them a secular justification. Therefore, all political arguments should adhere to the "principle of secular motivation."[3] An essentially neutralist position would ask that citizens refer only to shared premises about justice that would allow both religious and nonreligious citizens to discuss politics without addressing metaphysical or foundational issues. In this view, the requirement of secular reasoning imposes an equal burden on all citizens.[4]

It could further be argued that we should exclude religious speech from the public realm on grounds that the framers intended something more than mere state neutrality. In this view, the establishment clause entails the affirmative establishment of a secular political order. Therefore, public moral disputes can only be resolved on grounds that are capable of being articulated in secular terms. While religious individuals may feel unfairly hamstrung by this requirement, the asymmetrical treatment of religion in the public realm might be an intentional and unavoidable feature of the social contract to which we owe civil peace, and from which all religions benefit. According to this view, our Constitution intends to endorse a culture of secular liberal democracy.[5] In answer to the question of whether Rawls's "overlapping consensus" includes religious voices,[6] the answer would be "no." In its place, we might offer a more generous and lenient reading of the free exercise clause to offset the more stringent and restrictive reading of the establishment clause.

Those who regard themselves as more receptive to religious arguments by permitting them to be introduced into public discussion often attach the proviso that they meet the standard of "public accessibility" or intelligibility. They demand of the religious citizen a certain intellectual humility; that is, that he accept the fallibility of his position. This citizen must maintain an attitude of self-critical rationality and at least a bit of detachment. In other words, his convictions must not be unshakable. But this ideal is not, in the end, neutral. It would continue to exclude Lubavitch religious positions on many issues just as surely as the strictest readings of the establishment clause because Lubavitchers will not accept the fallibilist and accessibility criteria.

Excluding religious arguments of their sort would create two classes of citizens: those whose arguments are privileged in the public realm, and those whose are not because the substance of their speech fails the test of rationality, fallibilism, or accessibility.[7] Any version of the exclusivist position will favor religions that place a priority on individual autonomy and self-revising rationality. Why should "those who view pluralism and fallibilism as vices accept them as norms of civic virtue?"[8] The neutralist and exclusivist standards of public speech have a strong conservative, even elitist, bias that favors the mainstream religious establishment.

Finally, there is no greater likelihood of achieving political consensus by stripping language of all references to religion. Because a large part of our shared conception of justice is derived from religion, it might be easier to build a consensus starting there. Equality, the sanctity of life and property, economic justice, natural right and natural law may be expressed as secular concepts, but they have their origin in religious tradition. The abolitionist movement, the women's rights movement, and the civil rights movement all employed unabashedly religious language. Since no one has yet articulated a widely accepted secular theory of justice, we ought to continue to mine our religious traditions.[9] For those who see our religious traditions as the source of our highest political ideals, the prospect of a public square denuded of these ideals poses a much greater danger to democracy than does their presence.[10] A fully "inclusivist" position would go beyond welcoming bland "ecumenical" religious speech. According to this position, there is no reason to silence anyone, since all public laws, in the final analysis, have to be couched in secular terms. Moreover, we can be fairly confident that democratic processes will tend to sideline fringe groups.[11]

While the debate about public reason is far from resolved in either academia or the courts, it reveals, at the very least, that there is more than one conception of reason operating in our society. Some may count this epistemic pluralism as valuable to democracy; others may find it damaging. My view is that people should be free to offer whatever justification they wish for their political choices. It is certainly in most people's interests to make their position as accessible and appealing to the largest number of people. Democracy imposes the requirement that a victorious position muster a majority, and this in itself tames the most extreme political speech. The sensitive question is whether many of us would be willing to live with outcomes that were not liberal, but were arrived at through democratic procedures. The exclusivist position on political speech may then be understood as a way of exercising veto power over nonliberal, as opposed to undemocratic, outcomes.

If there is no obvious political solution to this problem on the horizon, how should we behave when we encounter an argument that seems alien or inaccessible? Does civility dictate that religious people curb their views or at least tailor them to the requirements of public reason? Perhaps civility and social solidarity dictate that we give our neighbors the benefit of the doubt even if their reasons elude us, as long as principles of justice are not at stake. I know people who do not believe that men landed on the moon. I know people who firmly believe in time and space travel, auras, reincarnation, and other things that I regard as, well, unlikely, yet when we discuss politics I find their reasoning to be impeccably logical, acute, and cogent. I never know what lies behind their political choices and views. They may distil them from voices in the air. But I am perfectly satisfied that they can articulate these views in accessible, if not always persuasive, terms. Now, this might be an argument against the position I want to defend. If people who hold views that do not conform to conventional standards of rationality are able to couch their political views in language that does, why can't everyone? Shouldn't this be a model for all political speech?

Several examples illustrate the impossibility of couching some issues in secular language. My time and space traveling friends are able to compartmentalize their lives in such a way that their "otherworldly" views rarely impinge on their assessment of political issues and candidates. They can find justifications for their political choices that are pretty mainstream and will not elude their neighbors' attempts to make sense of them. No secular justification can be provided, however, for the commandment to keep the laws of kashrut, yet Jews have asked the state to uphold these laws in the marketplace. Kashrut belongs to the category of mitzvot called *chukim*, which cannot be understood through human reason. In this category also belongs the prohibition against *sha'atnez*, or the wearing of garments that are a mixture of wool and linen by anyone but the high priest. Also in this category are the laws of *taharat ha mishpacha* (family purity), which mandate the strict separation of husband and wife for part of the month.

Some contemporary Jews have sought rational reasons for these chukim: practical or health-related justifications, say, for avoiding pork. But when unable to find a satisfying rational explanation for these commandments, many Jews have declared that they are no longer binding. For the Orthodox, chukim are binding for the simple reason that G-d declared them to be so, and for them that is a more powerful and compelling reason for obedience than anything relying on practicality or utility for its justification.

As for the other two categories of mitzvot, *eidos* (commandments to remember and observe various holidays, festivals, and miraculous events) and *mishpotim* (commandments that regulate human relationships), the rationale behind these is easily accessible to human reason. In fact, prohibitions against lying, cheating, stealing, murder, and adultery are not only accessible to human reason but one can imagine societies or individuals generating such prohibitions based on reason alone, with or without instructions from a deity. To Lubavitchers the beauty of chukim, in part, is that they are further evidence of the omnipotent "otherness" of G-d. If Jews were instructed only to obey rational mitzvot, they could also come to believe that these commandments, so accessible to human reason, were the product of humans and not G-d.

The chukim, by commanding Jews to fulfill seemingly irrational commands, lead the observant Jew to understand that obedience to G-d's will is the whole point of Torah. I have heard Lubavitchers say that even if the ful-fillment of mitzvot led to a miserable rather than a happy life, it would still be their obligation to do as G-d commanded. If the laws of kashrut demanded that meat and milk be consumed together, they would do that. As one Lubav-itcher put it, he was very grateful that G-d had not prohibited chocolate, though it would make dieting a lot easier if he had done so. Orthodox Jews are confident that there are reasons behind chukim and that these reasons will eventually be revealed. In this sense, they resemble people who remain con-fident that while a scientific explanation for a particular phenomenon may not be available to us at present, a scientific explanation does indeed exist and will be discovered eventually. In both cases, an element of faith is involved.

For the most part, whatever Orthodox Jews choose to do is not political in nature and requires nothing from, or has no impact on, their non–Jewish neighbors. But in several recent cases, Jews have found themselves in con-frontations with either neighbors or the law without the wherewithal to ex-plain their reasoning in secular terms.

In one case, Simcha Goldman, an Orthodox U.S. Army captain, found himself unable to convince his superiors, and then the Supreme Court, that the wearing of a *kippah* or *yarmulke* (head covering) is obligatory for Jewish men rather than voluntary.[12] It took Congress to override this Supreme Court ruling. In another highly publicized and controversial case involving the Satmar Chassidim's attempt to create a school district coextensive with their township, and yet another involving their refusal to permit female bus drivers on boys' school buses, the Satmar were unsuccessful in persuading the courts to their point of view.[13] A more permissive reading of the free ex-ercise clause might have remedied these problems, as might a more sympa-thetic attitude on the part of neighbors.

Orthodox Jews have been much more successful in getting the govern-ments of Canada and the United States as well as state and provincial au-thorities to back up the laws of kashrut by enforcing the use of *heckshers* (markings on wrappers), which certify a food product as kosher. In this in-stance, however, Jews were able to couch their needs in secular terms and to appeal to the state on recognized principles of fair trade, truth in advertising, and the prevention of consumer fraud. There was no need for the state to un-derstand the religious rationale behind the policy in question, as long as a sec-ular purpose was available. But success is always provisional when it relies on finding a secular rationale that persuades the court. A Brooklyn federal judge recently struck down a 118-year-old statute known as the "New York State kosher laws" as an unconstitutional entanglement of state with religion. If the decision, which is under appeal, stands, it will indicate that the court, no longer persuaded of the validity of the secular concern for consumer protection, is at a loss to find sufficiently accessible public reasons for maintaining the kashrut laws as they currently exist. In the face of the plaintiff's claim that state enforcement of the kosher laws inhibits fair market competition, a purely religious justification will surely fail.

Another example of an issue of great importance to Orthodox Jews, but which cannot be explained in anything other than religious language, and therefore might be inaccessible to the general public, involved the erection of an *eruv*. An eruv consists of nothing more than a string, thread, or wire that is run, usually across the tops of telephone poles, to symbolically enclose an area. In Jewish law, the eruv converts public space into private space. The distinction between public and private is important to observant Jews, particularly for Shabbat. Because it is prohibited to transfer anything in one's possession on Shabbat between public and private domains, Jews are unable to carry even a house key. They also cannot carry a baby or child, which means that a parent must either refrain from attending shul or prod a cranky toddler on what may be a long stroll between home and shul. By enclosing an area with an eruv, the enclosure is converted into private space, and suddenly strollers, keys, glasses, and the like may be carried. It would require a very long and esoteric explanation to persuade most people of the logic behind this. Arguments justifying the eruv are based on Jewish law or Halakhah, and while this may posit a nonnegotiable command in the minds of Orthodox Jews, it is unlikely that non-Jews would accept the proposition that civil law should uphold Halakhah.

In several cases in New York, New Jersey, Montreal, and north London,[14] neighbors have protested and even brought lawsuits over the erection of an eruv. In a north London neighborhood, several neighbors circulated a petition to prevent the erection of the eruv. The irony, here, of course, is that the non-Jews could couch their position in rational, secular terms, meeting the standard of "public reason." Their position, as they articulated it, was that while the eruv would have no tangible affect on their lives (in fact, had the Jews erected it under cover of darkness, it is unlikely that anyone would have ever noticed its existence), by making life more comfortable for Jews and the neighborhood, therefore, more hospitable to them, an influx of Jewish families might ensue, and, as a result, property values might fall. Ironically, this argument is completely accessible and rational. It has also been employed in one form or another in the other cases mentioned. The argument that the Jews used in attempting to persuade their neighbors is not.

In a community north of Washington, D.C., a different line of reasoning prevailed and a different outcome was achieved. Jews went from door to door asking their neighbors to sign a petition permitting the erection of an eruv. Interestingly, while the non-Jewish neighbors had no inkling of what their Jewish neighbors needed this string for, they signed off on the request without hesitation. I suppose they just considered it the civil thing to do—after all, the eruv neither "broke their legs nor picked their pockets." This case demonstrates that while our fellow citizen's form of rationality may not always be transparent to us, that does not mean that it is therefore inaccessible. I understand precisely what someone means when they say the world is flat. I can visualize a flat world. Their claim is not inaccessible, though it is unfounded. A person may accede to another's wishes or claims as long as the person is persuaded that there are reasons behind them, and that fulfilling them would not harm others or infringe on the exercise of their rights. It is possible to understand other peoples' reasoning processes, and grant their legitimacy, without granting their validity.

Reasoning as a Chossid

Liberal theorists have described how liberalism understands the world. Few people have described how Lubavitchers understand the world. Lubavitchers have no desire to explain themselves to others, and as a result there are no studies about Lubavitchers by Lubavitchers that would qualify as sociological, ethnographic, psychological, or political scholarship. The Lubavitcher press, Kehot Publication Society, sees its mission as the explication and dissemination of the classic writings of Jewish philosophy and Chassidus among Jews. While there are books that contain commentaries on these texts, they are intended to clarify, not criticize. There are also published histories of the movement; memoirs and letters of the most prominent rabbis and Rebbes; biographies of Chassidic leaders; daily meditations; guides to the laws of kashrut, holiday observances, taharat ha mishpacha, and the like; and the central religious texts: Torah, Talmud, Tanya, and the Siddur (prayer book). But they have no particular interest in writing or even reading about themselves. They are not indifferent to the outside world; in fact, they are completely current when it comes to technological, medical, and scientific developments. They also follow politics closely and listen in on a bit of baseball. But analyzing the culture of liberalism is not an interest. Writings on the culture of liberalism do exist, but mostly in the form of cautionary tales, often filled with hyperbole.

Lubavitchers understand themselves primarily in their own terms. Though they are not indifferent to how the outside world perceives them, the outside world is not critical to their self-definition because it is not a primary point of reference. In other words, a Lubavitcher's self-identity is not created in relation to the outside world; rather, his or her perception of the outside world, including the culture of liberalism, is shaped in relation to his or her Lubavitcher identity. This does not preclude a sense of citizenship and attachment to a particular country. Lubavitchers recognize and appreciate, for instance, the rights that they possess under the Canadian and American Constitutions. They are not the flag-waving sort of patriots, but respect and affection for their countries is widespread and genuine. One Canadian Lubavitcher rabbi repeatedly referred to Canada as the "country of kindness." Still, the world is perceived through the prism of Torah, and Torah commands their highest loyalty.

Lubavitchers assume two essential claims about the world: "the whole world is full of his glory" (Yeshayahu 6:3) and "for this thing is very near to you, in your mouth and in your heart, that you may do it" (Deuteronomy 30:14). These verses suggest that G-d is everywhere and constantly involved in his creation. Absent his constant oversight and continuous willing the universe into creation ex nihilo, the world would simply cease to exist and revert to *ayin* (the nothingness from which it came). This is a far cry from mechanical views of the universe in which a supreme being winds up, kicks into action, and then abandons his creation. In Chassidus, creation is contingent and completely dependent on G-d from minute to minute. G-d's creative energy and intervention are always present, holding matter in a state of existence and organization.

This view is similar to the Second Law of Thermodynamics, or the concept of entropy. If G-d did not constantly generate and organize matter, it would revert to a state of disorganization. To use the example of a car—the probability that a car would materialize out of a heap of metal is virtually nil. Once created, this car will, without constant upkeep, quickly revert to a heap of scrap metal. In the Chassidic view, the universe and all of its objects and inhabitants, from the simplest to the most complex, could only come into existence and continue to exist by the hand of G-d.[15] In this view, there is no place, no time, no action, including the movement of a leaf in the wind, from which G-d is detached. Nothing happens randomly and there are no coincidences or accidents in this universe. The Chassidic view should not be confused with pantheism, or the belief that G-d is consubstantial with the universe he created. The created world is not a direct manifestation of his being, as will be explained shortly through the Chassidic concept of *tzimtzum*, or the progressive concealment of the Ein Sof (G-d's infinite light).

The second verse explains that although G-d is omnipotent and far beyond our complete intellectual grasp, he is still accessible. Humans can connect with G-d using their physical and mundane capacities, if they make the effort. And a third important premise of Tanya is that any human is capable of achieving this communion with G-d. While the ideal might be a life in which every moment is devoted to the study of Torah, there are many opportunities for any person, no matter what his or her profession or schedule or education, to perform mitzvot—the link between G-d and humans. Accordingly, Lubavitchers refer frequently to the verse, "And you shall know Him in all your ways" (Proverbs 3:6).

The soul consists of *sechel* (intellect) and *middot* (emotion), which lead us to G-d when combined. For Lubavitchers, intellect has primacy over, and is actually the source of, emotion. Just as G-d possesses ten *sefirot* (emanations or attributes), humans possess ten intellectual and emotional attributes corresponding to these sefirot. This, by the way, is what is meant when Torah says that humans were created in the divine image. The first three sefirot are components of the intellect: *chochmah* (a flash of insight, conception, and inspiration); *binah* (understanding, analysis, application, development, and cogitation, a form of reasoning often associated with women); and *da'ath* (internalization of knowledge, attachment, union, and contemplation—da'ath is the word that is used, for instance, in the statement "Adam knew his wife"). Intellect is so central to the ability to grasp G-d through his Torah that the acronym for the three forms of intellect employed in this process, ChaBaD, has become a synonym for the movement, and is used interchangeably with Lubavitch. Lubavitchers are also called Chabadniks. If one attempts to understand the three levels of reasoning, it becomes clear that, taken together or separately, they do not correspond to critical rationality.

The additional seven sefirot that compose the human soul are emotional attributes derived from the third component of intellect, da'ath. The emotions are the "children" of the intellect. They give rise to the sensations of *chesed* (love and kindness), which lead humans to observe the 248 positive mitzvot, and to *gevurah* (severity and discipline), which leads to observation of the 365 prohibitory mitzvot. Stressing that humanity's desire to attach to G-d originated in the intellect is intended to counter the claim that Lubavitchers rely upon "blind faith" instead of "reason." The tendency of liberal theorists to treat faith and reason as polar opposites misunderstands the fact that the two are, in the eyes of Lubavitchers (and many other religious people, both Jewish and non-Jewish), mutually supportive.

The second chapter of Tanya elucidates the mystical kaballistic concept of *tzimtzum* (contraction), which represents the process of self-limitation through which G-d manifests his infinite essence (Ein Sof) in sefirot, which are his attributes. G-d radiates his essence throughout the various levels or worlds, but in each successive level of descent (*seder Hishtalshelut*), his essence becomes progressively more contracted, clothed, and concealed. These worlds, or levels of the creative process, are, in descending order: Atzilut (the world of emanation), Beriah (the world of creation), Yetzira (the world of formation), and Asiyah (the world of action). The physical world inhabited by humans is the very lowest world, in which G-d is most concealed. The Hebrew word for world, *olam*, is related to the word *he'elem*, which means concealment. But the purpose of creation could not be fulfilled if G-d were to remain concealed. He is described in some Lubavitch literature as a father who engages in a game of hide-and-seek with his children, hiding in order to be found. If the children give up the search, the father is greatly pained. The reason, according to Tanya, that G-d created this lower realm was so that he might "have a dwelling place in the lower realms" (Tanya, chap. 36). "The Holy One, Blessed be He, desired a residence below" (Midrash Tanchuma, Nasso 7:1).

The goal of making this world an abode for G-d is achieved through mitzvot of action (Tanya, chap. 37). Through humans transforming the darkness to light, recouping the sparks that have descended and dispersed, this lowest realm has the capacity to become the highest. G-d's holiness is most concealed in this world so that the darkness that pervades the lower world can be transformed. Humans are the agents of this transformation. Mitzvot, described in the Torah, allow humans, through physical action, to draw down the light of the Shechinah (divine presence) upon one's animal soul and body, rather than upon the divine soul alone. The divine spark of the soul is always pure, but the animal or corporeal part (passions) can be elevated and purified only through a practical or physical act. It is the nature of mitzvot to connect the material and physical to G-dliness:

> G-d created the universe and all physical objects yeish mei'ayin [something from nothing]. Jews must transform the "something" into "nothing," transform the material into spiritual. The avodah [service or work] of turning the physical into spiritual and making the physical into an instrument for the spiritual is a personal obligation. Every single person, individually, is required to do this.[16]

In short, according to Tanya (chap. 36), this descent of G-d's light from world to world, and its progressive concealment at each level, is not for the purpose of the higher worlds but for the purpose of the lowest world. This is the will of G-d because he finds pleasure when the *sitra achra* (the other side of creation and the source of evil, which is defined as the concealment of G-d) and the *kelipot* (physical husks or shells that hold and conceal sparks of holy light) are transformed into their opposite—goodness or holiness. When this occurs, finally, during the messianic age, the Ein Sof light of G-d will shine with greater intensity and superior quality than the radiance of the higher worlds because this is a light that emerges from darkness.

It may seem puzzling that Lubavitchers consider the world to be on the verge of redemption when we seem mired in greater spiritual degradation, discord, chaos, and self-absorption than ever before. The Lubavitcher dialectic posits that the lower the level to which we have sunk, the greater the effort required to elevate the world, the richer the possibilities, and the greater the rewards.

Lubavitch on Liberal Reason

As we have seen, even the esoteric or mystical writings of Judaism, such as Kaballah and Tanya, assume our reliance on reason in order to achieve union with G-d. The faculty of reason is not different among Lubavitchers; neither is it temporarily suspended when they engage in religious activities. It must operate all of the time, or never, because there is no aspect or moment of daily life that is not intertwined with Torah precepts and mitzvot. One cannot eat, drink, wash, or awake from sleeping without a special *brocha* (blessing) being required. There are blessings to be said immediately on waking in the morning, and at night before retiring. In between, there are three formal prayer services at shul: Shacharit in the morning, Mincha in the afternoon, and Ma'ariv in the evening. In addition, the holidays that occur throughout the year (only one month has no holiday or festival) and, of course, Shabbat every week, mean that there is no effective distinction between religious and practical time, religious and practical concerns, and, therefore, between religious and practical reasoning.

The most significant distinction, then, between the way the Chossid and the secular individual exercises his or her reason has little to do with cognition or the mental processes involved in processing information about the world; it has to do with the objective or purpose of this attribute or capacity called reason. For Lubavitchers, reason and intellect lead to *emunah* (faith). Both are to be exercised in the service of G-d, in such a way as to elevate and sanctify the physical world. Perhaps the best way of illuminating the relationship of faith to reason is by referring to the giving, or more properly, the receiving of the Torah by the Jewish people at Sinai. As Lubavitchers emphasize, Torah says that G-d asked the Jewish people if they would accept the

Torah. They spontaneously answered, "We will do and we will listen." This illustrates the Lubavitch view of the proper relationship of reason to faith. It is not that reason is subordinate to faith. The Jews did not answer simply, "We will do," which would have suggested blind obedience based on faith alone. Neither did they answer, "We will listen and we will do," which might have made performance contingent on a decision as to whether they liked the commandments or found them reasonable. Instead, the answer "We will do and we will listen" indicates a willingness to do as G-d commands on faith, accompanied by a willingness to study and understand those commands on the level of intellect and reason.

This practical approach of doing, and then studying and understanding, characterizes the Jewish view of the relationship between the physical performance of mitzvot, which can be done mechanically or habitually, and mitzvot performed with *kavannah* (inward intention and sincerity). While the mechanically performed mitzvah is sufficient, kavannah gives the mitzvah "wings." A mitzvah performed with kavannah is, therefore, superior to one performed without it. But kavannah alone, like mere intention absent the performance of a physical mitzvot, counts for almost nothing. There is no tradition in Judaism of hermits, recluses, or cloistered nuns or monks. Because it is the animal soul and corporeal body that require elevation, merely thinking about a mitzvah does not involve the body and cannot elevate it. For instance, silent meditation without speech and the movement of the mouth, because it does not involve a physical act, cannot elevate the physical to holiness the way spoken prayer can. (The swaying movement and chanting characteristic of Chassidim when they pray demonstrates this principle. It serves the dual purpose of giving prayer a physical aspect and focusing concentration.)

When Lubavitchers speak about the faculty of reason as it is employed by secular individuals in liberal society, they contrast it with their own conception of reason, which in their view leads both to the truth and to the good. Liberal reason as they understand it is an alien derivation of Protestant Christianity and the Enlightenment program, which leads to individualism, autonomy, situational morality or relativism, ceaseless demands for rights and entitlements, and a fixation on "me-ness" that impedes harmonious community life. When the liberal quest for universal reason was combined with modern democratic principles, they worked together to erode not only the meaningless social and political distinctions but some meaningful ones as well. In the Lubavitch view, for instance, distinctions based on race are foundationless, whereas distinctions based on sex are not.

Judaism is based upon making proper "rational" distinctions, which puts it in opposition to modern social trends. Proper distinctions do not imply inferiority. The very word and concept of "holiness" is related to "separation." There is a distinction between physical and spiritual, mundane and sacred, which must be overcome; a distinction between *niglah,* or public and exoteric knowledge, as in the Torah and Talmud, and *nistar,* or hidden and esoteric knowledge, as in Kaballah and Tanya. There are distinctions between the *tzaddik* (righteous one) and the *rasha* (evil one), the Rebbe and his Chassidim, the rabbi and the layperson, teacher and student, righteousness and sinfulness, man and woman, and between Jews and the nations, clean and unclean things, and the permitted and the prohibited.

Distinctions abound in Jewish life. For instance, during Havdalah, the ritual that signals the conclusion of Shabbat and holidays and the beginning of the workweek, one recites, "Blessed are You, Lord our G-d, King of the Universe, who makes a distinction between sacred and profane, between Israel and the nations, between the seventh day and the six work-days. Blessed are You, Lord, who makes a distinction between sacred and profane" (Tehillat Hashem, 234).

Similarly, the fifteen blessings that boys and men say each morning note the distinctions that G-d has made in three areas. A man thanks G-d for not making him a woman, a slave, or a gentile. The first of these blessings is often cited out of context by feminists as evidence that women are held as inferior in Judaism. As noted earlier, this blessing denotes the acceptance by a man of his obligation, not shared by women, to perform 613 mitzvot in order to perfect his soul and achieve union with G-d. All three blessings may, historically, have been intended as a response to Paul of Tarsus's claim in Galatians 3:28 that there were no differences between Jew and gentile, slave and free person, man and woman. The notion that there are no relevant distinctions was roundly rejected by Jews (not to mention slaves, I expect). Relevant distinctions serve to structure and give meaning to Jewish life.

Individualism and Autonomy

In addition to the retention of distinctions in a secular world where distinctions in principle are suspect, Lubavitchers do not share one of liberalism's central concepts, that of individual autonomy. The idea of atomistic selfhood is incongruous with Torah. The ideal that Chassidim hold to—which applies to both men and women—is *mesiros nefesh* (the subordination of the will to G-d); *bittul* (self-nullification before G-d); *kabbalos ol* (accepting the yoke of G-d); and *tsnius* (physical and intellectual humility). The ideal for which

Lubavitchers strive—in short, humility, restraint, and reserve, even to the point of self-negation—is diametrically opposed to liberalism's self-glorification, self-gratification, self-actualization, and self-absorption.

While humans should regard themselves as completely subservient to G-d, this does not mean that individuals are viewed as completely subservient to other humans. Nor are they expected to renounce physical pleasure; on the contrary, the major stream of Jewish thought opposes asceticism and mortification of the flesh. Although the Amidah, the central prayer of the three daily services, says, "let my soul be like dust to all," this suggests that one should not hold a grudge or feel superior to others. It does not require that one regard oneself as less than his or her fellows. If autonomy is understood in terms of individual self-gratification or "flourishing," particularly at the expense of others (which would inevitably be the result if an individual eschewed his or her obligations), this would clearly be incongruent with Chassidic thought. Self-interest or egoism is associated with the lower, or animal, soul. If, however, autonomy is understood as moral autonomy, Chassidic thought very much emphasizes this sense of individual moral sovereignty and responsibility for actions. This meaning is not lost when it is combined with the notion of the individual as a member of a community.

Contemporary liberal culture is contrasted with Jewish values (in a way that probably overstates the flaws of the former and the virtues of the latter), but there is more than an element of truth captured in the critiques of modern secular society and its moral code. As Rabbi Emmanuel Feldman puts it: "When a society is based on 'Me-ness' and on its corollary—'how much am I entitled to take?'—then it is reasonable and just that everyone should be able to take as much as possible. Since this is not feasible, society works out a system whereby everyone has equal rights to take."[17]

By way of contrast, it is pointed out that Hebrew has a word for obligation (*chov*), but despite modern Hebrew's effort to find a word for rights, the word that is used, *zechyot*, actually derives from the word *zechut*, or merit. Lubavitchers use the word *z'chus* frequently, as in the common toast, "May we have the z'chus to see Moshiach soon," or it was because of the "z'chus of the women that G-d gave Torah to the Jews." Here it is obvious that it would be nonsensical to translate z'chus as *right* or *entitlement*. Rabbi Feldman continues:

> The Torah is not a Bill of Rights, but a bill of obligations to G-d and other people. Torah does not mention the right to be treated decently; it stresses that we must treat others decently. In Torah we have no right to life, liberty, and pursuit of happiness; instead we have the obligation not to diminish someone else's life, liberty or happiness. Torah is not designed to make us feel good; rather it is designed to teach us how not to make others feel bad.[18]

Jewish legal tradition, going back over two thousand years, has its own way of expressing the dignity and worth of humans, but its categories are not the same as liberalism's. Jewish jurisprudence does not possess a concept of human rights. The closest analogue is mitzvah, which, as we have noted, means commandment or obligation. The concept of rights is linked in liberal thought to the social contract whereby individuals relinquish part of their freedom in order to gain security of person and property. This mythical voluntary arrangement provides legitimacy and justification for the state as well as for the limitations on its power. The community is the product of prudential artifice and the individual is the unit of analysis and the bearer of rights in the liberal formulation.[19]

Liberals have a problem understanding why individuals might saddle themselves with a set of ends and values that do not appear to serve their rational self-interest. The liberal notion of contract rests on the assumption that parties to the agreement are free willed and no one would enter into a contract that did not improve his or her situation or in some way benefit him or her. It would be a major departure from rationality to voluntarily enter into a contract that makes one worse off than before. If an individual did enter into an agreement that did not serve his or her interests, an observer would have to conclude that either the party to the contract had been coerced (that is, ceased to exercise his or her free will), or was irrational. Lubavitchers, according to this view, do not understand the basics of contract theory.

Actually, Lubavitchers, and Jews in general, are quite familiar with the idea of contract. After all, the original covenant between G-d and Avraham and then between G-d and the Jews at Mount Sinai was something of a contract. The central prayer of Judaism, the Shema, resembles the language of a contract, specifying that if Jews fulfil their obligations to G-d, he will grant them abundant harvests and a good life, whereas, if they neglect his commandments, they will suffer dire consequences.

But concepts of coercion, free will, and benefit play out in Jewish contract law in ways that liberal contract theory and law would find odd. For instance, in recent times, because of the declining authority of Jewish courts, men have been able to withhold divorces from their wives with some impunity. The problem is one of enforcement. In the close-knit Jewish community of earlier times, fear for one's reputation if not fear of G-d produced conformity to social and religious norms. Absent the social cohesion of the European shtetl, now when a man refuses to be persuaded by the court or rabbinical authority to "do the right thing," Orthodox communities will resort, when all else fails, to coercion to force a man to sign the divorce decree (*get*). Sometimes outright violence is used, but more often the threat of violence suffices.

Now, in liberal contract law, a divorce agreement (or any other agreement, for that matter) signed under duress would be considered invalid since it could not reflect free willed consent on the part of the signatory. In the Jewish understanding, however, the divorce agreement obtained this way still represents a valid contract. It is held to be binding and valid because the man is simply being helped to will what he otherwise would freely will if his best instincts were not being overruled by his *yetser hora* (evil inclination). Lubavitcher men express little reservation about helping recalcitrant husbands to liberate themselves from the inclination that has clouded their reason and free will.

Another example of how Jewish thinking about contract differs from the classical liberal conception is the *bris mila,* or the contract created between G-d and each Jewish male through circumcision. This *bris,* carried out at the age of eight days for every Jewish male, would certainly violate the liberal conception of contract. Here, an agreement is made on behalf of an infant who is in no position to understand or consent to it. It connects him to G-d, of whose existence he could not yet be aware. Moreover, the mark of the covenant in his flesh could put his very life in jeopardy, identifying him without his consent as a member of an often-reviled minority. Even when this danger is absent, the contract burdens him with the obligation to perform 613 mitzvot. How can a person be burdened without his knowing consent and the contract still be considered valid? Herein lies a crucial distinction between liberal and Jewish thought. Under Jewish law you may not burden someone against his or her will, but you may give someone a privilege or do him or her a good without his or her consent. Because the contract gives the child the wherewithal to connect to G-d, the mitzvot are not conceived of as a burden, but as a privilege. The same holds for the infant girl, who is born directly into a covenant with G-d and needs not even be formally initiated. The issue of free will simply does not pertain here.

The foundation of Jewish law and statehood was a collective experience, a collective contract. It occurred at Sinai with the giving of the Torah. Indeed, according to Chassidus, every Jewish soul ever to be born was literally present at this event, and therefore party to the contract. There is an enormous discussion among Talmudic scholars about whether the contract was voluntary, and, if not, whether it can be considered binding. The preponderant view is that while the acceptance of the law was initially voluntary, compliance thereafter was obligatory. There is also a charming *midrash* (allegorical interpretation) of the event at Sinai that says that the acceptance of the commandments was slightly less than voluntary. The precise Hebrew wording in the Torah implies that the people stood "under" Sinai, suggesting that G-d held Sinai over the heads of the Jews and threatened to drop it on them if they refused the Torah.

In the writings of the sages, there is a discussion about whether it is preferable for an individual to perform mitzvot out of a sense of obligation, or whether it is more laudable to perform them voluntarily out of love and free choice. Whereas most liberals would conclude that voluntary choice is loftier than obligation because it seems more consonant with individual autonomy, the rabbis conclude that the loftiest motive for the performance of the commandments is obligation. In fact, it is less worthy for an individual to voluntarily perform a mitzvah to which this individual is not personally obligated than it is for this same individual to enable someone else to perform a mitzvah to which he or she is obligated.

"Because G-d commanded" is the highest and most compelling reason to undertake an obligation: "Indeed, to be one who acts out of obligation is the closest thing there is to a Jewish definition of completion as a person within the community."[20] Adulthood is not regarded as the achievement of a state of autonomy or independence. On the contrary, when a boy becomes Bar Mitzvah at age thirteen and a girl Bat Mitzvah at the age of twelve, having reached the threshold of adulthood, the young man or woman is now expected to take on the responsibility and obligation of performing the commandments. Maturity means relinquishing the freedom of childhood. The Jewish adult does not see the fulfillment of his or her role as a "right," but he or she would not feel like a full member of the community if prevented or exempted from the fulfillment of his or her obligations.

Value Relativism

In another important respect, Lubavitchers view liberalism as an alien value system antithetical to Judaism. Liberalism, in their view, possesses a dangerous form of moral relativism or situational ethics. When right and wrong depend on whatever the current generation regards as ethical, then the content of morality will change by the minute. What appears as just today will be unjust tomorrow. Well-intentioned political leaders, parents, and teachers will revise morality to fit the current fashionable standard. No one will feel able to justify their standard of right and wrong with any conviction because the individual will be the arbiter of right and wrong, based on whatever subjective and shifting criteria he or she feels comfortable with at the moment. Against this, Lubavitch holds the Torah as the source of immutable, absolute, eternal, and unchanging truth and morality, issued by

G-d, who foresaw every human situation and condition that could arise to the last generation.

The relativism of values that is characteristic of liberal societies is derivative of the Enlightenment. Because values, as distinct from facts, cannot be verified empirically or intersubjectively, they are treated as provisional, historically and culturally contingent, situated, and fallible. No value can reach the status of a demonstrable truth. The self, as well as what the self values, is subject to revision. Although the freedom to revise our choices and our understanding of the world may lead to social and individual growth, progress, and freedom in the liberal conception, this constant revision is seen by Lubavitch as a vice rather than virtue. If something is true, it is always true. It appears to Lubavitchers that society is constantly announcing and then renouncing new social, ethical, and scientific truths. To them, this is not evidence of open-mindedness; it is evidence of intellectual floundering and confusion. The example of post-Enlightenment science's monumentally nonsensical and dangerous theory of eugenics, which lent credibility to Hitler's racist theories, stands out in the community's collective memory.

Lubavitchers respect science, particularly medicine and technology, but they enjoy stories about the latest scientific truth to be overturned. Cosmologists, they point out, keep revising the age of the universe. Scientists keep revising the age of the earth, the time when life first appeared on earth, the interpretation of the humanoid fossil record, and the like. To Lubavitchers, the fact that scientists are always exchanging one certain truth for another does not throw the whole enterprise into disrepute, but it does refute the claim that scientific knowledge is absolutely authoritative. If scientists still can't settle on the date of the earth, for instance, why accept any of their competing claims when the Torah has never changed its calculation about the age of the earth? A Lubavitcher who is also a professor at McGill University offered that it "is not my problem to reconcile Torah and science to the satisfaction of the so-called rational person. G-d can do what He wants."[21] He cited the sage's claim, "If I could know G-d, I could be G-d."

Lubavitchers, however, do not see a conflict in principle between science and Torah. They point to Shimon Bar Yochai's prediction in Kaballah that science and G-dliness will converge on the eve of redemption, with the former in the service of the latter. The great advances in scientific and technological knowledge in the past several generations are understood as a harbinger of the messianic age. In addition, the Rebbe, having been educated as an engineer, maintained a lifelong interest in technological developments and was always on the lookout for ways in which science confirmed Torah positions. Many scientists accept the fundamental indeterminism of nature, as in Heisenberg's uncertainty principle, which declares the unpredictability of both the position and velocity of subatomic particles. This acceptance of indeterminacy is used to support the Lubavitch claim that there is no absolute truth in science. For them, true science and true religion will ultimately be revealed as compatible. In the interim, the limitations of intellect must be compensated for by *emunah* (faith). The recognition of the deficiencies of reason should lead to faith. As Rebbe Menachem Mendel Schneerson expressed it, "Intellect, when left to its own devices, may well fail a man, whose self-love may ultimately blind him to the truth. By prefacing understanding with faith, one guarantees that his subsequent comprehension will be on the mark."[22]

Reason, understood as skepticism, can be a help or a hindrance in the human quest for the truth. There are times when Lubavitchers will avow that reason is helpless, as when we encounter a divine command that we cannot fathom with the intellect. The appropriate response in such a case is not skepticism, but faith.

Free Will

Torah, for Lubavitchers, possesses absolute truth and applies to every aspect of life. It is a complete blueprint with significance for everything a Jew does. Lubavitchers have more confidence in these revealed truths of G-d, as they see them, than in any form of contingent human wisdom. The Torah is not only the revealed word of G-d, according to Chassidus; the Hebrew letters of Torah contain the essence of G-d. *Anochy,* which begins the Ten Commandments, means, "I am the Lord your G-d." According to Chassidus, anochy is also an acronym for *Ana nafshi chetavit yehavit,* which means, "I Myself gave it [Torah] to you in writing," or, "I gave you Myself."[23] According to Lessons in Tanya, "G-d compressed His will and wisdom in the 613 commandments of Torah and in their laws, and in the letter combinations of Scripture."[24] In the Chassidic view, the very letters and words of the Torah contain G-d's holiness and wisdom. This makes the Torah, in the eyes of Lubavitchers, not simply a handbook or metaphor but a vessel of divine revelation. Because G-d has revealed his wisdom in every letter of Torah, all parts and all commandments are of equal importance, and none can be disregarded as trivial, dated, or irrelevant.

> As explained in the Zohar, Torah and the Holy One, blessed be He, are truly one. . . . The wisdom of Torah expresses G-d's wisdom; its practical application and laws—e.g., whether or not a particular object is kosher—expresses

His will. . . . The Torah, being G-d's intellect, is thus one with G-d, Himself, and when a Jew understands and unites himself with it, he is united with G-d, Himself.[25]

This obviously, would not satisfy an individual who did not believe in G-d, or a G-d whose purposes define and subordinate the purposes of individual humans. If G-d is omnipotent, omnipresent, and omniscient, how can there be any room for the exercise of human free will or free choice, they will ask. And how can there then be any room for individual moral autonomy and sovereignty? Is there not a contradiction in claiming that G-d is all powerful yet humans are responsible for their own behavior, even to the point where the balance of the entire human community can hang on their performance of a single mitzvah?

What room is left for freedom if intellect and reason are devoted to the discovery and understanding of divine truth? The Perkei Avot ("Ethics of the Fathers") says that "only a Jew who studies Torah is truly free" (6:2). This freedom differs from the liberal conception of "unimpeded motion" or "absence of restraint." In fact, without the constraints of mitzvot, humans would be in a state of slavery to their baser nature and passions. The "yoke of Torah" (*kabbalos ol*) is not intended to make humans miserable but to enable them to achieve joyful union with G-d. If it is in the essence of what it means to be a Jew to fulfill Torah mitzvot, then straying from this obligation would be the same as straying from one's essence, which for Lubavitchers is the antithesis of freedom. Moreover, our interaction with the Divine is reciprocal. When humans fulfill a purpose other than what was intended, they disrupt G-d's orderly creative process.[26] When humans fulfill their roles and obligations, they bring down the messianic age more quickly.

The process of concealment (*tzimtzum*) makes the world appear to our senses to be a rudderless ship. Daily existence seems to be no more than a string of disconnected, meaningless, and random events. It is often the case that the logical, the apparent, and even the obvious are false. For Lubavitchers, the Torah provides the roadmap for making sense of this evidently chaotic world. Chassidus reveals the universe is not only the product of design but that "the entire creation is fashioned the way it is so as to confer cosmological significance on our seemingly ordinary lives."[27] Accordingly, "the loftiest esoteric concepts in Kaballah and Chassidus . . . are therefore, of real and immediate relevance to the ordinary, bill-paying, car-driving, working Jew."[28]

The tension between revelation and concealment "is essentially designed to provide growth opportunities for His children."[29] The other purpose of concealment is to afford humans free will. How this is so is not immediately apparent. After all, the fact that G-d may conceal his actions in the world does not make him any less controlling than the puppet master who stays out of view of the audience. The concept of *hashgacha protis* (divine providence), one of Maimonides' Thirteen Principles, states that nothing in the world happens by accident; everything happens according to divine plan, even the most insignificant event. Can this be squared with free will, or is human freedom simply an illusion?

It is written in the Ethics of the Fathers that "All is foreseen and freedom of choice is granted" (Perkei Avot 3:15). Raavad (Rabbi Avraham ben Dovid, c.1120–1198) offers the explanation that G-d knows what humans will choose, but this knowledge has no effect on our choices. According to Maimonides, G-d and his knowledge are one, and he is not governed by the laws of time. There is not past or future, only perpetual present. There is no paradox between G-d's knowledge and human freedom. G-d does not exist in linear time, according to Chassidus, so his foreknowledge does not obliterate human free choice. A stone does not fall to the ground because I predicted it would. The opposite of free choice is not foreknowledge but coercion.[30]

That G-d may know what a person will do does not mean that he controls or interferes in that choice. Each individual, according to Chassidus, is responsible for his choice to do good or evil. It is within the individual's power to choose good and refrain from evil. According to the author of Tanya and founder of Lubavitch, Schneur Zalman, each man has the potential to root out (as opposed to merely repress) every evil thought, action, and deed. If he succeeds, he is considered to be on an even higher level than an angel because an angel has no freedom of choice between good and evil. "And their [angels] fear and love [of G-d] is natural to them; they need not create fear and love of G-d through intellectual contemplation of G-d's greatness."[31]

According to Rebbe Menachem Mendel Schneerson, this emphasizes "the lofty level of Torah and mitzvot that are motivated by intellectual love and fear of G-d. So sublime is this form of service that it transcends the service of angels."[32] Free will, then, is a capacity that G-d gives humans in the hope that they will use it to find him. This is the same reason that he keeps his plans concealed. For instance, were G-d to reveal the precise date of the coming of the Moshiach, there would be no incentive for humans to continue choosing to perform mitzvot. The analogy used among Lubavitchers is of a person waiting for a plumber or repairman to show up. If he were to give you the precise time of his arrival, you would go about your business for the rest of the day, thinking nothing of him, only preparing for his arrival at the specified time. On the other hand, if you do not know when he is going to arrive, you spend the whole day anticipating and preparing as if he might arrive any moment.

The objective of concealment, then, is to allow humans free will. The purpose of free will is to choose good; for Jews, to perform mitzvot. The purpose of mitzvot is to elevate the sparks of G-dliness that are concealed in matter and physicality. By infusing the physical with spirituality and holiness, the arrival of the Moshiach is hastened. Human freedom, then, is an integral part of human nature, according to Chassidus.

Political Reason

To Lubavitchers, there is no special skill or type of reason involved in deliberating about political issues and assessing candidates. Most agree that the real distinctions among citizens lie not in citizens' different reasoning capacities but in their different levels of interest in politics. Common sense is the form of political reasoning that Lubavitchers recognize. "Critical rationality" would not strike them as being fundamentally different from or superior to the form of political deliberation that they employ.

There is increasing empirical support for the thesis that styles of reasoning are culturally determined or situated in one moral tradition or another. While Western culture has produced a penchant for linear, analytic reasoning that seeks to resolve polarized contradictions, other cultures are more at ease with seeming contradictions.[33] This being true, there would be no compelling reason to prefer the Enlightenment-derived version to what we might call "Lubavitch reason" unless it could be demonstrated that the former was essential to the exercise of democratic citizenship and that the latter was not adequate to this task. Whether one possesses critical rationality or just plain common sense is not likely to set citizens apart in terms of political competence or commitment to democracy.

In the next section, I will examine liberal feminist perspectives on Lubavitcher women, to further illustrate the problems that arise when we insist on imposing the liberal ideals of autonomous individuality and critical rationality universally. These women make sense of both their world and the liberal world in ways radically different from those to which liberal thinkers are accustomed. Even more than Lubavitcher men, they test the ability of liberalism to appreciate nonliberal perspectives and values.

CHAPTER SEVEN

Lubavitcher Women and Liberalism

Moses ascended to G-d and Hashem called to him from the mountain,
saying, "So shall you say to the House of Jacob and relate to the Children
of Israel."

Shemos 19:3

The House of Jacob refers to the women of Israel. Why did G-d
approach them first, before the men, to receive the Torah? It is answered that
G-d understood that since the young children would be the guarantors of the
covenant, in each generation the women would be the ones to teach them.
G-d enjoined Moses to speak gently to the women because they would accept the Torah without prodding, spontaneously out of love for G-d, and
teach their children with gentle patience. He enjoined Moses to speak to the
men firmly, even harshly, because his expectations of them were, well, apparently a bit lower.

This passage from Exodus suggests to Lubavitchers that women and men
have both a different manner and a different role. But unlike the portrayal of
women as essentially defective men by classical Greek and early to medieval
Christian thinkers, there is no sense of inferiority implied by the distinctiveness of women in Jewish thought.

Women are depicted in Jewish writings in various capacities: matriarchs,
prophets, political leaders, military leaders, and scholars. It was a woman who
established the model demeanor for prayer (Channah) and women who established the model of the appropriate way to challenge authority (the daughters of Tzelaphad). Tamar and Ruth took the initiative to ensure the survival
of the line of the House of David; Judith and Yael took up arms to defeat enemy generals; Esther intervened with a king to save her people from destruction; and Ima Shalom, Yalta, and Bruria were respected scholars nearly
two thousand years before the world had heard of feminism. Jewish history
is full of celebrated women who lived their lives and made their contributions
publicly. It is also full of women who made their contributions to Jewish survival, often under incredible hardship, in more private ways. The ideal Jewish woman, whether a private or a public figure, is called by the title "a woman
of valor."

Liberal feminists and Lubavitcher women have quite a bit to say about each other, some of it harsh, some of it pitying. Both groups share the tendency to use the other as a foil. Many Lubavitcher women are *ba'alot teshuva* (voluntary returnees), well acquainted with liberal secular society. Even the most sheltered Lubavitcher women cannot avoid constant contact with the larger society. Therefore, Lubavitcher women know more about their liberal counterparts than liberal women know about them.

Liberal feminists, to the extent that they can even hear Lubavitcher women's assertions of satisfaction with their lives, feel the need to dismiss these assertions as inauthentic. The fact that women who seem so obviously oppressed and controlled actually express happiness with their situation clearly irritates many feminists. For their part, Lubavitcher women see liberal women as having allowed themselves to be duped and denatured, contending that sexual liberation and careerism have only increased the opportunities for exploiting women.

At the heart of the mutual incomprehension and unwillingness of each side to grant the authenticity of its opponent's perceptions and experiences are the philosophical and epistemological differences that were outlined in the preceding chapters. Liberalism, with its emphasis on individualism, critical rationality, and autonomy, finds nonliberal worldviews nearly incomprehensible as opposed to merely unattractive. This incomprehension is magnified when the question of women arises because almost all women, secular or religious, deviate rather dramatically from the liberal model of personhood. In other words, the problems created by holding individuals to the liberal standard of autonomy and critical rationality become pronounced as soon as we depart from the model of an abstract, generic male citizen. Giving an individual some ascriptive characteristics, say, making him a Chossid, compounds the problem. Turning from this male Chossid to a female Chossid may be one of the most dramatic departures from the model liberal individual.

Jewish feminists have had as much difficulty as non-Jewish feminists with understanding traditional Jewish women such as Lubavitchers. Most of them have been struggling with Jewish law, which they view as unjust to women. Some find the injustice in Halakhah (Jewish law) itself, others in the overlay of customs and interpretations that men have given it through the ages. Some would ignore or radically reinterpret the law, demanding access to traditionally male roles; others would respect the sanctity of the law while attempting to change the image and status of women and to expand their roles within the parameters of law. Cynthia Ozick represents the latter, in wanting a bigger piece of the pie for women, while Judith Plaskow represents the former, in wanting to bake a whole new one.[1] Some radical proponents of Jewish feminism find the problem in the "otherness" of women and the "maleness" of G-d. They would eschew the male imagery and replace it with their own "goddess imagery."[2]

In short, feminist critics of Jewish law have generally rejected it on much the same grounds as liberal Jews. Far from accepting it as G-d-given, they see it as made by men, with men's interests in mind. It is artificial and oppressive, anachronistic and irrelevant. On the other side, Jewish law has been defended as nourishing and sustaining the deep relationship between men and women, and between humans and G-d. While these defenders are likely to be regarded with suspicion by liberal feminists because they stand firmly within Halakhah, they regard themselves as feminists, in a truly Jewish sense.

Tamar Frankiel argues that simply giving women the same roles as men would miss the point. Women have never been portrayed as inferior in intellect, wisdom, ability, or determination in Judaism. We may not be doing women a service if we restructure Judaism in the image of contemporary liberal society, which is itself flawed. Frankiel asks, "Can we in good conscience submit our spiritual tradition to the dictates of modern culture?"[3]

The evaluation of liberal society heard among Lubavitcher women shares more with the essentialist feminist critique of liberalism than the liberal feminist critique of liberalism. It carries strains of prefeminist and postfeminist consciousness as well, resembling both Jane Addams's and Carol Gilligan's feminine ethos of caring. Their appreciation of the traditional role of Jewish women is portrayed with sensitivity in the works of Tamar Frankiel, Blu Greenberg, Debra Kaufman, Bonnie Morris, and Lynn Davidman. Yet few Lubavitcher women have spoken in their own voices in public.

Therefore, although they would be unlikely to characterize themselves in this way, Lubavitcher women can be characterized as countercultural critics of liberalism in their rejection of the commercial, or market, mentality, and their recognition of the nongendered aspects of oppression and exploitation in liberal society. Feminist studies that examine whole relationships, thus departing from the liberal fixation with the autonomous individual who is supposed to represent both male and female, expose this assumption. Similarly, Carol Gilligan exposed the male bias in the theories of Jean Piaget and Lawrence Kohlberg, which judged the more relationship-oriented morality frequently displayed by girls to be defective compared to the abstract moral reasoning more often displayed by boys.[4]

This sort of evidence has led some more radical feminists, within a framework of feminine essentialism, to argue for remedies ranging from the voluntary withdrawal of women from the male-dominated world, to revaluing the traditional roles that women perform, to "feminizing" the norms of the public realm. The creation of a semiautonomous women's world, by some accounts accomplished by Lubavitcher women, is probably unachievable beyond the confines of similarly small, insular communities, defined either according to religion, sexual orientation, ethnicity, or race.

The alternative, liberal remedy, which has traditionally focused on the elimination of legal barriers to equality, has probably run out of steam, having pretty well eliminated legal discrimination against women in the workforce and in public life. The model appears to have exhausted its proposed strategies. It has been most successful in bringing well-educated middle class women up to the starting line in the race of life. These are the women who are best positioned to take advantage of "equal opportunity." But many women cannot make good on the promise of legal equality. It did not take long for feminists to recognize that the liberal dichotomy between public and private realms and behaviors was forestalling the liberation of women. Liberalism shields powerful sources of inequality in the private domain of the family, securely beyond the reach of legal remedies. This led to the battle cry, "The personal is political."

Since the inequalities of the private sphere overflow into the public sphere—affecting the distribution of rights, opportunities, and power—the family, it was claimed, should be scrutinized, like any social institution, in terms of injustice and justice. This led to demands in some quarters that the family be revamped or even neutralized. Some feminists refused to give up on the institution of the family, hoping to reform it by eliminating its dependence on the traditional, sexually determined division of labor. Others regarded the traditional family as the permanent, incorrigible repository of reactionary and oppressive practices. But here, the opponents of public intervention into the private realm included most women as well as men.

That many women seem to side with their oppressors has been a sore point for feminist theory. Lubavitcher women would seem to them to be a case of this par excellence. Women who belong to minority cultures raise a particularly thorny problem because of the already sensitive relationship that exists between minority and majority cultures. When the rights of minority cultures are measured against the rights of individual women, which set of rights should prevail? Should our sensitivity toward minority cultures and our desire as a liberal society to tolerate diversity force liberal feminists to close their eyes to what they would regard as violations of women's rights?

Understandably, many feminists can find much to despise in the lives of traditional women in which the cultural barriers to equality seem to make a mockery of the formal, legal equality that feminists have worked so hard to

achieve. For these theorists Lubavitch typifies the traditional, patriarchal society. Unmoved by arguments that make cultural diversity an integral component of liberal theory, they have no sympathy for groups that seem to be
flouting liberal principles under the guise of cultural self-preservation. For
them, the issue of collective rights and diversity should remain subordinate
to the issue of individual rights. Granting rights to groups is likely to reinforce traditional male power structures that result in the subcultural oppression of women. As Susan Moller Okin puts it, "In general, the defense of
'cultural practices' will have a bigger impact on women than men since
women spend more time in the private sphere. . . . Discrimination against
and control of the freedom of women is practiced . . . by virtually all cultures,
past and present, but especially religious ones and those that look to the
past—to ancient texts and revered traditions."[5] It would be better if such
groups "became extinct or were altered."[6] Oppression exists in any culture
that deviates from liberal norms of autonomy, individuality, rationality, and
equality. Many feminists contend that most cultures have as one of their principal aims the control of women by men. Patriarchal groups will only have
that power enhanced if we grant special rights or protections to cultural, ethnic, or religious minorities.

What of the claim that people, presumably including women, need a culture to provide them with the building blocks of their identities? For Rawls
and Kymlicka, we have a higher-order interest in achieving self-respect, and
this is best served by membership in a "rich and secure cultural structure,"
whose point is to create a backdrop for meaningful individual choice. If a
group does not provide this, then there is no other justification for it. Kymlicka contends that we must investigate the internal workings of minority
groups before we confer rights on them. He would have liberals accept external protections for beleaguered minorities in order to promote justice between groups, but these groups, for their part, must reform internal practices
that restrict the freedom of their members, again, presumably including
women.

A liberal feminist will argue that women cannot be free and equal as long
as they are not granted all the rights, duties, and opportunities that are given
to men. In principle, they favor gender neutrality. All aspects of life must be
governed by principles of liberal justice whether they are part of the private
or the public realm, the sphere of "good" or the sphere of "right." They do
not regard themselves as advocating that society treat women as if they were
men; rather, they would advocate treating everyone as if they were generic,
genderless individuals. In her important book, *Justice, Gender, and the Family,* Susan Moller Okin concludes that "If we are to be true to our demo-

cratic ideals, moving away from gender is essential." In the just world, "all social differentiation among the sexes vanishes."[7] The just future would be one without gender in which sex would have no more relevance than eye color.[8] Childbearing and child rearing would be distinct enterprises, the former inescapably a woman's role, and the latter capable of being equally shared, with social and economic institutions forced to accommodate this.

Why not simply accept that different cultures view freedom and equality through different, though equally valid, lenses? Why not say that cultures determine sex roles without implying that these roles are in any way natural? The problem here is that any willingness to accept sexually differentiated roles risks not only lending them legitimacy and credibility but also admitting that they may be natural simply because they are so prevalent in so many cultures. This is particularly touchy when most cultures saddle women with less attractive and personally fulfilling roles. The extreme version of this anxiety about the sexual division of labor maintains that women should not even be permitted privileges or exemptions based on natural physiological traits, lest these traits and exemptions be used to bar them from some desirable opportunity in another situation.

To many liberal theorists, treating women differently automatically implies treating them as inferior. It is probably healthy and good to view all distinctions and categories set up by law and custom with suspicion, even those that are intended as protective rather than restrictive. The Fourteenth Amendment reflects the correct assumption that putting people in different categories and subjecting them to different treatment almost always implies superiority or inferiority and reinforces relations of dominance and oppression. Of course, we have discovered in the history of the application of Fourteenth Amendment stipulations that treating people equally can require treating them the same or treating them differently. It depends whether the goal is to create equality of opportunity (equality at the starting line) or equality of outcome (equality at the finish line).

Treating people the same when they are the same will result in rough equality, but treating people as if they were the same when they are not will only engender more inequality. An example might be the standard of living of men versus women after a "no-fault" divorce. In divorce court in most states, men and women are treated the same, but this formal equality is immediately subverted by the fact that men and women are differently situated with respect to employment and income. As Aristotle discussed in Book V of the Nichomachean Ethics, the temptation to obliterate all categories in order to achieve equality, and thereby justice, is understandable but misconceived. It should probably be presumed that treating people according to different standards is an injustice, unless the standards and the categories they create are based on "right reasons." Michael Walzer's version of this principle maintains that what is to be considered as just within a given sphere depends on what that sphere is all about. His "separate spheres test" permits inequalities in a given sphere only as long as they do not flow into an unrelated sphere.[9]

Putting men and women in separate categories, if done for the "right reasons," would not automatically constitute an injustice. For instance, taking into account the physical differences between men and women may not always be irrelevant to the performance of a given task. But misunderstanding this has led to many ironic policies, such as a Vermont court overturning a company's policy of prohibiting women of childbearing age from working with chemicals that had been proven to be toxic to fetuses. In the judgment of the court, a woman should not be singled out or defined by her reproductive capacity and therefore the company's policy was judged to constitute illegal discrimination.

The line between oppressive and protective treatment may be a fine one and distinguishing between the two may be a matter of perception. Many practices are perceived differently from within than from without. For instance, liberals find the veiling of Muslim women oppressive, but many Muslim women regard it as empowering. Polygamy, seen by liberals as degrading, may create solidarity among the women involved while monogamy is just as often an instrument of male domination. In many cases, what liberals want to present as the clash of liberating versus oppressing forces is really no more than the clash of liberal and nonliberal values. While well-meaning liberals may see themselves as knights on white horses, rescuing helpless damsels in distress, the damsels themselves may not want to be rescued. Herein lies the dilemma for liberal theorists. If the damsels not only find their lives attractive, but find life in the liberal, secular society unattractive, do we have the right to assume, as many liberal feminists do, that the damsels are too cowed to be regarded as rational? Do they, therefore, forfeit the right to have their choices granted the same respect that the liberal doctrine of neutrality would have us grant all other individuals in determining and pursuing their conception of the good?

If sex discrimination produces internal norms of subordination, then the "exit" remedy that many advocates of multiculturalism suggest as a safety valve is insufficient because women are unable to scrutinize their own practices from the inside. This problem is compounded by government's asymmetrical treatment of religion, giving it more latitude to discriminate than would be permitted to nonreligious groups. This leads some theorists to ar-

gue that there should be no general barriers to the application of antidis-
crimination remedies simply because a religious group is the offender. They
question whether the preferences of religious women can be taken seriously
when "they are adaptive to unjust background conditions. In such conditions it is not even clear whether the relevant preferences are authentically
theirs."[10] Women who choose to subordinate themselves to such conditions
are guilty of reproducing norms of inequality for other women.

While this claim seems to admit that women have a role in establishing and
reproducing the norms of their communities, this is not understood as a sign
of women's power or control over their lives, as it would be in other settings.
Is this as true for the women who participate in the current fads of body pierc-
ing, tattooing, cosmetic surgery, and self-starvation as it is for the women who
perpetuate foot-binding and genital mutilation? These are all harmful practices, and I do not want to make a case for respecting any of them. But it would
be dangerously arrogant to assume that the choices of Third World women
are culturally determined, while those of First World women are freely chosen. Once we begin to question the "authenticity" of individual choices we
might have to understand in a whole new light the people given to watching
professional wrestling or daytime television. Lubavitcher women may coun-
tercharge that liberal, secular society with its media- promoted images is the
society that truly exploits, oppresses, devalues, and objectifies contemporary
women.

While we are not always perceptive about our own culture's impact on
women, we are often ignorant about other cultures. According to Sander Gilman, "Western bourgeois women claim to speak universally for all women."[11]
When we focus on "disparities of power," we implicitly raise objective, external standards that come close to a "full-blown articulation of objectively
defined gender roles."[12] This happens whenever we evaluate a cultural norm
by whether it promotes or restrains individual autonomy.

The prevailing view of Lubavitcher women tends to combine ignorance
and bias. It is patronizing to see these women as indoctrinated victims or as
"deluded." In applying the liberal standard of freedom to Orthodox Jews, we
miss the fact that Lubavitcher men are even less free in the liberal sense than
Lubavitcher women, and no more capable of scrutinizing the internal norms
and practices of their community. In this case, one could not accuse men of
conspiring consciously to preserve their prerogatives. Nor is it clear why men
benefit more than women from the traditional division of roles except to
people who value the public life over the private, and think that true self-
actualization is only possible in the former. For women who prefer to challenge
male definitions of success and repudiate male culture, instead of strategiz-

ing to become part of it, the life that liberal feminists condemn as oppressive may be perceived as liberating.

A willingness to put aside preconceptions can have a dramatic impact on the way we perceive unfamiliar practices. This became very apparent in an interview I conducted with Chantal Pilon, the former assistant to Robert Keiffer, the Quebec MP who represents a district north of Montreal that is home to a large community of Tasher Chassidim. As a feminist, at first she felt very hostile toward the community because the women seemed to marry young and then be saddled with enormous families. As she began to spend more time in the community, she began to realize that women were active in generating and maintaining the norms of their community. She noticed the tradition of female solidarity and mutual assistance. She noticed the joy and spirituality of their lives. She began to reappraise her understanding of what freedom meant, incorporating the idea that it might include the freedom to walk around one's neighborhood at all hours without fear. She noticed the respect for women, for mothers, and for children. She noticed the active involvement of the fathers with the children.

Meanwhile, as she entered her thirties, she began to experience new pressures in her own life as she added motherhood to her roles of wife, lawyer, and legislative assistant. She asked herself whether she was as happy as the Tash women she knew. What were the values of her own society? Were they really superior? No longer so quick to judge or repudiate, Chantal Pilon came to recognize the pleasure of being in the society of women. She wonders why we don't experiment more with women-only experiences and activities within our own community. Although one could claim that Pilon's views had simply swung like a pendulum from hostility to affection, and that both extremes probably partly misunderstand the reality, it is clear that our perceptions about the oppressiveness of women's lives in nonliberal cultures are at least in part a product of our own culturally produced predisposition to rush to judgment based on what we think gives life value.[13]

Liberalism has its agenda, and its own sacred cows. As Joseph Raz writes, "Our culture is rife with injustice and intolerance. Before we criticize other cultures, we might want to hold a true mirror to our own."[14] The ideology of liberalism and individual rights does not solve the problems of the postindustrial market economy, the sexual division of labor, the lack of adequate child care, the lack of public family support policies, or the lack of enforceable child support laws. Legislative reforms did not solve these problems, nor did they penetrate the private realm to change the norms, roles, and behaviors of men and women.

It is no wonder that some women want to abandon the fast track for a life of community, self-restraint, dedication, virtue, and strong family life. Debra Kaufman, in her interviews with *ba'alei teshuva* (returnees to Orthodox Judaism), identifies a recurring theme, which is the failure of liberal feminism.[15] These failures, as detailed by the women she interviews, caused many of them to revise their earlier feminist views and expectations. The features of contemporary life as they impact women are difficult to ignore. They include a 50-percent divorce rate, the frequency of sexual assault, and, for those who make it into the high-paying upper strata of the economy, a corporate climate that is hostile to mothers. The "feminization of poverty" points up the failure of both liberal feminists' hopes and the general ethos of acquisition and materialism.[16] As Martha Minow writes, "In short, these were reforms that took the male norm and simply extended it to women, ignoring the array of social institutions and practices that have made women different and subjecting women to the burdens of that difference."[17]

No one would argue that the remedy for the deficiencies and failures of liberal feminist reforms would be a return to the status quo ante. But it is fairly clear that the liberal model of the autonomous individual, to the extent that it characterizes the human ontological and existential condition at all, describes men better than women. (In fact, my female students through the years have been quick to recognize that Hobbes could not have been a woman and written about humans in the state of nature as he did.)

The claims of women who flee "liberal patriarchy" must be assessed against this background of unkept promises and disillusionment. We might do well to listen to what Lubavitch women say, as insiders, about their world of meaning—which derives from Torah, Talmud, the writings of the Rebbes, the Rabbonim (the writings of the rabbis), and the sacred mystical texts that comprise Kaballah and Tanya—and perhaps most important, about their everyday lives and experiences in their world and ours.

What Lubavitch Women Say

Lubavitchers emphasize the cooperative rather than the competitive nature of their relationships. The different natures of men and women were intended by G-d to complete and complement the other. Therefore, obliterating the distinctions between men and women will make this complementarity and completion impossible, disrupting the natural and social order well beyond the confines of the individual marriage.

The basis of the distinct roles accorded to men and women is to be found, according to them, in differences that go back to Creation. The male and female are two halves of one being who was divided at Creation. Originally, Adam is created as the pinnacle of G-d's design. Up to that point, G-d had declared each segment of his creation to be good. Each part of his creation was brought into being ex nihilo and for no other purpose than to please or serve him. But when Adam was created, G-d looked at him and realized that it was not good for this creature to be alone. Eve was the only part of creation that was added to perfect it, to make it complete. She was therefore the only being who did not need to "become" because she was already as G-d intended her to be.

According to Rabbi Manis Friedman, the dean of Bais Chana (a seminary for women) and one of the more public figures in Lubavitch, the essential differences between male and female character trace back to their different origins. Because Adam was created from dust, men retain that primordial memory of nothingness, which makes for a fragile ego. Women, on the other hand, having been created from humanity, retain no subconscious memory of their nothingness, and therefore, while a woman may fear abuse or injustice, she does not, like the male, fear annihilation. According to Chassidus, the male striving to build and acquire is the product of his ego desperate to go from nothing to something. He is in the process of becoming, whereas women, having been created in a state of completeness, can afford to give and nurture others. Men's ability to nurture is limited until he gets beyond his own need to be the biggest and the best, until he silences his disturbing sense of nothingness, which Friedman calls his "masculine demon": "When a nothing becomes a something because he has faced his demon with the proper guidance, he becomes a man. Only then is he ready to meet a woman."[18]

This explains, in part, the different blessings that men and women recite in the morning. Much has been made of the fact that men thank G-d for not having made them women, while women thank G-d for having made them according to his will. While this has been used to demonstrate the inferiority of women in Judaism, the insiders' explanation supports an entirely different view. Men can only be perfected through the fulfillment of the 613 mitzvahs. By doing mitzvot, men are given the opportunity to refine their nature. Women are exempt from fulfilling many of the time-bound mitzvot in part because of their pressing obligations to their children. But there is more to it than that. Lubavitchers believe that women are also freed from many mitzvot because of the merit of their foremothers.

This is expressed in a number of passages: "In the merit of the righteous women our ancestors were redeemed from Egypt" (Talmud Sotah 11:B); "The women did not participate in the sin of worshipping the golden calf" (Talmud Pirkei De Rabi Elazor, chap. 45); "G-d first offered the Torah to the women and only afterwards to the men" (Exodus 19:3, Talmud Mechilta Mishpatim); "The women were the first to volunteer and donate towards the building of the Divine Sanctuary" (Exodus 35:22, Talmud Shmos Rabbah 48:7); "Unlike the men, women did not believe the lies of the twelve spies" (Numbers 26:64, Talmud Tanchuma Pinchos).

Women, in short, do not need to rise above and perfect their natures in the same way that men do. Men need the structured environment of the shul with its rules, prayers, and public, communal performance of mitzvot. They need to "do," whereas, according to Chassidus, women need only to "be" in order to connect their essences with G–d. Men gain access to G–d through the performance of external mitzvot, which are physical acts; women are connected, as one Lubavitcher woman told me, "essence to essence" with G–d. Boys need to be inducted into the covenant through the bris milah; girls are born directly into it.

On the cosmic level, the universe is understood to contain a balance of male and female elements. Time, or process, is associated with the masculine, whereas space and place is associated with the feminine. Since the task of humans, as Chassidus understands it, is to "make a home for G–d in the world," this means bringing him into time and space. In the Jewish calendar, the six weekdays are masculine, full of work and activities in the public realm. Shabbat, represented as a queen or bride, is associated with a place—the private realm of the home. In *geulah* (redemption), after the arrival of the Moshiach, the world will become eternal Shabbat. According to Chassidus, it is the merit of women that will bring the Moshiach, and the ultimate "feminization" of the world. Time or process will stop, and become place, or home. Six days of the week we are preoccupied with doing; on Shabbat, we are preoccupied with being. "In the messianic era the female will *tzovev* [surround, transcend] the male" (Jeremiah 31:21). The feminine is associated with Shabbat in another regard. Because, according to Chassidus, "Eve was G–d's final creation," and he created her immediately prior to Shabbat, "The final act is the very first thought" (Friday night liturgy). These are understood as references to the spiritual stature of women.

In Kaballah, of the ten *sefirot* (emanations of the infinite and transcendent G–d), it is the final one that channels his power to the human world. This sefirah, known as *malchut* and as *Shechinah*, is the feminine aspect of G–d. Malchut represents sovereignty, nobility, and rulership, and Shechinah is the form of divine presence or spirit that hovered over the Tabernacle. The feminine essence will be given its full due in the messianic era.

The Rebbe Menachem Mendel Schneerson emphasized this vision: "After thousands of years of male dominance, we now stand at the beginning of the feminine era, when women will rise to their true prominence, and the entire world will recognize the harmony between man and woman."[19]

Lubavitcher women established a women's organization called N'shei u'bnos ChaBaD in 1952. It holds annual conventions in cities around the United States and Canada. The organization publishes a journal and several newsletters, and sponsors a variety of classes for women on spiritual and practical matters. Having followed the journal and attended many classes and lectures, I can attest to the seriousness of purpose and rigor of these classes, which gives Lubavitcher women their reputation, at least among other Chassidic courts, for intellectualism. Women are not only permitted to study Torah, it is required of them.

When it comes to challenging law, there are accepted principles that apply equally to men and women. Torah law is considered inviolable, whereas rabbinical law, meaning the compendium of Talmudic interpretations of Torah law, is compelling but not as authoritative. It can be challenged, but only with caution. Custom (*minhag*) may, in some cases, become binding, but it is more susceptible to challenge. In the words of the sages, one should consider, "Is the controversy in the name of heaven?" In other words, does the impulse come from a holy urge or is it prompted by ego? Is it a quest for truth or something less sublime? An incident involving women found in the Torah (Numbers 27) is often taken as a model for contemporary men, as well as women, of the correct way to raise a legal question in the face of authority (in this case, no less of one than Moses). This passage describes how the daughters of Tzelaphad, who had died without sons, petitioned Moses to inherit their father's land, thus establishing to this day the principle of female inheritance and emphasizing the equality of women with men in G-d's eyes. The daughters are not only honored by being mentioned in Torah individually by name, but by being called models of wisdom, virtue, logic, learning, and sincerity. They are praised as righteous because they put the search for the right and true outcome ahead of their personal interests in the case.

Lubavitch holds that there are real differences between men and women that go beyond the physical. They also think, speak, and behave differently. No Lubavitcher will believe that all of these differences are a product of socialization, or even biology; rather, they will tell you that these differences are inherent in a person's essence. But they will also tell you that there is no spiritual distinction between men and women, only a distinction in the manner of their service to G-d.

Women, in fact, are credited with strengths: "Sarah was superior to Abraham in prophecy" (Genesis 21:12, Talmud Tanchuma Shmos); "Women were given an extra measure of understanding" (Talmud Nidah 45); "The wisdom of the woman builds her home" (Proverbs 9:1); "Redemption comes only in the merit of righteous women" (Yalkut, Shimoni Remez 606). Because they feel secure in their roles, Lubavitcher women are puzzled by what they see as the contemporary crisis in secular society in which the sexes seem to want to change places. Each sex wants to sacrifice its uniqueness in the pursuit of equality, but in their view there is nothing positive to be gained in this denial of one's nature. To them, liberal feminism bears the imprint of self-absorption and self-destruction, damaging to both sexes.

The central question of liberalism, and therefore, liberal feminism, seems to Lubavitchers to be, "How can I fulfill my needs, realize or discover my true self, enhance my prestige and status, exercise my rights against others and express my individuality?" When such women ask, "Is Halakhah being fair to me?" they are trying to turn Torah into yet another instrument of self-gratification.[20] But Torah standards for both men and women are not congruent with the liberal ideals of autonomy. Instead of self-aggrandizement, Torah demands subordination to the will of G-d by both sexes. Torah also demands putting the community ahead of the self. In terms of the relationship between husband and wife, it demands complementarity rather than competition.

While outsiders might perceive distinctive sex roles as a sinister plot to reinforce male dominance, Lubavitchers emphasize the misery caused to women in liberal society by forcing them to deny their nature. Anecdotal evidence leads them to understand the secular world as having distorted and manipulated both men and women's natures through materialism, egoism, power, consumerism, and personal ambition in the public realm. Men receive most of the blame for bringing their will to dominate into the home. The culprits that corrupt contemporary family life and make the feminist response appear appropriate are the products of liberal values: excessive individualism and the culture of ambition and self-interest.

When men bring home business tactics rather than wisdom and sensitivity, women take the brunt of it, and respond in kind. But this form of liberation is ultimately an illusion. According to Lubavitch, "True women's liberation does not mean seeking equality within a masculine world, it means liberating the divine feminine aspects of a woman's personality and using them for the benefit of humankind."[21] Instead of seeking validation on male terms, women are enjoined, along with men, to introduce spiritual values into their lives. Lubavitch is fully cognizant of the reality of financial needs, and neither men nor women are asked to forfeit careers. Both men and women are enjoined to place their career at the service of their family. The private realm is considered superior to the public realm.

One of the areas of greatest satisfaction expressed by both men and women within traditional Jewish life is the strength and stability of the family. In this community, marriage is accepted as the natural adult state. Interestingly, women are not obligated by Torah to marry and produce children, whereas men are. There are two explanations for this. First, one cannot be compelled to enter into a contract that has the potential to cause one harm or even death. Because childbearing is (or was) dangerous, a woman can only enter into marriage voluntarily, not under compulsion. Second, by making marriage and childbearing voluntary rather than obligatory, we are prevented from regarding women as mere sexual partners or childbearing vessels. Remembering that surrounding cultures viewed the rationale for women's very existence in purely physiological or reproductive terms, the Jewish understanding that a woman's purpose is not biologically determined is rather impressive. Indeed, when Rachel cried to her husband, "Give me children, for if not I shall surely die" (Bereshis 30:1), Jacob chided her for failing to recognize that her value was not solely as a mother.

Men who remain unmarried are regarded with even more pity then unmarried women. An unmarried woman can fulfill her mitzvot or commandments, but an unmarried man cannot. A man is commanded to "be fruitful and multiply" and he must have a wife in order to do so. The wife, therefore, is an enabler. In the Jewish understanding, there is great merit in enabling one who is commanded to do so to perform his or her mitzvah. The husband is indebted to his wife. Once married, the man is commanded by Torah to take responsibility for the education of his children. The woman is not similarly obligated.

Lubavitcher men seem to take this obligation quite seriously, and in large families father's help at home is essential. I met many men in the Montreal community, including my downstairs neighbor, who had carefully designed their careers so they could work from the home, and therefore be available to help with the small children. Men and boys can be seen pushing strollers and walking with children, learning with them, and drilling children on the weekly *parsha* (section of the Torah). The yeshiva *bocherim* (young men still in their teens) take responsibility for running the *messibos Shabbos* gatherings, in which boys, grouped by age, are collected from their homes on Saturday afternoons with the twin purpose of reinforcing the week's learning and giving the mothers a break. (This is an institution that both my boys and I came to appreciate very much.) The teenage boys do not balk at this infringement on their very limited free time. They see it as both a mitzvah and good preparation for their future roles as fathers and teachers. My own boys are as delighted as my daughter to be asked to watch younger children, and quarrel over who gets to hold the neighborhood babies. It is charming to see how competent and willing both boys and girls are when it comes to looking after younger children.

Marriage is seen not as a union but a reunion, in which two incomplete halves, each searching the world for his or her *bashert* (intended), finally fuse into a single, complete being in marriage, reflecting the two forms of divine energy. As the Torah notes, Adam was originally both male and female, like G-d. G-d thought the better of this arrangement because Adam would be too self-sufficient and egotistical. By separating the male and female aspects of Adam, man would have to go in search of what he had lost. The Hebrew word for bride, *kallah,* is related to the word *completion.* The word for marriage, *kiddushin,* means sanctification or elevation to completeness. The first bridge that the man builds to the rest of humanity would be to his partner in marriage. The language employed is "*ehehseh lo eger kenegdo*" (Bereshis 2:18) or G-d created women not as a helpmeet "for" man but as a helpmeet "against" man. The word suggests her position as opposite him; that is, as fully equal rather than subordinate.

From this relationship, in concentric circles expanding outward, the couple is intended to connect with the larger community. In the marriage, as in the public sphere, the man's role is to use his aggressive energy to refine the material world. The woman's more subtle energy, often mistaken for passivity or weakness, is her inner dignity and her power to reveal the innate G-dliness in all that exists. Each must access the other's energy, each must combine, but each must first understand his or her true self, in the Lubavitch view. According to Talmud, man and woman are like two fires. When they have G-d between them, they unite. When they don't, they consume each other (Talmud, Sotah 17a). Marriage at its best is understood in Chassidus as the human's opportunity to participate in divine creation, and each family unit is conceived of as a tiny world. The sages commanded that a man is to honor his wife above his own self and to love her as himself (Yevamot 62b; Maimonides, Hilchot Ishut 15:19). The union between a man and woman is depicted in the mystical writings as a metaphor for the union of G-d and Israel.

Unfortunately, not all marriages match the ideal. But the Orthodox community no longer ignores the problems that occur. The increase in divorce and domestic violence is probably a product of modern life, and so modern remedies are sought. The establishment of Auberge Shalom, a shelter for Orthodox Jewish women in Montreal, signals an attempt to combat the problem. I was surprised to hear the rabbi of the shul that I attend use the forum of his Shabbat talk to support Auberge Shalom and to address head-on the problems of domestic abuse. Abuse, in his view, includes not only the obvious physical forms, which are rare, but also the withdrawal of affection and respect, since marriage is intended to serve the emotional as well as material needs of an individual. The community now produces its own counselors, social workers, and psychologists, and offers a range of courses to support stressed young mothers of large families. There is an abundance of self-help tapes on family concerns, particularly child rearing.

Saying extra *tehillim* (psalms) and prayers and giving extra *tzedakah* (charity) is always the first recommendation when someone is faced with difficulties, but this does not exclude recourse to divorce. Women do not feel the need to endure miserable marriages, but neither do they seek divorce frivolously. I met a number of women who were divorced, and in every case they received support and sympathy from both men and women in the community. The assumption seems to be universal, if unfair, that men were at fault when marriages went bad.

Separation of the Sexes: Lubavitcher Women Create Their World

Critics of Orthodox Judaism cite the separation of the sexes as a symbol of female servility. The obvious examples of the differentiation of sex roles include *tsnius* (modesty, dignity); *mechitza* (the curtain or wall between men and women during prayer); *taharat ha mishpacha* (laws of family purity, the monthly separation of husband and wife); sexually segregated education and different curricula; and the *get* (document of divorce issued by the husband according to Jewish law). To outsiders, these institutions reflect women's low status in Judaism; to insiders, they protect and elevate both sexes, in addition to fulfilling G-d's commands. Both sexes recognize the power of sexual desire and are careful not to incite it. In keeping with Chassidic thought, an action or relationship that has the capacity to be the most sanctified when carried out appropriately also can become the most degraded when it is not.

The segregation of the sexes begins at about the age of three with separate schooling, separate sections of the shul, and same-sex playmates. This pattern holds throughout life. Beyond family members, boys and girls will have very little contact with each other. Men and women are cordial, but praying and socializing tend to be done with members of the same sex. At the dinner table, female friends tend to congregate together, and men do likewise.

When it is time for a young man or woman to marry, usually in their early twenties, a family member or friend may suggest a *shidduch* (match). Sometimes a professional *shadchan* (matchmaker) is used. If the girl and boy agree, a meeting will be set up and the couple will spend time together. If it is apparent that it will not be a match, it is incumbent upon the parties to break off the meetings before time is wasted or feelings hurt. Social dating with no intent of marriage is not permitted; further, it is not desired by either boys or girls. If the prospects appear good, more dates will take place until the couple agrees to become engaged. Long engagements are not the norm. There is some fear in the community that young people, especially boys, are being inadequately prepared for the responsibilities of marriage. Still, divorce rates are extremely low compared to the average population. There is no concrete data available, but estimates within the community put it at about 5 percent.

Tsnius

The principle of *tsnius* is often translated as modesty, but it actually means something closer to dignity, inwardness, and self-restraint. It finds support in Psalm 45, which says, "the glory of the king's daughter is within." Though tsnius applies equally to men and to women, because the requirements pertaining to women's dress, head-covering, and demeanor are more familiar and visible to outsiders, they have been interpreted by some feminists as an indication that Judaism is either fearful of or repulsed by women's bodies and sexuality.

The code of behavior that regulates the contact between the sexes is regarded as restrictive and demeaning by outsiders, but as protective by insiders. Tsnius is not an indicator of women's second-class status, but is designed to protect her from unwanted male attention. If anything, it may be demeaning to men that Chassidim assume the male to be less able to restrain his impulses, to the point where a woman's physical beauty and even voice are considered to create turmoil in the male soul. Men are as much subject to a dress code as women are, but for different reasons. Dress gives a woman control over when, where, and to whom she reveals her attractiveness. For men, dress is more of a boundary-setting device, which reminds them constantly of who they are and what behavior is expected of them. (I have certainly noticed that my post-Bar Mitzvah son changes his behavior when he dons his black suit and hat.)

Dark suits, white shirts, and covered heads set men off from secular society even more dramatically, and remind them constantly of their role. The *tzitzis* (fringes) that hang out from under their shirts are intended to remind boys and men of their constant obligation to G-d. The uniform is part of their identity, and creates a boundary between them and outsiders in a way that women's dress does not. In fact, Lubavitch women are quite fashionable. Their longer skirts, hats, or wigs do not make them visible or distinctive in the outside world, as does the clothing of the men.

The noticeable lack of demonstrativeness and public displays of intimacy and affection has led to many false assumptions and stereotypes. The assumption that sex is regarded with distaste or even revulsion, and that women are regarded as evil or unclean, is based on a misunderstanding of the external behavior of one of the few remaining groups in society to live their lives inwardly with modesty and self-restraint. Anyone who knows anything about Jewish marriage laws understands that the sexual part of the relationship is an important and ongoing commandment found in Torah and stipulated in the most ancient form of the marriage contract, or *ketubah*. One of the three fundamental obligations of a husband, in addition to providing for his wife's sustenance and clothing, is his duty "to gladden his wife." This is quite separate from the duty to procreate. The importance of sexual intimacy is underlined by the fact that it is mandatory even during pregnancy or after menopause when procreation could not be its goal. Additionally, women possess a right to sexual relations (the man has no such right) as part of the marriage contract.

Lubavitchers sense that the reason for the obsession with sex in the outside culture is that reading, watching, and talking about sex has become a substitute for the real thing. Although outsiders accuse Chassidim of prudery, Lubavitchers pity outsiders for their unsatisfying sex lives. Finally, Lubavitchers believe that if young people of both sexes are able to say "no" emphatically before marriage, they will be more able to say "yes" after marriage without reservation and without the jaded and blasé attitude that is so prevalent in secular society. Sexual promiscuity and inappropriate or misdirected intimacy makes it more difficult for both husband and wife to derive the maximum happiness and intimacy from the special nature of married life.

Upon marriage, women are required to cover their hair. This is read by outsiders as yet another demeaning restriction. Although some young brides express regret at having to cover their hair, all do so after marriage and going to have the *sheitel* (wig) made is a big event. Female friends and relatives are ready with opinions and suggestions about color, style, and the like. A new sheitel will be immediately remarked upon by the neighborhood girls. One becomes quickly adjusted to wearing a sheitel, though every woman has an amusing story of some awkward moment in high winds or the like. (My moment involved having a large iguana get his claws hooked in mine.)

The rationale for covering the hair comes not from anything having to do with a woman's inferiority, but from ancient kaballistic writings that suggest the mystical power that a woman's hair achieves after a woman marries. The sheitel was described to me by Lubavitch women as the modern equivalent of a crown. Because it does not invite touch and because it allows the woman to reserve showing her hair for the privacy of her intimate relationship with her husband, it gives her a sense of dignity and the power to regulate the setting and the beholders of her attractiveness. The requirements of tsnius are not suspended when a woman reaches old age. Her womanliness is avowed throughout her life. Womanliness is not equated with youth as it is in contemporary society.

Interestingly, recent voices in the mainstream community have been picking up on the modesty issue. Using Orthodox Jews as her model, Wendy Shalit notes the positive results of modesty laws and the connection between them and women's happiness. She sees modesty and self-restraint as the source of women's power, not of their oppression. Sexual liberation has not served women well; rather, it has left them vulnerable. Women have been debased by pornography, advertising, and fashion. They have been the victims of sexual freedom, not the beneficiaries, and have responded in record numbers by engaging in self-destructive behaviors and eating disorders. Modesty, Shalit states, not only preserves the erotic better than licentiousness does, it provides a woman with the armor or shield that is, in fact, a power equalizer.[22] Lubavitchers echo this sentiment, "People who are close when they should be distant will end up being distant when they should be close."[23]

Taharat Ha Mishpacha

Critics of Orthodox Judaism often target the laws of family purity, or *taharat ha mishpacha*, as a prime example of Judaism's contempt for women, because they require the separation of a man and wife during her menstrual period and for a week thereafter, until she submerges herself in the *mikvah*, or ritual bath. While outsiders see this as a sign that women are regarded as unclean, traditional Jewish women understand these laws as giving them power and control over their body and their sexuality, especially for those women who had experienced their sexual freedom in the secular world as exploitative rather than fulfilling. In addition, women claim that the family purity laws have meant that their husbands cannot regard them simply as sex objects, or take access to them for granted.

The separation for two weeks each month, many women testify, respects the natural ebb and flow of sexual interest, restores passion, and makes them feel like brides again each month. Additionally, it reinforces the spiritual or "platonic" side of the relationship; for part of the month, at least, the husband must not regard his wife in a sexual way. The sages excluded a purely objectified love of wife or a love based on self-gratification or any other self-serving motive. "Any love that is contingent upon a specific consideration—when that consideration vanishes, the love ceases; but if it is not dependent upon a specific consideration, it will never cease" (Perkei Avot 5:16). The ideal is a marriage in which the sensual element is the expression of a spiritual bond. Torah says that man and woman were created to be companions to one another. The sexual union serves this purpose as much as it serves procreation.

The fact that Lubavitcher women have as many children as health permits, making families with ten, twelve, and even more children quite common, strikes many outsiders as appalling. After all, having a large family makes no economic sense in an urban society and in terms of liberal values appears quite irrational. Every Lubavitcher woman I met had a story about a non-Lubavitcher woman asking her whether she was "permitted" to use birth control, or whether she had all of her children "on purpose." The Lubavitcher women find it very funny that outsiders think they are too simple or too cowed to control their reproductive lives. In fact, they do rely on G-d to send them as many children as he intends, but the use of birth control, or at least prolonged nursing in order to space children apart, is widespread. Birth control is mandatory if pregnancy would jeopardize a woman's health. Families seem to greet each child with love and great celebration. It is not at all unusual to see relatives coming from other continents for the birth of a child, even though that child might be the fifth or the tenth. Moreover, a birth in the community is greeted as an event of collective good fortune. Hearing the news, even people unrelated to the family will respond with "*mazal tov.*" People gather at the home after a birth and before the bris milah for the Shalom Zacher (the welcoming of the child). The bris [circumcision] is a community celebration as is the naming of an infant girl.

In Chassidus, the arrival of the Moshiach is predicated upon the performance of mitzvot; the more souls on earth to perform them, the sooner his arrival. The women, then, although not obligated in the way that men are to procreate, see themselves as having a very direct hand in bringing the Moshiach, both by bringing down these souls and guiding them in the performance of mitzvot. In addition, names possess great significance in Judaism, and giving the name of a deceased relative confers honor on the relative and the child. Naming a child or grandchild for a relative lost to the Holocaust has particularly poignant significance.

The Home: Sanctuary and Altar in Exile

The women I interviewed stressed that they are agents rather than victims of Judaism, emphasizing the critical role that women play in shaping and transmitting the norms and practices of the religion. Jewish women have always worked outside the home and exercised control over the family's economic resources (which, at least in Marxist terms, gave them the real power), but the home has always been their major preoccupation and their domain. Men commonly defer to their wives on matters related to the household. The energy and strength of Jewish women is celebrated each Friday night as the family gathers around the table to welcome the Sabbath. Before the man makes Kiddush sanctifying the wine, he chants the ancient hymn of praise, taken from chapter 31 of the book of Proverbs (attributed to Solomon), called "Aishes Chayil," or "A Woman of Valor," to his wife. This tradition recognizes that historically it was the women who kept the tenuous thread of Judaism alive by preserving the family, despite poverty and persecution. The woman is praised on Shabbat because this is the holiest day of the week. Shabbat is traditionally referred to as the "bride" or "queen" and is ushered in with joy in the home, the realm of feminine values and power. Because both men and women, and children from the earliest ages, hear the repetition of this hymn weekly, it stands as the clearest enunciation of female virtues:

> Who can find a wife of excellence? Her value far exceeds that of gems. The heart of her husband trusts in her, he lacks no gain. She treats him with goodness, never with evil, all the days of her life. She seeks out wool and flax, and works willingly with her hands. She is like the merchant ships; she brings food from afar. . . . She considers a field and buys it; from her earnings she plants a vineyard. She girds her loins with strength, and she flexes her arms. She realizes that her enterprise is profitable. . . . She holds out her hand to the poor, and extends her hands to the destitute. . . . Strength and dignity are her garb; she looks smilingly toward the future. She opens her mouth with wisdom, and the teaching of kindness is on her tongue. . . . Her children rise and acclaim her, her husband praises her. Charm is deceptive and beauty is naught; a G-d-fearing woman is the one to be praised. Give her praise for her accomplishments, and let her deeds laud her at the gates.

This is a far cry from Paul instructing wives "to be subject to your husbands as to the Lord" (Ephesians 5:22–24). In the traditional Jewish hymn, women receive praise for their industriousness, competence, and devotion to the family, the poor, and to G-d. There is no virtue to be found in being submissive or passive; rather, the ideal woman is independent. She is entitled to praise for her initiative and skill. There is no sense in which her contribution is less valuable or her activities less desirable than those of her husband in the sight of G-d, her family, and the community.

Lubavitcher women are quite frank about their feeling that women should not seek careers or professions as an end in themselves, but then neither should men. Both men and women who work should confine themselves to *parnoseh,* or earning a living in a field, which will allow them to live according to the stringent requirements of daily prayer, Torah study, and the upbringing of the children. Careerism, or single-minded devotion to making money and getting ahead, is as frowned upon for men as it is for women. In addition, Chassidic culture is probably the least macho culture in the world. Scholarship, piety, charity, and devotion to family and community are the standards of masculinity, rather than wealth and athletic or military prowess. Pride, ambition, and conquest are all viewed as vices. The "masculine ethos of aggression and self-importance is replaced by the feminine ethos stressing modesty, humility, and a collectivist orientation."[24]

Lubavitch not only revalues the domestic, it invokes the feminine principle in many sacred contexts. The home, the domain of the feminine, is much more than a house. The Midrash (a body of commentary and stories intended to explain Torah) teaches that the Patriarchs envisioned Mount Moriah, the location of the Temple and abode of the Shechinah, or divine presence, in different terms. Avraham called it *har,* or mountain, a lofty place full of awe. Yitzhak referred to it as a *sadeh,* or field, a place of solitude and reflection. But Yaakov, the father of the Twelve Tribes, called it *bayit,* or home.

To this day, the most sacred spot in Judaism is called "home" or Beit Hamikdash, reflecting the centrality of the home to Jewish practice. Until the Temple is rebuilt in the time of the Moshiach, the home is like a mini-Beit Hamikdash, and the women are like the Kohenim, or priests that served in it, re-creating in the home the sanctity and the center of Jewish life. The family table is the equivalent of the *mizbayach,* or altar. In short, the women, in this understanding, are the architects of the "most sacred spaces on earth— our homes." The home is seen as "pivotal factor in our national survival and the key to the redemption of our people." For religious women, the question may be expressed this way:

> How is it that we allowed this most remarkable agency, the home, to become devalued in our time? How is it that we allowed the role of women, the home's primary force, to be denigrated? How have we permitted the secular world with its idolatry of self to convince us that there can be a more worthwhile calling than creating places of loving, caring, and belonging?[25]

Mechitza

The *mechitza* (separation) between the sexes during prayer in the form of a partition, wall, or curtain, is another practice that has been misinterpreted as implying the inferiority or uncleanness of women. For Orthodox women (and for many radical Jewish feminists) this separation takes seriously the need for privacy and freedom from the distraction of the opposite sex in order to turn one's attention to G-d and express one's devotion without inhibition. For these women, the mechitza is liberating rather than oppressive, and suggests to them the full spiritual equality of women and the seriousness with which their prayers are taken. Moreover, this separation creates a space and an opportunity for women to interact independently of men and take control over their spirituality, just as the separation from their husbands once a month allows them to take control over their sexuality. Being in a community of women is not understood by these women to be demeaning; rather, it is understood as affirming. And just as in the case of the laws of family purity and tsnius, the mechitza confirms the power of sexual attraction in both directions. For Lubavitchers, the fact that men and women in secular society can be in close proximity and not be affected by the erotic tension is a sad reflection on the desensitizing and denaturing impact of the constant bombardment of sexual imagery.

Education

As for the dual educational systems, girls' and boys' schools do have very different curricula, with the boys receiving the bare minimum of required secular courses up to seventh grade, when they begin the exclusive study of religious subjects. Girls, on the other hand, receive a much stronger secular education in addition to their religious studies. Although their education in Halakhic matters, or matters of Jewish law, emphasizes those laws that relate primarily to women, family life, and kashrut—on the understanding that women are the protectors and transmitters of Judaism to the next generation—it is not restricted to those concerns.

The history of women's education within Judaism is a mixed one. Talmudic scholars have debated whether fathers have the same obligation to educate their daughters as they do their sons. Some have argued that it is permitted but not obligatory. A minority has argued that it is not even permitted. One sage, frequently cited by feminist critics of Judaism, asserted that anyone who teaches his daughter Torah is to be considered as having taught her *tiflut,* translated as either "distortions" or "wantonness." The concern he voiced had to do with the dangers posed by superficial understanding. On the other hand, Lubavitch has taken the contrary view: Failing to teach one's daughter Torah will lead to tiflut in the modern age, when it can no longer be assumed that a girl will passively absorb Torah from her family or surroundings.

Lubavitch history, in fact, is replete with women scholars of great accomplishment. Edel, the daughter of the founder of Chassidic Judaism, was legendary. Her father, the Ba'al Shem Tov, applied to her the verse from Torah "at his right hand was a fiery law unto them," which was the Hebrew acronym of her name (*eish dalet lamo*) (Deuteronomy 33:2). Freida, the eldest daughter of Schneur Zalman of Liadi, the founder of Lubavitch Chassidus, was responsible for compiling her father's manuscripts and produced several manuscripts of her own.

The sixth Lubavitcher Rebbe gave his blessing to formal education for women in prewar Poland, throwing his support behind the Beth Jacob movement. The seventh Rebbe, Menachem Mendel Schneerson, pioneered in teaching women not only Torah but Talmud. He stated that this acknowledged the changing role of women in society, and recognized the reality of mother as teacher. In addition, he said the world could not progress toward redemption without including the entire Jewish population in the mastery of the law.

One area in which Lubavitch might have been regarded as backward is now being viewed in some circles as progressive. The benefits of sexually segregated education for girls are becoming more widely recognized. The Beth Rivka girls learn to exercise leadership in addition to focusing on their academic studies without the distractions or the social pressures that can undermine girls' academic performance by the time they enter high school. This complicates the claim that girls receive an inferior education to that of the boys.

Imagine the opposite scenario, in which the boys were given a full secular education, taught the language of the land, permitted to enter secular institutions of higher learning, and prepared to succeed in the secular economy. Meanwhile, imagine that the girls were being tutored in the sacred texts and ancient language of the community, deprived of almost any secular training after the age of thirteen, left unable to communicate in the language of the land, and therefore denied opportunities to succeed in any profession outside of the religious community. If this were the policy of the Lubavitch community, feminists would be up in arms, and with justification. But this scenario is the opposite of the Lubavitcher reality. The women, in fact, because they have the superior secular education, are often more gainfully employed than their husbands. In short, while there is great value and honor attached to being a Talmud scholar, there is no financial remuneration attached to this role. Prestige, in this case, does not translate into power, which complicates the situation for theorists who want to argue that men subjugate or undervalue women in traditional Judaism.

The Get and the Agunah

The Hebrew word for marriage, as noted, denotes holiness, elevation, and completeness. The consent of both parties has always been a requirement of marriage. The contract, or *ketubah*, which took on its standardized, modern form in the first century BCE, is a unilateral document of women's rights, held in the possession of the woman. At the marriage ceremony, it is read aloud and signed by two witnesses. It obligates the man to provide for his wife even in the event of divorce or death. The rights of women are, therefore, not dependent on the good will of men. They are enumerated specifically, including the right to conjugal relations. If a husband withholds this right, the wife has grounds for divorce. The husband has no reciprocal right. If he approaches his wife against her will it is considered rape.

Divorce can be instigated by the woman for a variety of reasons, including finding her husband repugnant. On the other hand, hurdles and costs for instigating a divorce are imposed upon the husband. Complicated procedures were intended to prevent capricious divorces and protect women; however, in modern times, these procedures have backfired. When Jews lived in insular settings, the power of both the religious court (Beth Din) and community norms prevented men from abusing these procedures by willfully withholding the divorce decree, or *get*. The rules that were intended to protect women have, ironically, left some women in legal limbo. Unable to persuade her husband to grant her a divorce, a Jewish woman may be unable to extricate herself from a bad marriage. She then becomes an *agunah*, or chained woman.

Lubavitchers will not abrogate Halakhah, but when a particular law seems to impose an unequal or unfair burden on women they will certainly seek remedies within the law. Groups began to form in the United States, Canada, and Israel several years ago to help *agunot* obtain their divorces. They have received widespread support from men (including rabbis) as well as women. They seek rabbinic enforcement of the legal provisions that are already in place to remedy the problem. Rabbinical and social pressure, formal and informal, is brought to bear against the recalcitrant husband. I found no sympathy for such men among other men in the community. I was surprised by the intensity of the condemnation and outright disgust expressed toward husbands who refused to give their wives a *get*. If anything, the men were more adamant than the women, and more likely to suggest that coercive, even less-than-legal, measures be used against them.

As the head of the Beth Din of Canada told me, the regrettable situation of the agunah weighs heavily on all of the rabbis of the Beth Din. The problem, as he understands it, is one of enforcement which, ironically, has been created by trends in modern life well beyond the control of the Jewish community. Accompanying the rise of the nation-state and the idea of individual rights of citizens was the decline of the *kehillah*, the semiautonomous Jewish community that had been part of the corporate structure of medieval Europe. In the days when the kehillah enjoyed undisputed power within its locale, it could enforce Jewish norms, contracts, and divorces quite easily. It could, in many regions, even call upon local non-Jewish authorities for backing. The phenomenon of the agunah, therefore, is a recent one, created in the vacuum left when the kehillah dissolved and the state declared itself unwilling to enforce religious law. Ironically, the agunah is a victim of the fall of communal, and the rise of individual, rights.

Another aggravating factor has been the rise of secularism and the entrance of Jews into the wider society. The threat of being ostracized by the community no longer imposes unbearable social, economic, or psychological costs. The recalcitrant husband either no longer cares or simply removes himself from the range of the communal Beth Din. He has the choice now of joining a different synagogue or leaving the fold altogether, in response to the pressure exerted by a rabbi to grant his wife a *get*. In short, community norms no longer have the power they once did. In response, the community has begun to collectively bribe and even to use coercion to force a husband to give a *get*. I know of rabbis who have traveled hundreds of miles to persuade recalcitrant husbands. This problem is not likely to be resolved in the near future. In Canada and a few states in the United States, women have had some limited success in enlisting the civil courts in their efforts to obtain *gets*. In England, a court recently rejected entanglement in religious controversies.

Although the husband retains the power to withhold a *get* in modern times, women's rights trump men's with respect to custody of the children. In one important respect, and perhaps the most important as far as mothers are concerned, the presumption in Jewish law is that the children belong squarely with the mother. Judaism recognizes that the bond between mother and child is on a different level than that between even the most devoted father and his child. According to Kaballah, the mother, by dint of having carried and given birth to the child, develops a mystical connection with the child, which transcends, or goes deeper, than mere love or sentiment. This understanding may make some liberal feminists uncomfortable because it clearly regards women as having a natural and spiritual proclivity toward childbirth and child rearing. While men may make loving and attentive fathers, they are not regarded as possessing a corresponding "parenting instinct." In the eyes of traditional Jewish women involved in divorce proceedings, this presumption gives them real power.

Finally, although the situation of agunot is distressing and cries out for a remedy, Jewish women were among the first, historically, to be contractually granted the right of divorce. This contract is a remarkable statement about the status of women in Judaism, particularly in light of the status of women in the surrounding cultures until well into this century. Jewish women were among the first to possess rights, dignity, economic power, and spiritual equality.

The Teshuva Phenomenon

Liberal feminists often contend that "insiders" are less able to understand their own cultures than outsiders because they are deprived of an external, objective vantage point. In addition, because they have nothing against which to compare their own cultural norms, they are likely to accept them blindly, rendering their acceptance unautonomous and inauthentic. There are many women in the Lubavitcher community whose attachment to their culture ought to qualify as autonomous and authentic. These are the women referred to as "ba'alot teshuva," literally, "masters of return." Their voluntary acceptance of Jewish law is all the more disturbing to some feminists because it fits the model of autonomous choice.

The teshuva phenomenon goes back to the 1960s, the decade that began the erosion of our common civic religion. The bland mush of distilled shared values, symbols, and meanings had evolved into what Robert Bellah termed "narcissistic and privatized" spiritual experiences, fringe religions, and cults. Many of the teshuvas had cut their spiritual teeth on the civil rights movement, the antiwar movement, and various strands of the counterculture. They had had their fill of the sexual revolution, drugs, and other religions. Their return to Judaism represented the discovery of their own roots, and their rejection of alien cultures.

Many of these returnees encounter Lubavitcher *shluchim* (emissaries) on their college campuses where they were on their way to becoming successful,

professional, secular Jews. Most are products of educated, middle-class, and
not particularly observant families who found their new lives mystifying. Liberal theorists would likely find their choices as mystifying as the teshuvas'
parents do. After all, why would someone throw away the opportunities that
their parents had worked so hard to provide them, trading in an "open" future for a "closed" one? I will leave it to psychologists and sociologists to
probe the inner workings of the mind of the teshuva, but my guess is that they
will try to apply some version of the "true believer" model or the quasi-
fascist-longing-for-security model. My experience is that while there may be
a small percentage of teshuvas who are in a pathological flight from freedom,
most are not.

The ba'alot teshuva come to Lubavitch in search of a moral community in
which both public and private virtue means something. They are unhappy
with the pluralistic and relativistic values of modern secular life and their return to Orthodox Judaism reflects a fully conscious rejection of this culture.
They are looking for a sense of community to counterbalance the meaningless individualism of postmodern culture. In Lubavitch, they find the community that they are looking for. They see themselves as having reclaimed
and repossessed their ancient inheritance. These women make sense of the
traditional division between male and female activities and systems of meaning by emphasizing the vital importance of their sphere. The women's sphere
is a place where they are free to create personal, intellectual, social, and political relationships; where they can find the resources to build a community
of meaning and action.

These women feel able, for the first time in their lives, to claim control over
their own bodies and sexuality and marital lives. According to Debra Kaufman, "They seem to transcend the domestic limits set by patriarchal living,
not by entering a man's world, but by creating their own."[26] In a sexually segregated world, male domination has less, rather than more, significance. This
claim runs counter to the contention that women, when relegated to the private realm, are even more subject to male domination. Most Lubavitch
women are very "woman-identified" in their attitudes, celebrating their
closeness to each other, to nature, culture, spirituality, birthing, and child-
rearing activities. Like radical cultural feminists, they celebrate their gender
differences, whereas in secular society they had felt devalued as women.

Another contingent of ba'alot teshuva voice a different set of motives.
Their perspective is rooted not in the rejection of freedom or equality but in
the view that liberal feminism is an alien and distinctively Protestant Christian product, at odds with Jewish values. In response to women's criticism
that Lubavitch forces women back into the home, Lubavitch women answer

that it is not Protestant-derived feminism but spiritual Judaism that frees Jewish women from having to define themselves according to the Christian majority culture. Their concern is more for the survival of their minority group than for liberating themselves from Jewish men. By upholding the virtues of the Jewish home as a separate realm from the mainstream secular or Christian realm, Lubavitcher women are already liberated. They are "intentionally reproducing the difference between Jewish and non-Jewish versus unintentionally reproducing their own oppression."[27]

Although the articles in the Lubavitch women's journal, *Di Yiddishe Heim* (The Jewish Home), sometimes take a rather defensive tone in rebutting liberal feminist criticism, it is because they often read these criticisms as just another vehicle for the expression of anti-Semitic sentiments. Just as many African American women have not been drawn to liberal feminism because they were more inclined to focus on external rather than internal oppression, Lubavitcher women do not see their men or their religion as the enemy.

Lynn Davidman's 1991 study[28] of ba'alot teshuva was based on interviews with students at Bais Chana, the seminary run by Lubavitch in Minnesota for women returning to traditional Judaism. The dean of Bais Chana is Rabbi Manis Friedman, who has introduced nonobservant women to Judaism for many years. In her interviews with these women, Davidman discovered that many of them emphasized that, in becoming observant, they were really just becoming "themselves." These were primarily college-educated, middle-class women who had experienced the fluidity and openness of contemporary life and were now in search of some stability, in gender roles and in relationships. Dissatisfied with their previous relationships, many were looking for a strong family life and a community of people living life with a shared purpose. They understood that Jewish law, or Halakhah, is not just another lifestyle, but their true "home." In weighing the costs and benefits of liberal freedom and individuality, and the modern view of women's roles, against the traditional view of women's roles, they opted freely for the traditional. Orthodox Judaism, they claimed, conferred a higher status on women than did secular society.

Debra Kaufman's study of newly Orthodox Jewish women confirmed that these women felt that Judaism, by giving equal spiritual weight to women, grants them equality with men. The women interviewed did not seem to display the self-doubt or lack of confidence so common among women in the general population. Kaufman pondered the paradox that these women feel fully valued in an Orthodox setting. Is this a reactionary or a radical stance, she asks? How can we account for women's commitment to laws and traditions that they did not make? Are these women victims of false consciousness? Are they victims at all? In the end, Kaufman wrote, "Theoretical categories cannot distinguish between an 'authentic' and an 'alienated' woman's experience."[29] Practices perhaps devised by men to set women apart may be used by women as the basis for female solidarity.

The aggressive efforts to counter liberal feminism, and to draw in secular women who had become dissatisfied with their lives, have been seen by some critics as opportunistic. They accuse Lubavitch of being disingenuous in appropriating feminist concerns and terminology, and exploiting the overlap between some of the more extreme feminists and the traditional separation of the sexes as practiced in the strictest possible way within traditional Judaism.

In fact, the Lubavitcher message has an audience that extends well beyond its own members. Attempts by nontraditional Jewish feminists to incorporate greater spirituality into their practices have created an area of mutual receptivity with Lubavitcher women, leading to the revival of ancient women's celebrations and rites, such as the observance of Rosh Chodesh (the new month) as a special day for women to gather, study, and rejoice. There has also been a revival of interest outside of the Chassidic and Orthodox community in the *mikvah* (ritual bath of purification) as well as in the period of privacy and separation during menstruation. Some secular feminists have adopted these traditional practices, recasting them in a feminist light. Lubavitchers have not discouraged this and in fact have been quite happy to publicize these practices and their benefits, using feminist terminology.

The stature of historical Jewish heroines and scholars has probably been deliberately and consciously elevated as a response to the secular feminist movement. In the cycle of holidays and festivals, women are featured prominently during Pesach, Chanukah, Purim, and Shavuot, providing girls with models of strength, ingenuity, and courage. In addition, Lubavitch has begun to encourage the public celebration of a girl's Bat Mitzvah, which occurs at the age of twelve. Although girls are not called to the Torah as boys are at thirteen, a girl is expected to give a *dvar torah* (scholarly talk) on a portion of Torah. Girls are raised to feel that they are an integral part of the community and crucial to its survival. As my own daughter prepares to become Bat Mitzvah, it is very clear that she feels very secure in her role.

Even if the motive behind all of these adjustments is to "keep women in their place" (in fact, the consequences of the improvement in Lubavitch education for women have perhaps reinforced, rather than threatened, traditional roles), the fact that women have used their education to increase their power and status in the community is also a consequence—one that appears to be neither unanticipated nor regretted by men. The scope for positive action and full participation by women is authentic, in the view of the women who occupy this world.

Autonomy may require that we be aware of various choices open to us, but not that we necessarily exercise all of these choices. If the only proof we have of our autonomy is that we not only examine but periodically revise our choices, then anyone who remains entrenched in one lifestyle from childhood would be suspected of nonautonomy. Yet, when the child of a liberal, secular family opts to adopt the lifestyle that she received from her parents, liberal theorists do not seem to raise an eyebrow. They would be much more concerned if she exchanged her secular or liberal lifestyle for a traditional one. Is this a bias in favor of liberal projects and ends? In any event, some notions of liberal freedom and autonomy are an illusion. Are we free to do what we want, or what we can? Is our self-definition a matter of choice? Without our roles are we free or merely abstractions? If we are really free to do everything and anything, we may discover that we really do not want to do anything at all.

Finally, the sort of freedom of choice associated with contemporary liberalism does not serve women or children very well. "Liberalism, by endorsing male irresponsibility, self-indulgence, and detachment from the claims of others," encourages the flight from family commitments. Family life yields to the individual pursuit of self-actualization and personal fulfillment. The marriage contract, like any other, is binding only as long as it satisfies. Liberal autonomy, in short, "works well for men, but not for the women and children who are dependent upon them."[30] The celebration of individual autonomy, combined with the eradication of gender roles, has created as many problems as it has remedied.

Women may well applaud the triumphs of the liberal women's movement in this century. In fact, in many respects, all women are feminists today. But while many women may define "liberation" in liberal terms, others do not. According to Debra Kaufman, "Orthodox women reconstruct the sex/gender system to enhance their status and to bring men's culture, aspirations, and values into line with women's values and interests. Therefore, while they may seem to reject liberal feminism, they raise women's status, power, enhance self-esteem . . . engage in female institution building, insure community survival, and create a woman-centered world."[31]

Lubavitch women, instead of attempting to mimic male roles, have achieved what they feel to be closeness with G-d, prestige, power, and status by living according to the dictates of Torah and their womanly nature. They feel that they can only serve G-d by being themselves. These women claim that liberal, secular women, or religious women who adopt male religious practices and roles, are denigrating women and devaluing their unique accomplishments, rather than raising their status. The message of liberal feminism, as read by Lubavitch women, is that without women being able to mimic male roles and accomplishments, women are nothing.

Their reading of the messages and meanings of their own world is that women play a pivotal role in the expressed, shared goal of the community— bringing the final redemption, or *geulah*. They see their roles as equal, though separate. From outside of their world of meaning, it is easy to read the messages that women receive as part of a sinister plot to convince them that they are of equal value to men while keeping them in their inferior and subordinate roles. Labeling these women deluded is not merely condescending. It highlights the fact that outsiders can only judge these women if they are willing to raise, and then defend, an objective standard of happiness, one that invalidates the Lubavitcher woman's standard of happiness and sense of satisfaction with her life.

Cultures give messages to their members. If Lubavitcher women are constantly told from childhood that they are valued and respected, if they are treated with dignity, if they absorb these messages as part of their self-definition and identity, does this not become reality? Words and deeds mean something. Lubavitcher women, in believing and living this reality, make it true, whatever the motive behind the message might have originally been. In short, even if we suppose the most nefarious of male plots, the plot has back-fired. Conspiring to make women believe they are equal seems a pretty foolish way to keep them down. Moreover, the conspiracy theory assumes that men are the sole creators and purveyors of meaning, when in fact women are very much involved in the creation and interpretation of community norms.

If Lubavitcher women believe themselves to be equal and behave accordingly, on what basis can an outsider claim that these women are subjectively equal but objectively subjugated? Eventually the distinction between authentic and inauthentic experience dissolves because there is no way to support this judgment except by relying on the majority's status as the majority, that is, on the weight of popular opinion and prevailing custom. This is especially true when those beyond the borders of a culture claim that what they happen to find unintelligible, is in fact, inexplicable. A Lubavitcher might respond to a liberal critic in the words of Isaiah, "For My thoughts are not your thoughts" (Isaiah 55:8).

CHAPTER EIGHT

Subgroups and Citizenship

There are several current strands of scholarship that reconsider classical liberal theories of associational life and the role of subgroups in a democracy. Some theorists have questioned the ontological premises of liberalism, specifically, the conception of humans as atomistic individuals, emphasizing instead that humans are naturally constituted to live in groups. For them, associational life is the source of values and identity. Other theorists focus on associational life as the incubator of democratic habits such as trust and mutual respect. In both cases, the group is seen as a vehicle for self-realization and citizenship.

But there is a third group of theorists who examine associational life from a different perspective. They see these groups as sources of law and authority for their members. To an extent, these groups will necessarily compete with the state for the loyalty of the individual. This is a disturbing idea for traditional liberal thought, in which abstract, generic citizens give their loyalty to the state. Liberal theory seems most comfortable with either individuals or states as the basic units of analysis. Even the family poses problems for liberal theory when a contest arises over which institution has ultimate authority over children. Substate loyalties defined by class, religion, gender, race, or ethnicity are problematic in a political system that responds primarily to abstract individuals. To one extent or another, this third category of theorists challenges the right of the unitary state to claim a monopoly on constitutional interpretation and lawmaking. They would welcome the proliferation of subnational sovereigns and worlds of normative meaning.

Perspectives on Subnational Groups

Subnational groups may either support the state or compete with it. The benefit to democracy of factions, as described by Madison in "Federalist 10" and by de Tocqueville, lay not in themselves but in their ability to fragment and disperse power and thus check the pretensions of the state. It was for later theorists to describe how associations serve democracy by fostering certain politically salutary attitudes and behaviors. The thicker the layer of associations making up civil society, it is claimed, the healthier and more vital the democratic state that plays host to them because subgroups and associations complement the state by eliciting civic behavior from citizens.

Political theorists such as Benjamin Barber, Robert Putnam, and Kent Greenawalt consider religious groups particularly salutary for democracy. According to Robert Putnam, "Faith communities in which people worship together are arguably the single most important repository of social capital in America."[1] Half of all associational membership in America, he points out, is church-related. Religiosity is a powerful correlate of civic engagement as well as voluntary and philanthropic behavior. But not all religious associations serve democracy equally well. Those that are too individualistic or privatized and those that are too fundamentalist, fervent, and insular do not provide the same level of direct or indirect civic benefits to the wider society. It is not clear where Lubavitchers would fall on this continuum. They may fall outside of his framework altogether: Like most political theorists, whether classical liberals or communitarians, Putnam seems to be referring exclusively to those associations in which members conceive of their affiliation as voluntary.

While associational life is considered to be natural and necessary for both the individual and democracy, membership in any specific group is viewed ultimately as a matter of individual preference. Members can choose their affiliations, entering and exiting more or less at will. Even theorists like Will Kymlicka, who not only share the communitarian premise that humans are at home in groups but openly advocate for the recognition and protection of minority cultures' rights, are not entirely comfortable with groups that do not understand membership as a voluntary choice. They share with classical liberals the view that the group should create the preconditions of individual autonomy by serving as the locus of value formation.

There is a difference between being a Chossid and becoming a member of a bowling league, to adopt Putnam's famous example. Despite the fact that communitarian theorists promote the idea that humans are social beings who do not independently manufacture but rather find their identity and "discover" their values in a social and cultural setting, they would not necessarily see Chassidim as a model. While communitarian theorists view humans as communal beings in private life, they expect people to behave as liberals in public life. Communitarians complain about the assimilative impact of the dominant culture upon constitutive communities, but they share the tendency to treat liberal values as synonymous with civic virtue, and are just as apprehensive about the impact of nonliberal groups on democracy as the liberal theorists they criticize.

Therefore, neither traditional liberals nor communitarians celebrate Chassidim as their ideal. Associations are deemed valuable to democracy by theorists such as Robert Putnam and Benjamin Barber because they are, in Barber's words, "the civic soul of democracy."[2] In other words, associations may serve their members' social, spiritual, and recreational needs, but it is their ability to serve democracy that validates their existence. For political theorists who believe that democracy is best served when there is a high level of congruence between political culture and political institutions, private and public norms, civil society and the state, private individual and public citizen, the existence of groups that are not aggregates of otherwise autonomous individuals will raise ambivalent feelings.

Groups like Lubavitch may seem to compromise the political process. Although they cast individual votes, they appear to vote, or engage in other forms of political activity, in order to strengthen group cohesion and further the group's interests. The pursuit of individual interests is considered a valid expression of one's citizenship, and the pursuit of the common good is considered a civic and noble expression of one's citizenship, but the pursuit of an interest that is shared by an insular group is troubling to many liberal theorists. This is so even if its insularity is a survival strategy that does not, in itself, put the group at odds with other "shared democratic purposes."

Most Jews, within a generation or two of arriving in Canada or the United States, assimilated into the pattern of voluntary associational life: "In a society that promoted autonomy and voluntarism and that promised liberation from the obligations and traditions of the Old World, the case for communal solidarity had to compete against many other options. . . . Jews could not come across as motivated by a narrow particularism, by a sovereign preference for peoplehood over citizenship."[3]

Unlike most Jews, Chassidim, including Lubavitchers, came to Canada and the United States in order to exercise associational freedom. But to refer to the Chassidic courts as voluntary associations would miss the mark. Chassidic identity is not organized around the individual but around the family, hence around descent and upbringing. Continuity and community form the basis of their identity in a world that is much more hospitable to voluntary associations.[4] Chassidim are out of step with the Lockean and Kantian understanding that individuals undertake obligations through free-willed contracts and that no one is bound by a set of loyalties, ties, or obligations that were imposed upon him or her without consent from birth.

Groups whose membership is defined in ascriptive terms, such as race, gender, religion, or ethnicity (as opposed to shared interests, hobbies, or concerns), are not considered associations in the liberal sense. According to the liberal conception, members of associations remain individuals. They vote as individuals, enter and exit as individuals, maintain multiple memberships and loyalties as individuals, exercise their rights as individuals, and conceive of themselves as individuals. The association has no independent existence apart from its members. For Chassidim, their court, or community, is conceived of as greater than the sum of its parts. Although the individual is not completely subsumed within the community, leaving the court would be tantamount to shedding his or her identity.

The issue of nonvoluntary affiliation is troubling to many theorists, all the more so because it is usually part of a cluster of nonliberal practices and values. The anxiety that many people feel is understandable when the discussion turns to nonliberal groups that hoard weapons and express the desire to overthrow the government. But even loathsome groups, as long as they are law abiding, may serve democracy by taming their members' undemocratic urges and violent proclivities, and harnessing them to group life. Very few groups, with the exception of avowedly subversive ones, would be counted as beyond the pale by Nancy Rosenblum. She reminds us that groups are constituted with the interests of their members, not necessarily the state, in mind, meaning that we should not evaluate groups exclusively on the basis of the service they provide to the state. But as Martha Minow attests, nonliberal minority groups are likely to find their practices subjected to much closer scrutiny than those groups that adhere to the values of the majority. Chassidim have certainly experienced this.

Groups as Political Actors

It is one thing to argue that there is room in a liberal democracy for groups that do not subscribe to liberal values, but it is another thing to argue that these groups should be welcomed as political actors, bearers of rights, or units of formal representation. Yet, some argue that many groups that make up society have the capacity to better serve the needs of their members than the universal state can. For them the idea of universal citizenship is abstract to the point of meaninglessness. Iris Marion Young contrasts it with the "politics of difference."[5] Here, the goal would be to work out a new division of labor between groups and the government, revamping representative democracy to accommodate cultural diversity. Groups as well as individuals would then be recognized as real, rights-bearing political actors.

Despite increasing academic attention to pluralism, diversity, and formal group rights in both the United States and Canada, the United States does not grant special rights to minority ethnic, racial, linguistic, or religious groups, with the exception of aboriginal tribes. Canada recognizes group rights to a greater extent, but does so in a limited way. There are many implications arising from the fact that "neither the U.S. nor Canada has a constitutional mechanism that explicitly allows religious communities to articulate their notions of childhood, membership, and co-existence."[6]

While the First Amendment to the U.S. Constitution does not explicitly protect the right of association (as the Canadian Constitution does), the assumption that it is a full-fledged right by corollary or by implication is universal. According to the liberal model, associations are best understood as voluntary aggregates of individuals. Religious groups, in keeping with this model, are usually regarded as voluntary as well. The U.S. Constitution has no provisions for recognizing religious groups in any other terms. Even the Canadian system, which allows Jews to identify themselves according to either religion or ethnicity, does not expect a Jew's political and religious identities to be coextensive.

As Michael Walzer contends, "Democracy can be accommodating to groups, as long as it deals only with individuals. . . . The primary function of the state and of politics generally is to do justice to individuals, and in a pluralist society, ethnicity is simply one of the background conditions of this effort."[7] The state can provide a framework for groups to flourish, but it cannot actively intervene to guarantee a group's continued existence. This depends on the vitality and efforts of the group itself. In any event, Lubavitchers would not fit well into this schema since they do not aspire to group representation or agitate for group rights in either Canada or the United States. On the contrary, in both countries, much like more mainstream Jews, they are among the strongest supporters of individual rights.

In this section, we will leave aside questions about group rights, multiculturalism, and diversity because they do not promise to further our understanding of groups such as Lubavitch, nor do Lubavitchers make use of these concepts in understanding their world. Conceptually, they are the bridge between the literature on associations and democracy and the literature on what is variously called "legal pluralism," "nomic diversity," or "overlapping sub-federal sovereignty." This literature is sensitive to the problems faced by groups that determine that, in order to flourish, they must be selective in their interactions with the society and the state. Should it be up to the state or the group to decide the nature and scope of the interaction?

Unlike group rights theorists, most legal pluralism theorists do not propose revising our system of representation in order to create a formal role for groups as political actors within the system. Rather, they bemoan the reduction of all law to state law and see subgroups as multiple, nonstate sources of law. They support those beleaguered enclaves that continue to struggle for legal autonomy, and thereby continue to mount a challenge to the supremacy of a unitary source of law for all members of society. Lubavitch fits in this category fairly neatly, though its relationship with the contemporary liberal state is rarely as confrontational as those groups that most often draw the attention of legal pluralists.

Legal pluralism and Chassidim hearken back to a similar historical and political setting. Both draw their political insights from premodern Europe where vestiges of semiautonomous corporate entities survived and fought for authority in the face of the burgeoning system of unitary nation-states. Eventually, nation-states won out, subordinating and domesticating all other entities that might have served their members as alternative sources of meaning and authority. The Jewish *kehillah* or *kahal*, which throughout medieval Europe had enjoyed a certain quasi-sovereign legal and legislative autonomy, succumbed to a similar fate. Of course, the power and very existence of the kehillah had always depended entirely on the goodwill of the local non-Jewish rulers, which made its existence precarious. For better or worse, Jews as a community enjoyed privileges, and Jews as a community suffered expulsion and murder.

The rise of the nation-state and the conceptualization of individual rights of citizenship had an enormous impact on the Jewish corporate structure. The emancipation movement, which eventually encompassed the Jews of Europe, offered the rights and duties of citizenship to Jews as individuals in exchange for communal autonomy. This is not the place to evaluate the deal, but the changes wrought upon individual Jewish self-identity by modernity and the entrance into secular society were accompanied by the demise of the kehillah. All that remains of the traditional communal structure of Jewish life is represented in the contemporary world by Chassidic courts such as Lubavitch. These last vestiges of Jewish communal life struggle to maintain their values and their authority over their members in the face of an overwhelmingly powerful and not always tolerant unitary state.

In examining the interaction between normative communities, specifically Lubavitch and the state, legal pluralists ask whether the boundary-maintaining activities of these nomic groups, aimed as they are at ensuring the survival of the group, compromise the role of the state as the guarantor of individual rights? Do these nomic groups seek to establish a system of *polynomia,* or multiple sources of authoritative law, and thus challenge the state's monopoly over the propagation of laws? By seeking to establish the parameters, boundaries, and rules regulating the interaction between the nomic group and the state, does the nomic group challenge the assumed right of the state to determine the nature of the interaction and participation of groups and the wider society? Are nomic enclaves more problematic from the perspective of the state when they participate in politics than when they remain politically passive?

If we were to free the legal imagination from structuralist thinking and from Weberian formal rationality, universalism, positivism, certainty, and order, we could reconceive the polity as an infinite number of overlapping systems of law that both structure and compete for the loyalty of its citizens. There is no reason, according to this view, to imbue the state's legal system, or any other for that matter, with transcendent virtue. This model raises the possibility of regarding nonconformist behavior by enclaves such as Lubavitch as a reflection of an alternative conception of legal normativity rather than a case of "Constitution flouting." This perspective acknowledges that "Jewish law is a system which intersects with state law in uneven and dynamic ways, such that, for Chassidim, one system may take priority over the other in certain contexts, and with respect to particular issues."[8]

Lubavitch corresponds closely to what Robert Cover called *paideia,*[9] or "nomic communities." A nomic group is by definition an enclave. It is bent on preserving its own values and norms, which are usually significantly different from those of the surrounding community. Its aim is survival. Its members may feel beleaguered and threatened, although not necessarily because they perceive the outside world as hostile. On the contrary, in the United States and Canada, the outside world is all too attractive and inviting, in some respects. Some way of cloistering themselves from the distractions of the outside world is sought. This does not require removing themselves to a remote setting, though for some groups like the Amish, Hutterites, and Tasher Chassidim, physical isolation has been the preferred method of self-preservation.

William Shaffir, in writing about the Montreal Lubavitch community,[10] adopted Frederick Barth's concept of "ethnic group boundary" as a device for maintaining identity and fostering self-preservation in the face of external forces that might otherwise absorb or sweep away the group. Boundary maintenance is a counterassimilation tactic. It does not necessarily require isolation from the wider society, but may instead include a host of measures such as the careful oversight of education; the filtering of media; distinctive clothing, customs, and behaviors; and a separate calendar and language. These are devices that allow Chassidim to structure and control the nature and scope of their interaction with outsiders.

The idea that the state is merely one contender for supremacy in creating and interpreting law is another aspect of Cover's theory. His sympathies clearly lie with the underdog in this competition—the nomic community as opposed to the state. For Cover the nomos is a small, integrated normative universe with its own system of meaning. "A nomos is a present world constituted by a system of tension between reality and vision"[11] with a narrative linking the two domains. The nomos is held together by the strength of its members' commitments rather than by coercion. Cover describes two models or systems, the "world-creating" community, and the "world-maintaining" community.

The first ideal type, the world-creating nomos, possesses a "common body of precepts and narrative," a common education, and a common sense of direction and purpose for the individual and the community. Chassidim approximate this ideal type. The Torah, according to Cover, is pedagogic. It requires study, interpretation, and projection—that is, its precepts need to be carried into the real world of action. Its "discourse is initiatory, celebratory, expressive, performative, rather than critical and analytical."[12] It is also a narrative in exile. The point of reference for the community is not the contemporary world and its understanding of reality but the Torah and its understanding of reality. This brings it into conflict with the state's attempt to inculcate its citizens with the critical and analytical mode of thought, which itself expresses and initiates them into the paideia of liberalism.

A "world-maintaining" community is imperialistic about its norms and its narrative, which it seeks to impose and enforce. "The universalistic virtues we have come to identify with liberalism are system maintaining 'weak forces.' They are virtues that are justified by the need to ensure the coexistence of strong normative meaning."[13] Because liberalism is the quasi-official doctrine of the state, the state has the role of maintaining the liberal world of meaning. According to Cover, "interpretation always takes place in the shadow of coercion."[14] How much leverage it has or chooses to exercise against the world-creating nomoi in its midst is restricted by its constitution. But since the state exercises something of a monopoly with respect to constitutional interpretation, this gives it a fair amount of latitude, and certainly the upper hand, in defining the relationship between it and the various nomoi. When faced with the problem of multiplying worlds of meaning, the more remote or alien the values of a given nomos, the more likely it is to come under state scrutiny and to be perceived as a rival.

The ability to create and interpret law requires the corollary ability to suppress other law-creating bodies. According to Cover, this tension is not trivial. The state and the nomos are bound to come into conflict because they are bound, at some point, to offer conflicting interpretations of the law. There is a radical dichotomy between the social organization of law as power and the organization of law as meaning. From the nonstatist viewpoint of the nomic group, this is a competition between two equal nomic worlds. The perspective that says that only the state can create law "confuses the status of interpretation with the status of political domination."[15]

In the case of conflict, states Cover, the nomic community must decide whether to offer resistance or whether to withdraw. Most groups, like the Amish and Chassidim, are both lawful and nonviolent. The Amish have historically avoided confrontations, entering the legal system, as in the *Yoder* case, only when it is essential, and otherwise opting for withdrawal. Chassidim similarly do not seek out confrontations with the state, but they have shown themselves ready and able to use the legal system defensively as another boundary-maintaining technique.

According to Cover, various insular nomic communities have established their own interpretations of the U.S. Constitution, and are locked in a constant struggle with the state to retain their independent authority. These communities, be they Amish, Mennonite, or Chassidic, are likely to emphasize the right of association, freedom of religion, and freedom of conscience, claiming that they trump other public policy goals, no matter how noble. The First Amendment, then, becomes a boundary, marking off and protecting the community from civil coercion. Groups that are constituted on the basis of shared religious practice have a leg up provided by the First Amendment. While most theorists do not believe that religious groups ought to be given carte blanche, many applaud the asymmetrical treatment that religious groups receive.

For nomic groups like the Chassidim, separateness is constitutive and jurisgenerative. There can be no Chassidic Judaism apart from the Chassidic community. Lubavitchers would share Cover's view that the state should not intervene in the internal life of the community for capricious reasons merely to assert its will. They would share Cover's conclusion that "we ought to stop circumscribing the nomos; we ought to invite new worlds."[16]

The recent narrow defeat in the Supreme Court of an attempt by one group of Chassidim to press its jurisgenerative claim evoked a flurry of reactions. Political and legal theorists divided over whether to condemn or defend the constitutionality of the school district created by the state of New York to accommodate the Satmar Chassidim.[17] The New York legislation was applauded by some as a model of how the state could respond positively to the challenges of multiculturalism. Thomas Berg saw it as "a happy instance in which the political and cultural majority protected the practices of an unconventional minority without imposing any costs on other citizens."[18]

But when the school district was struck down by the Supreme Court, Martha Minow charged that the legal order was forcing the Chassidim to choose between separatism and assimilation because, in order to become eligible for the same benefits and rights extended to other citizens, the Chassidim had to sacrifice their distinctive religious practices. She asked, "Does the secular, democratic state require assimilation as the price of membership?"[19] Abner Greene also criticized the ruling, maintaining that our constitutional order should recognize "permeable" sovereignty, which allows semiautonomous nomic groups to exercise public as well as private power, as long as they do it in conformity with the Constitution. He concluded that "the flourishing of these nomoi is central to the liberal democratic project."[20]

The ruling revealed "a salient feature of liberalism's deep structure," according to Robert Lipkin. "Liberal political theory can explain and justify toleration of nonliberal cultures only in the following circumstances: when nonliberal cultures are sufficiently like liberal cultures so as to avoid deadly conflict or when the liberal culture derives instrumental benefits in tolerating the nonliberal culture."[21]

Other political and legal theorists have not been as sympathetic to the sort of nomic diversity that Chassidim contribute to the polity. According to Christopher Eisgruber, assimilation is a constitutional value. His view is that liberal society should only tolerate those subgroups that provide benefits to an "invigorated constitutionalism." Retreating into segregated enclaves does not serve this purpose. Only by living their differences in full view can these groups foster self-critical reflection on the nature of the good life by their fellow citizens.[22]

Jeff Spinner shares this view. He would have government promote "pluralistic integration," using education and any other means compatible with the Constitution to reform nonliberal groups.[23] Although the state, in Spinner's view, is restricted from working overtly to dismantle groups such as the Amish or Chassidim, "it would not be a terrible loss if [they] were to disappear."[24]

In his view, unlike the Amish, who are not good citizens, Chassidim are bad citizens. The distinction is that the Amish exercise what he calls "complete exit" from the political sphere, which is relatively harmless to the liberal state, whereas Chassidim attempt to exercise "partial exit." He complains that they want cultural exit, but not political exit. He counts Chassidim as a "liberal paradox, in that they vote, run for office, serve on local political boards and commissions, make deals and deliver block votes to politicians who come to curry favor and endorsements."[25] It irritates him that Chassidim use the rules of democratic political engagement as a strategy for fortifying themselves against the liberalizing influences of the wider society.

Ira Lupu is similarly unsympathetic to the self-segregating lifestyle of the Satmar Chassidim. Rather than a voluntary affirmation of a separate life, he sees their "exit" more as a (cowardly) flight from social ostracism, a form of defensive huddling. Their motivation is not principled, in Lupu's view; rather, their actions are prompted by covert, sectarian, and ultimately unconstitutional considerations. Worse, the Satmar Chassidim want to maintain their own identity without severing their ties with the state. Such a grant of "partial exit" would essentially implicate the state in a grant of sovereignty to a community that could not be counted on to exercise its power consistent with constitutional norms. Lupu sees more similarities between Chassidim and the Branch Davidians, Bob Jones University, and the Montana militia than between Chassidim and genuine nomic enclaves.[26]

Judith Failer condemns Chassidim as "unhealthy for democracy, especially when they exercise political power."[27] This is because when they "make claims on government as citizens, it is not a true exercise of rights or citizenship as Americans, but it is based on Halakhic considerations."[28]

That most of us make rights claims only when they are violated, with no higher principle in mind but to solve our specific problem and live as we choose, does not appease those for whom legitimate engagement in the political realm requires that some larger purpose is advanced. Apparently, the state should foster social diversity only insofar as it enriches "our" lives. From this perspective, the question is, "What benefits do we reap by tolerating the presence, and especially the political activism, of enclave groups that do not share our liberal values?"

It is improbable that Chassidim could undermine democracy either through the manipulation of democratic procedures or through the demonstration effect. Moreover, the harshest critics of nonliberal groups should probably welcome their political involvement because it structures a group's behavior according to accepted norms.

The rules of political engagement apply to Chassidic citizens just as they do to other citizens. Exposure to the values of the wider society is an unavoidable side effect of political participation. Politics achieve for Chassidim what rural isolation achieves for the Amish: the maintenance of boundaries and the survival of a world of meaning. Why should we begrudge minorities the only means that they have to ensure their survival? Why should we hold them to a standard of citizenship that most interest groups also fail to meet? Since when is it out of bounds to enter the political realm to further a special interest?

As for the isolation and homogeneity of the Chassidic communities, how different is it, in effect, than the self-isolation of gated communities and wealthy enclaves, in which interaction with those unlike themselves is just as limited? Why should Lubavitchers elicit more intense scrutiny for their impact on democracy than enclaves based on class? Why suppose that the citizens of Scarsdale serve democracy better than Lubavitcher citizens?

Groups, Boundaries, and Membership

Boundaries are a practical necessity if Lubavitch is to survive as a community. The traditional political theory of the Jews in exile has always included the principle, *dina di malchuta dina,* or "the law of the land is law." But in previous eras, the host governments were willing to permit a demarcation between the functions of the imperial or regional ruler and the kehillah, or Jewish communal authority. This represented, in a sense, a form of shared sovereignty, or the toleration of subnational sovereigns. The Jewish community related to the law of the land, to an extent, as foreign law. The U.S. Constitution is prepared to confer rights and duties exclusively upon individual, private citizens. It is obviously not prepared to cede power to semisovereign groups.

Liberalism's awkwardness with respect to the idea of community derives in part from the desire of the state to exercise its authority without competition from other would-be sovereigns, and in part from the still-potent Enlightenment ideal of a universality in which one big society becomes one big community. Even though intentional communities have always been part of the American landscape, there has always been an uneasy relationship between the gemeinschaft and the gesellschaft in our social self-image. The ambivalence about communities also derives in part from concerns about the impact of subgroups on their neighbors.

This is well illustrated in a series of controversies that came before the courts over the placement of an *eruv* in several American neighborhoods. An eruv, as was mentioned in an earlier discussion, is a thread or wire attached to preexisting telephone poles or the like, in order to completely enclose an area and thereby convert it, according to Jewish law, from a public into a private space. Since Jews are prohibited from carrying any object into a public space on the Sabbath, the erection of an eruv permits one to push a stroller, carry a key, and the like.

The eruv is almost always invisible from the ground and its very presence is undetectable to anyone who is not specifically looking for it. An eruv in no way creates a physical impediment or eyesore. If anything, the Jewish community, which is solely responsible for funding and maintaining the eruv, will spruce up the physical barriers to which it is attached. An eruv does not create a physical nuisance to the neighbors of the Jewish families that benefit from the enclosure.

The cases of *Smith v. Community Board No. 14* n66, 491 N.Y.S. 2d 584 (Sup. Ct. 1985) and *ACLU of New Jersey v. City of Long Branch*, 670 F. Supp. 1293 (D.N.J 1987) were granted standing as raising First Amendment, specifically, establishment clause issues, but in reality what was at stake was the meaning and boundaries of community, of exclusion and inclusion. In the *Smith* case, local authorities granted permission to construct an eruv. There were already more than thirty existing eruvs in the state of New York and nine in New Jersey. But non-Jewish residents charged that the permission constituted a violation of the establishment clause. The plaintiffs maintained that the eruv would create a "metaphysical" impact on the area, giving it a "religious aura." The *Smith* plaintiffs claimed that the injury to them consisted of an intangible impact. In fact, in both cases the courts ruled that the eruv did not constitute a violation of the constitutional prohibition against the establishment of religion in that the eruv, besides being invisible, was not a religious symbol.[29]

The best way to make sense of the plaintiffs' claim is in social and psychological, rather than religious or constitutional, terms. The non-Jewish residents believed that the eruv created a community, and simultaneously altered a preexisting one. Somehow, the placement of a thread at treetop level would make the plaintiffs feel "alien." In other words, the flip side of the Jewish community that was symbolically created by the eruv was the noncommunity of resident "outsiders." The solidarity of the Jewish community, it was feared, would provoke the opposite sense of fragmentation and alienation among the neighbors. These cases should probably also be understood in terms of the dynamic of neighborhood succession and the tensions over this phenomenon that are being played out in numerous neighborhoods nationwide. One such case has taken the form of a zoning conflict between the established residents of Beachwood, Ohio, and newcomers who are Orthodox and Chassidic Jews. A similar conflict is ongoing in the Cotes St. Luc and the Outrement sections of Montreal. At the heart of these conflicts is who gets to determine the character and the membership of the community.[30]

The willingness of neighbors to respect both diverse cultures and insular communities relies on reading the boundaries established by such communities as intended to shelter their culture rather than exclude their neighbors. It tests the ability of society to distinguish between communities that intend to exclude on the basis or race or class and those that intend to perpetuate a distinctive world of meaning, tradition, and law.

Liberalism has neither come to grips with the challenges posed by groups seeking to share jurisgenerative power, nor comfortably accommodated an alternative to the prevailing model of citizenship based on geographical and individualist political identity.

CHAPTER NINE

Normative Citizenship

The role of the Jewish citizen is to take a good system and give it a soul.
Rebbe Menachem M. Schneerson

Are Lubavitchers good citizens? There are two theoretical issues related to normative citizenship. The first has to do with the virtues of democratic citizens: What are they and how do we foster them? The second has to do with the loyalties or allegiances of democratic citizens: Does democracy require patriots?

The first issue is about capacities and skills; the second is about sentiments and identity. One could imagine two axes. On the vertical we might arrange "high" citizenship skills against "low" citizenship skills and on the horizontal we might arrange "particular" or "local" loyalties against "universal" or "cosmopolitan" loyalties. That done, we might attempt to locate Lubavitchers on the "good citizenship" scale in terms of their sentiments and capacities. But the question of whether or not Lubavitchers (or any of us) make good democratic citizens would not be resolved because we do not know, as a society, what it means to behave as a good citizen or even whether democracy requires skilled and patriotic citizens.

Democratic Virtues and Skills

In this section we will discuss several possible models of citizenship and see whether any of them can accommodate the Lubavitcher Chassidim. When we speak of citizenship, it will be in the normative rather than the legal definition, that is, "citizenship as a desirable activity."[1] The focus will not be on the classic issues of rights and freedoms, but on the dimension of the duties, loyalties, rules, virtues, and responsibilities of citizenship. The latter issue has taken on a new sense of urgency in the scholarly literature as concern for the stability of democratic institutions is expressed in terms of whether we are producing citizens with sufficient competence and commitment to keep these institutions afloat.

Politicians and social scientists are sounding the alarm over the disintegration of our families, schools, churches, and civic organizations, which are supposed to be the incubators of democratic behaviors and norms. The classical laissez-faire approach to citizen virtues has produced what would rate as "low" citizens on our scale. We can no longer be confident that individuals motivated by self-interest alone will function, in Robert Dahl's terms, as "good enough" citizens.[2] "Free rider" citizens may not expend the energy necessary to get to the polls if there does not appear to be a personal payoff. We could leave our democratic institutions in the hands of those citizens who are interested in politics, but the decline in voter turnout has been so precipitous that it raises the possibility that the outcome of our elections may not even reflect the majority's preference. This would not satisfy even the minimalist definition of democracy for most political theorists. Democracy may be a low-maintenance regime compared to others, but it is not a no-maintenance one.

This recognition has led to a revival in some circles of the classical republican model of citizenship, and attempts to reconcile this more demanding model of public life with the liberal model, which emphasizes privacy and individualism. Few would return to the Greek ideal, but they are closer to the "high" citizenship end of our spectrum, which is represented by Pericles' view that private concerns be made subordinate to public ones.[3] It would be difficult to convince modern citizens that public life is superior to private life. Our attachment to our private lives may be "a result not of the impoverishment of public life but the enrichment of private life."[4] Whatever the causes and consequences of the contemporary political malaise, public-spiritedness is not the defining characteristic of contemporary democratic citizens.

Meanwhile, the relative lack of political mobilization and intensity may account for the relative civil peace that Americans and Canadians have enjoyed. In previous eras, it was not political passivity but excessive mobilization of diverse factions that posed the greatest challenge to both rulers and political theorists. A remedy for incessant strife was found through the adoption of new civic virtues: toleration and civility. Good citizenship, redefined as civility, demanded that individuals keep their moral and religious convictions to themselves. The government would maintain an aura of neutrality toward people's private commitments, and it would be the role of private institutions like church and family to see to the moral training of citizens.

The market, against the backdrop of private institutions and associations that provided moral tutelage, could be amoral, doing the job of coordinating private interests so that the greatest good for the greatest number resulted, with a minimum of governmental interference or supervision of individual activities. But it wasn't long before it became clear that the market could not direct self-interest in completely constructive ways. As private institutions such as family and church began to lose their authority over the individual, and as immigrants from diverse backgrounds began to arrive in force, the public schools became the vehicle for inculcating the moral and civic values of a unified American culture.

Civic Education

The influence of associations, be they churches, families, unions, charitable organizations, or Putnam's bowling leagues and bird watching clubs, certainly helps foster democratic values and behaviors. They continue to serve as "seedbeds of civic virtue." Yet, their influence is indirect and passive. Moreover, not all associations are internally democratic or liberal. What is the mechanism whereby they serve a civic function? Would the Lubavitcher community qualify, in this case, as a passive transmitter of civic virtues? If it fails the democratic structure and liberal values test, would not most of the associations of civil society, if scrutinized, also fail? For instance, the most prevalent form of association, the family, has been characterized by Susan Moller Okin as "a school of despotism." Perhaps we demand too much of these groups. If the associations and groups that make up our society are not necessarily reliable cradles of democracy, then, as many theorists are convinced, the state must take a more direct and active role in inculcating the necessary skills and virtues of democratic citizenship. They contend that democracy cannot be expected to chug along, indifferent to the underlying political culture or to the private values of its citizens. Reviving the old common school tradition of deliberate civic education is one proposed remedy for our current civic malaise.

Theorists such as William Galston, Richard Rorty, Benjamin Barber, Amitai Etzioni, and Amy Gutmann contend that the democratic state can infuse its future citizens with common purposes and civic virtues through civic education. The Character Education Partnership of the early 1990s, which created a curriculum for schools, is an example of such an initiative. Congress has funded several character education pilot programs in the schools. The problem is that there is no obvious consensus as to what virtues and character traits are required of the democratic citizen. Here, any list, no matter how abstract and general, is likely to run afoul of some culture or religion. Whatever consensus there might have been about what constituted our common culture broke apart by the 1960s.

In fact, the idea of cultural consensus was probably always an illusion.

While the original intent behind the common school movement was to forge a unified national identity and public philosophy, focusing on patriotism, morality, discipline, self-restraint, and assimilation or "Americanization," well before the turn of the century the Catholic Church broke ranks with the strongly Protestant overtones of the program and opted out of the public school system by creating a parallel private system.

Some advocates of civic education, undaunted by the multiplicity of moral and religious views in our society, insist that a value-free curriculum can be developed that focuses on the structure and function of our political institutions. Others insist that the core curriculum must inculcate specific liberal values, among which are toleration and respect for law and the equal rights of others. These are arguably critical to civil peace and coexistence as well as to democratic politics. William Galston outlines four categories of citizen virtues: 1) general virtues of law-abidingness and loyalty; 2) social virtues such as independence and open-mindedness; 3) economic virtues such as a work ethic, the ability to delay gratification, and the ability to adapt to technological changes; and 4) political virtues including respect for the rights of others, willingness to demand only those social services that can be paid for, the ability to evaluate the performance of elected officials, and willingness to engage in public discourse.[5] These are arguably uncontroversially salutary for society.

Other theorists raise the hurdle for citizen competence by demanding that the democratic citizen possess "critical thinking skills." A citizen, according to their definition, is a "democratic deliberator." The duty to prepare children for their role as citizen of the state trumps even the parental right of free exercise of their religion as well as their rights over their children.[6]

Critical rationality, by definition, means more than open-mindedness, clear-headedness, or common sense. It demands that one be willing to question all received knowledge; ready to step outside of his or her world of meaning and treat its norms, values, and truth claims as provisional and relative. This is a more controversial demand, and it is challenged by people who do not believe that the skeptical stance is a requirement of democratic deliberation. In asserting that responsible participation in the political process requires the exercise of a particular form of rationality that is both "critical" and "autonomous," liberal reason is made to appear synonymous with democratic reason.

If only liberals are judged competent to deliberate about politics, then citizens who do not adhere to the liberal mode of reasoning might be deemed incompetent to participate. While no one has suggested disqualifying non-liberal voters, it has certainly been suggested that a curriculum be formulated that has, as a component, civic education and citizenship skills. This education, more than family upbringing or the exercise of individual conscience, becomes the vehicle for democratic character formation.

According to Maya Stolzenberg, there are basically three strands of liberal theory to be found in the contemporary literature, each with a corresponding model of citizenship: liberal individualism, civic republicanism, and communitarianism. Liberalism and civic republicanism converge in accepting liberal principles as civic virtues and in embracing as a civic good the use of education as a method of inculcating liberal values. They see the schools as playing an essential role in socializing future citizens into the "critical analytical" mode of thought. Although communitarians deplore what civic republicans advocate—that is, the assimilative impact of exposure to liberal culture and values—they accept most of the principles of civic education enunciated by liberals.

Stolzenberg finds it ironic that liberal individualism, civic republicanism, and communitarianism all share the same disposition to treat the principles of critical rationality, uncertainty, and subjectivism as axiomatic. Accordingly, she sees liberal education as a form of indoctrination. By denying that political deliberation may require no more than the sort of common sense that most people possess, and by claiming that citizens must be taught a special form of reasoning that happens to support or conform to liberal premises, groups such as the Chassidim can be defined as bad, or at least inadequate, citizens.

Diversity and Citizenship

Liberalism may be unable to account for society's "deep diversity."[7] Cultural and normative diversity is likely to produce different views about what constitutes good citizenship, many of them potentially constructive from a democratic standpoint. It is argued by some that diversity is the only principled formula on which the state can remain united. But the liberal model erects a transcendent ideal that is supposed to supersede particular differences and group affiliations. This ideal has in practice excluded groups not willing to adopt the general point of view. These groups are then condemned by the majority as nonrational. Women and, in this case, Lubavitchers might serve as examples. Something akin to Young's model of "differentiated citizenship" might be adopted, although not, as Young might want, to ameliorate past exclusion and underrepresentation, but to grant legitimacy to diverse concepts of citizenship. The most radical version of this model understands the state as obliged to serve the particularistic identities of subgroups, rather than the other way around. Minorities and immigrants would be under no reciprocal obligation to conform to a national political identity.[8] Respecting diversity would be not only a chief virtue of the liberal state, but its obligation.[9] Our cultural identities would be understood to coexist in a nesting fashion with our identity as citizens.

But other theorists worry that such a model of citizenship might fragment the polity into an aggregate of subnational ghettoes and create a "politics of grievance" in which groups compete for entitlements and reparations on the basis of shared victimization at the hands of the majority.[10] Will Kymlicka attempts to reconcile political integration and social pluralism using three categories of group rights (reflecting Canada's situation). The first would offer disadvantaged groups special representation, the second would offer multicultural rights for immigrant and religious groups, and the third, under rare conditions, would grant political autonomy and self-governing powers to geographically concentrated national minorities, such as native tribes or the Quebecois.

According to Kymlicka, the consequences of this form of differentiated citizenship would be integrative rather than disintegrative, because most individuals, especially those covered under the second category, would want to use their special rights to assimilate politically and economically. He does not worry that Canadian identity will be squeezed out by Anglo or French or native or immigrant identities. He is willing to grant subnational minorities a fair amount of latitude, and even to use state resources to bolster the cohesion of minorities, giving them roughly equal chances at survival with other groups, with the proviso that they conform to liberal norms in their internal practices.

Michael Walzer declares himself to be sympathetic to the vision of a pluralistic civil society, but in practical terms the state and the demands of citizenship must take precedence over more local loyalties. Multiple identities must all be encompassed within the bounds of citizenship.[11] All individuals are called on to conform to a model of civic or national political unity to which parochial ethnic, religious, and cultural allegiances must be subordinated. This unified political allegiance to the Constitution arguably will not do any significant damage to other important identities and loyalties they may cherish.[12]

Patriotism: The Sentiment of Citizenship

In addition to defining democratic citizenship in terms of a set of practical skills and behaviors, some theorists contend that democratic citizenship requires a set of sentiments, particularly the willingness to subordinate all loyalties and allegiances to the state. Does democracy require patriots? The pendulum has swung historically between two ends of the spectrum: particular, local loyalties versus universal, cosmopolitan loyalties. In the contemporary debate, Martha Nussbaum argues in favor of educating American students to be "world citizens," while Richard Rorty argues for a renewal of national pride.[13] This debate echoes the classical tension between the loyalty of Pericles to the polis and the loyalty of Diogenes to the world. In Socrates' relationship to Athens, his cosmopolitan loyalty to philosophy is pitted against his local loyalty to the polis. In the case of the fictional relationship of Antigone to Thebes, the tension is between loyalty to the polis and loyalty to her particular family.

Centuries later, the Enlightenment project fostered a universal outlook, culminating in the ultimate universalizing philosophy of Marxism. The dismal collectivity that it produced has been countered by revivals of nationalism, many of them virulent and invidious. Patriotism has its ugly side: chauvinism and intolerance. Is the alternative a "healthy" form of patriotism or is it cosmopolitanism? Perhaps we should place our primary allegiance with something closer to home than the world or the state. Where should a democratic citizen locate himself on the spectrum of loyalties? What should a citizen do with her other loyalties? Should we arrange our allegiances hierarchically, or in concentric circles, or like a nesting doll? If patriotism is a natural sentiment necessary for good citizenship, how does it rank against our other natural loyalties? Is it the case, as Lawrence Kohlberg suggested, that more abstract and universal attachments are of a higher moral order than more particular or concrete attachments?

The question of where we should locate ourselves on the spectrum of loyalties, from local to universal, ultimately yields no logically satisfying answer. If universalizing moral reason leads us ever outward, beyond the boundaries of local attachments, why stop at the nation state? Why not cast ourselves as world citizens? The contrary also holds. If our moral reasoning leads us in the other direction on the continuum, again, why stop at the nation-state? Why not bestow our highest loyalty on some subnational unit like clan, family, or finally, the atomistic self? In the postmodern world the self may seem the most common and legitimate repository of our loyalty.

In Favor of the "Low" Citizen

Not all theorists share the premise that something is terribly wrong with the behavior or sentiments of contemporary citizens. They believe that the urgent warnings that the political sky is falling are overwrought and exaggerated. They see no reason to impose a "supercharged" model of civic virtue on contemporary citizens. Richard Flathman draws a distinction between two models of citizenship: "high" and "low." "Low" citizenship corresponds to the "bourgeois" and "high" to the "*citoyen*." According to the "low" model of citizenship, the individual looks after his own needs and interests and requires little from the state except the enforcement of laws and contracts in order to maintain the environment of free transactions and exchanges. The "high" model of citizenship is closer to the classical ideal associated with Pericles, Aristotle, and Rousseau. Here, citizens find their fullest gratification when engaged in the business of the polis. Flathman sees the revival of normative theorizing about citizenship as a throwback to this tradition.

Unlike the civic republicans and communitarians, Flathman rejects the "high" model of citizenship. His worry is not that particularistic identities or loyalties will scuttle a common political identity. Nor does he worry that incompetent citizens will fail to deliberate rationally about political issues and candidates, and thereby sink the polity. He worries about the revival of citizen virtues of the "high" sort because these virtues encourage citizens to identify too strongly with authority. He fears strong government more than he fears poor citizenship; or else he defines good citizenship as requiring suspicion of authority. Rousseauian citizens come dangerously close to the Jacobin or totalitarian model in which individuals are stripped of any other identity besides that of public citizen. Citizens who are too virtuous, too good, and too public may be a greater danger than today's typical, merely adequate citizen.[14]

Religion and Citizenship

Given his conception of the ideal citizen, it is no accident that Rousseau saw religion as a potential threat to the social unity he sought. He argued for harnessing religious sentiments to public purposes in the form of a single, state-regulated civic religion. Religious sentiment necessarily competes with patriotism because the religious person is, ultimately, a citizen of the "City of G-d." Spiritual citizenship, unlike physical citizenship, cuts across territorial boundaries. While spiritual citizenship does not preclude patriotism, the state is revealed as contingent. The traditional "wandering Jew" has been used historically as the stereotypic antithesis of patriotism—the ultimate, rootless cosmopolitan. He was the recipient of the universal law that went forth from Zion, and he went forth as well. Sojourning in many lands, he remained the quintessential outsider, always in physical and spiritual diaspora. In Jewish thought, any excessive attachment to tangible things or entities runs the risk of violating the prohibition against *avodah zarah* (idolatry), but nothing in Jewish thought precludes local commitments or patriotism.

Judaism, patriotism, and cosmopolitanism are not at odds if they are properly arranged. According to the sage Hillel, the self is the starting point of natural attachments. He said that first one must be for himself. But if he is only for himself, he is a moral failure. One must proceed outward from the self in order to be a moral person. Similarly, the account of the creation of Adam and Eve provides a model for marriage as a bridge from wife to husband, and then from family outward to the community and the world. The first attachments and loyalties are immediate, concrete, particular, and close to home. Local attachments are the prerequisite for being able to reach out to more distant and abstract places.

There are a variety of principled allegiances that are capable of coexisting rather than competing. We have a primary residence, but many homes. Torah lays claim to a Jew's ultimate loyalty, but it is commonly held that if one were to live according to Torah law, one would simultaneously be a good person, a good Jew, a good neighbor, and a good citizen.

Lubavitchers as Citizens

Lubavitchers are very much like other citizens in many respects. They are taxpaying, law-abiding members of the community. They have a higher rate of voter turnout than the general public, and they have gone beyond electing sympathetic representatives to becoming candidates for local political positions. In addition, Lubavitchers, like other Chassidim, achieve the kind of communal solidarity and self-help that democrats ought to find admirable. Yet, they are also different in many ways from mainstream citizens. These are people who regard themselves as in exile. Exile, in Chassidic thought, has both a spiritual and territorial dimension. Diaspora means that Judaism had to take on a supraterritorial aspect if it was to survive. Bereft of a physical homeland, the Jews made the Torah their spiritual homeland. It has held together the communal structure even in the absence of the physical borders and means of coercion exercised by true political entities.

Living a Torah life is the meaning a Lubavitcher attaches to freedom. That is why, ironically, a hospitable culture may be as dangerous as a hostile one. Physical exile is less of a problem than spiritual exile, meaning exile from his true nature and from his heritage, which occurs through assimilation. The

Chossid cannot function as a Jew outside of his community. He transforms his neighborhood into sacred space, where private religious observances spill over into the streets. It is simply impossible for religion to be restricted to the private sphere. To be stripped of membership in his community is to be stripped of identity and self. Assimilation would make his exile total. Because Lubavitchers define self, community, and the whole purpose of life in a distinctive way, it is no surprise that their view of citizenship is distinctive as well.

The physical place is always seen as temporary and provisional, even when it is comfortable and welcoming. But if he is living according to Torah values, then he is not living in spiritual exile; he is merely living, for the time being, in a foreign country, hopefully a friendly one. This is because all countries are, by definition, foreign. Lubavitchers appreciate liberal democracies because, although the values are alien, and despite the threat of assimilation, the net gain over other regimes, in terms of the ability to live a Jewish life without impediment, is considerable. Canadian and American Lubavitchers are fully cognizant that they live in what they refer to as a "country of kindness" and believe that they reciprocate with good citizenship.

Lubavitchers do not conform perfectly to the liberal, communitarian, or civic republican models. They are vexing to theorists not because they withdraw from politics, but because they are politically active. Some fear that they are injecting their alien, nonliberal values and political reasoning into the system, creating a threat to our democratic institutions. Yet, in a system in which most citizens view themselves primarily as taxpayers and consumers; in which many citizens hold illiberal views such as racism, sexism, and homophobia; and in which interest groups are free to lobby for everything from guns to tobacco, why be concerned with groups like Lubavitch?

They engage in political activity for many of the same reasons that other citizens do. They care about their political leader's skills, character, and ability to represent their constituents' interests with sympathy and accuracy. They love to tell deprecatory political jokes, just like their neighbors. For the most part, just as for the vast majority of citizens, their concerns are local: the crack in the sidewalk, local garbage pick-up, neighborhood security and safety, school funding, and the like.

If Lubavitchers participate in politics, why wouldn't they be considered model citizens, instead of being vilified as unhealthy for democracy? After all, unlike the Montana militia or the Branch Davidians, with which they have been grouped, no Chassidim have been known to stockpile weapons. They do not spread a message of hate for other races or religions; they do not commit violent crimes. Lubavitchers do not foment revolution, nor do they encourage disobedience to the law or disrespect toward the Constitution.

The complaints against Lubavitch voiced by liberal political theorists fall into three general categories: (1) Lubavitch is not internally structured along democratic lines; (2) Lubavitchers do not share society's liberal values; and (3) the political activism of Lubavitchers is aimed at reinforcing their group solidarity, insularity, and autonomy. These three alleged shortcomings lead to the conclusion that Lubavitcher citizens do not serve democratic purposes.

The first complaint, that Lubavitch is not democratically structured, is difficult to assess. If anything, Lubavitch, which is a loosely and nonhierarchically organized community with no officially recognized leadership, may be suffering from excessive democracy, even to the point of anarchy. Rabbi Manis Friedman, one of the most public and widely recognized figures in the Lubavitch community, feels that this extreme democracy is a political liability.[15] Each community and each ChaBaD House is quite independent in its decision making and fund-raising. Each year there are several inclusive conventions in which Lubavitchers make their preferences known and discuss the direction that the movement should take, but there are no formal voting procedures and no formal elections. While it is alleged that women have no part in these discussions, women have separate conventions where they make decisions about their objectives and their agendas. But again, there is no formal mechanism for registering member preferences. The outcome, in terms of policy statements and guidelines, seems to be arrived at by consensus. What becomes of dissenting opinions is hard to ascertain.

The second complaint, that Lubavitchers do not share liberal values, is partly on the mark. Lubavitchers, as individuals, tend not to behave as "rational maximizers." They also accept a sexually circumscribed division of labor and roles in public life that limit the interaction between men and women. More disturbing to liberal theorists is the respect that Lubavitchers afford their Rebbe, even after his death. His leadership conforms roughly to Weber's model of charismatic leadership, which is seen as a throwback by its critics to pre-Enlightenment, prerational forms of social organization and reason, yet Lubavitchers seem quite able to assess the skills and agendas of politicians.

The third complaint is that Lubavitchers pursue the political objectives of the group rather than pursuing some more refined democratic purpose, and that these political objectives are really driven by theological goals, in violation of the principle of shared public reason. If Lubavitchers allow their foundational beliefs to influence their political judgment, and reciprocally use their political judgment to protect their foundational beliefs, how much more is this an abuse of democratic citizenship than using one's vote to secure economic and material goods?

It is no mystery why Lubavitchers appear to vote as a bloc. Part of it is simply a misperception based on critics' expectations rather than concrete exit polls. When Lubavitchers do vote the same, it is not because they are incapable of deliberating independently, and it is not because they get the word from above. In fact, most Lubavitchers told me that they discuss politics and read the papers, and then decide how to vote, just as other citizens do. It is no surprise that people who share values, live in close proximity, and most important, share concrete interests, would tend to vote the same way. Many American husbands and wives often do, without raising suspicions. In fact, the last presidential election split the Lubavitch community's vote, indicating that there is more variation and more independence of political opinion than critics have been willing to acknowledge.

In short, the stringent, high-hurdle standard of citizenship probably cannot be met by the vast majority of American or Canadian citizens, religious or otherwise. Much of the information we have about how the average citizen formulates his or her preferences suggests that voting is often irrationally determined by factors unrelated to politics, such as the candidate's personality or physical appearance. While there may not be a host of Pericles-style citizens in their ranks, against the backdrop of the average American or Canadian voter, Lubavitchers come off as solid citizens.

Most importantly, despite their distinctive "comprehensive conception," Lubavitchers really do adhere to Rawls's model of fair play and respect for procedures and the rights and equality of other citizens. In short, they by and large adhere to his "political conception" of justice. Lubavitchers play by the rules, and allow other citizens to do the same. They accept the outcomes of elections or legal proceedings with equanimity. They pursue their rights within the parameters set out by the Constitution. If this isn't good or at least adequate citizenship, what is?

Recognizing that some of the antipathy expressed toward religious enclaves actually expresses the clash of comprehensive moral doctrines might ease some of the tension. But liberalism is the dominant ideology. Its adherents are often unaware of, or deny, its nonneutrality. It is probably in the nature of hegemonic ideologies to strive to suppress both ends of the loyalty spectrum—particularistic, subnational loyalties and cosmopolitan, supranational loyalties—accusing both of being incompatible with good (patriotic) citizenship.

CHAPTER TEN

Conclusion

The purpose of this book is to demonstrate that the basic attributes of democracy can be distinguished from those of liberalism, and that the exercise of democratic citizenship does not require adherence to liberal values. Accordingly, democracies can afford a tolerant approach to a range of culturally diverse groups and a variety of models of citizenship.

But liberal democracy is ambivalent, at best, not only about enclaves that do not share liberal norms and practices but also about the status of subgroups per se in liberal society. When these enclaves use the procedures of democratic politics to fortify their autonomy, they raise questions for the rest of society, including, "Is the toleration of political activity by nonliberal cultures the fulfillment of liberal principles, or is it the negation of liberal principles?"

The liberal account of public reason and personhood is not shared by groups like the Lubavitcher Chassidim. Autonomy and individualism are not central tenets of Lubavitcher thought. Public policies and laws based on these premises may pass as facially neutral among liberal theorists, but will strike Chassidim as anything but. For liberal political and legal theorists, this raises several important questions: To what degree is national unity predicated on shared cultural values or comprehensive conceptions of the good? How much national unity is required to ensure stable democracy?

Related to these questions is what some theorists regard as the urgent and pressing question about normative citizenship: What is actually required of the democratic citizen in terms of convictions, skills, and virtues? Some theorists have raised the bar quite high. In addition to being informed voters and at least occasional participants in political processes, they would like to demand that citizens deliberate and articulate in a particular way, specifically, as critically rational, autonomous individuals. Many of these "high hurdle" theorists of citizenship would impose requirements that would constitute a burden on, and even threaten the survival of, nonliberal cultures.

Much of what political theorists think they know about nonliberal enclaves like the Lubavitch and other Chassidim contains several misconceptions and stereotypes—the natural result of adopting a statist perspective, rather than making the effort to step into another world of meaning. From the inside, many of the beliefs and practices that appear alien and even oppressive may begin to appear reasonable or at least intelligible.

Critics also overestimate the fragility of both liberalism and our democratic institutions. It is possible to find ominous symptoms of the moral and political decay of our culture and political system, which might cause the erosion of our democratic institutions and ideals. To the extent that the concern is not overstated, measures should be taken that improve the moral and political climate without undermining citizen freedoms. The Lubavitcher Rebbe was a strong supporter of civic and character education. If anything, Lubavitchers safeguard rather than threaten the values of self-reliance, honesty, family, and community service that undergird our democracy. It is important to distinguish between liberalism and democracy. Lubavitchers demonstrate that democratic competence does not depend on liberal attitudes.

Finally, liberal theorists claim that humans thrive on "intellectual discomfort" and the ceaseless revision of life plans and values. This belittles those who hold to absolute truths, making such people seem ignoble, insecure, reactionary, unadventurous, or small-minded. It is probably true that some people of weaker fiber cling to religious life rafts out of intellectual laziness or the understandable desire to make sense of a fragmented, chaotic world of competing values and an unnerving array of choices. The world of endless possibilities and eternal becoming is not for everyone. In the postmodern world, the search for an anchor, a safe harbor, or a haven may lead in pathological directions. But not every longing for home, for purpose, for meaning, for a "return to the sacred" smacks of parochial or fascist leanings, or signifies a weak character.

Historically, the proliferation of spiritual movements has spawned some that are ridiculous, but also some that are profound. Lubavitchers are attached to their source, Torah. Their universe is neither shattered nor meaningless; rather, it is infused, down to the smallest detail, with sanctity. They are not alienated. If the sensation of exile has become part of the modern human condition, it has always been central to the Jewish experience. But they experience their exile as physical, not spiritual. Perhaps we should feel a touch of envy for people who have found a "home in exile."

Arguably, it is the hallmark of liberalism to treat one's own version of the truth as provisional, and one's conception of the good as mutable. Lubavitchers provide us with the opportunity to assess our values in light of a distinctive alternative. Their presence in our midst may, therefore, represent the fulfillment of liberalism's highest ideals even though they are not liberal. But whether or not they advance liberal purposes, the democratic project is not synonymous with the liberal one. Several models of citizenship can and do coexist, each making a special contribution to democracy. Our polity requires citizens of good will and democratic inclination. Lubavitchers, as well as many other nonliberal individuals and groups, fit this description admirably.

NOTES

Preface

1. Among the questions I asked were: What does "women's equality" mean to you? What are the most important things that you would like your children to learn from you about how to live their lives? Why do you think most *ba'alei teshuva* (voluntary returnees to the faith) are drawn to the Chassidische life?

2. Avrum Ehrlich supports the contention that a search of the Sorbonne's graduation records does not list Menachem Mendel. Avrum M. Ehrlich, *Leadership in the HaBaD Movement* (Northvale, N.J.: Jason Aronson, 2000).

Chapter 1. Does Democracy Need Liberals?

1. Robert M. Cover, *The Supreme Court, 1982 Term—Forward: Nomos and Narrative*, 97 Harvard Law Review 4 (1983).

2. William Galston, "Two Concepts of Liberalism," *Ethics* 105 (April 1995): 520.

3. Jeff Spinner, *The Boundaries of Citizenship: Race, Ethnicity, and Nationality in the Liberal State* (Baltimore: Johns Hopkins University Press, 1994).

4. Christopher Eisgruber, *The Constitutional Value of Assimilation*, 96 Columbia Law Review 87 (1996).

5. Judith Lynn Failer, *The Draw and Drawbacks of Religious Enclaves in Constitutional Democracy: Hasidic Public Schools in* Kiryas Joel, 72 Indiana Law Journal 383 (1997).

6. Ira Lupu, *Uncovering the Village of Kiryas Joel*, 96 Columbia Law Review 104 (1996).

7. Michael Specter, "The Oracle of Crown Heights: Rabbi Menachem Schneerson," *New York Times Magazine*, March 15, 1992, 32–45.

8. Stephen G. Bloom, "Strangers in a Strange Land," *Chicago Tribune Sunday Magazine*, January 28, 1996, 10.

9. Nomi Maya Stolzenberg and David N. Myers, *Community, Constitution, and Culture: The Case of the Jewish Kehillah*, 25 University of Michigan Journal of Law Reference 633 (spring/summer 1992): 643–44. Same source is also cited in Martha Minow, *The Constitution and the Subgroup Question*, 71 Indiana Law Journal 1, 10 n. 25 (winter 1995).

10. Amy Gutman, *Democratic Education* (Princeton: Princeton University Press, 1987). Stephen Macedo, "Transformative Constitutionalism and the Case of Religion," *Political The-*

ory 26, no. 1 (February 1998): 56–80, and "Liberal Civic Education and Religious Fundamentalism: The Case of God against John Rawls," *Ethics* 105 (April 1995): 468–96.

11. Benjamin Barber, *A Passion for Democracy* (Princeton: Princeton University Press, 1998).

12. Robert D. Putnam, *Bowling Alone: The Collapse and the Revival of American Community* (New York: Simon and Schuster, 2000) and *Making Democracy Work: Civic Traditions in Modern Italy* (Princeton: Princeton University Press, 1993).

13. Nancy Rosenblum, *Membership and Morals: The Personal Uses of Pluralism in America* (Princeton: Princeton University Press, 1998) and Nancy Rosenblum, ed., *Obligations of Citizenship and Demands of Faith: Religious Accommodation in Pluralist Democracies* (Princeton: Princeton University Press, 2000). Benjamin Barber, *A Place for Us: How to Make Society Civil and Democracy Strong* (New York: Hill and Wang, 1998) and *Strong Democracy* (Berkeley: University of California Press, 1984).

14. Kent Greenawalt, *Private Consciences and Public Reasons* (New York: Oxford University Press, 1995).

15. Jeremy Waldron, "Rights and Majorities: Rousseau Revisited," in *Majorities and Minorities*, ed. John Chapman and Alan Wertheimer, Nomos 32 (New York: New York University Press, 1990): 44–78.

16. Richard E. Flathman, "Citizenship and Authority: A Chastened View of Citizenship," in *Theorizing Citizenship*, ed. Ronald Beiner (Albany: State University of New York Press, 1995).

17. Susan Moller Okin, "Is Multiculturalism Bad for Women?" *Boston Review* 22, no. 5 (October/November 1997): 25–40.

18. Judith Plaskow, *Standing Alone at Sinai* (San Francisco: Harper and Row, 1990).

19. Martha Minow, *The Constitution and the Subgroup Question*, 71 Indiana Law Journal 1 (winter 1995).

20. Kenneth Karst, *Paths to Belonging: The Constitution and Cultural Identity*, 64 North Carolina Law Review 303, 331 (1986).

21. Roderick A. Macdonald, "Critical Legal Pluralism as a Construction of Normativity and the Emergence of Law," in *Theories et Emergence du Droit*, ed. A. Lajoie (Montreal: Themis, 1998), and *Metaphors of Multiplicity: Civil Society, Regimes, and Legal Pluralism*, 15 Arizona Journal of International and Comparative Law 69 (winter 1998); Robert M. Cover, *The Supreme Court, 1982 Term—Forward: Nomos and Narrative*, 97 Harvard Law Review 4 (1983); Martha Minow, *Making All the Difference: Inclusion, Exclusion, and American Law* (Ithaca: Cornell University Press, 1990); Nomi Maya Stolzenberg, '*He Drew a Circle That Shut Me Out': Assimilation, Indoctrination, and the Paradox of Liberal Education*, 106 Harvard Law Review 581 (1983); Robert Justin Lipkin, *Liberalism and the Possibility of Multicultural Constitutionalism: The Distinction between Deliberative and Dedicated Cultures*, 29 University of Richmond Law Review 1264 (December 1995); Marc Galantar, *Justice in Many Rooms: Courts, Private Ordering, and Indigenous Law*, 19 Journal of Legal Pluralism and Unofficial Law 1, 1 (1981).

22. Shauna van Praagh, *Changing the Lens: Locating Religious Communities within U.S. and Canadian Families and Constitutions*, 15 Arizona Journal of International and Comparative Law 125, 125–141 (1998).

23. Cited in Tamar Frankiel, *The Voice of Sarah* (San Francisco: Harper San Francisco, 1990), xiii.

Chapter 2. Chassidim

1. The first estimate is from an interview with Rabbi Levi Shemtov, head of American Friends of Lubavitch, Washington, D.C., August 2, 2000. The second is from Yigal Schleifer, "Chabad's Messiah Complex," *Jerusalem Report*, June 21, 1999, 1.

2. Jossi Klein Halevi, "Schneerson: Accessible, Beloved, Controversial," *Jerusalem Report*, April 7, 1994, 1.

3. Jordon F. Lubetkin, "Chabad in Cyberspace," *Cleveland Jewish News*, May 16, 1997.

4. Jerome Mintz, *Hasidic People: A Place in the New World* (Cambridge: Harvard University Press, 1992), 45.

5. Related to me at the Shabbos dinner table, Montreal, Canada, September 1999 (anonymous).

6. Simon Jacobson, *Toward a Meaningful Life: The Wisdom of the Rebbe* (New York: William Morrow, 1995).

7. Mintz, *Hasidic People*, 352.

8. Lecture by Rabbi Moshe New, Montreal, Canada, May 8, 2000.

9. Living with Moshiach homepage (www.moshiach.net), August 27, 2000.

Chapter 3. Lubavitch and American Politics

1. Kenneth Wald, *Religion and Politics in the United States* (New York: St. Martin's, 1987), 344.

2. Jonathan D. Sarna and David G. Dalin, *Religion and State in the American Jewish Experience* (Notre Dame, Ind.: University of Notre Dame Press, 1997), 2.

3. Daniel J. Elazar, *Community and Polity* (Philadelphia: Jewish Publication Society, 1995), 146–47.

4. Wald, *Religion and Politics*, 321.

5. Avrum M. Ehrlich, *Leadership in the HaBaD Movement* (Northvale, N.J.: Jason Aronson, 2000), 305 n. 6.

6. Interview with Rabbi Zushi Silberstein, Montreal, Canada, October 14, 1999.

7. Simon Jacobson, *Toward a Meaningful Life: The Wisdom of the Rebbe* (New York: William Morrow, 1995), 166.

8. Ibid., 161.

9. Ibid., 163.

10. Edward Hoffman, *Despite All Odds: The Story of Lubavitch* (New York: Simon and Schuster, 1991).

11. Ibid., 27.

12. Sarna and Dalin, *Religion and State*, 215.

13. Reported to me in an interview with Rabbi Manis Friedman, Burlington, Vermont, November 14, 1999.

14. Interview with Rabbi Levi Shemtov, head of American Friends of Lubavitch, Washington, D.C., August 2, 2000.

15. Ibid.

16. Interview with Nathan Lewin, legal counsel for Lubavitch and COLPA, Washington, D.C., August 3, 2000.

17. Jerome R. Mintz, *Hasidic People: A Place in the New World* (Cambridge: Harvard University Press, 1992), 189.

18. Sarna and Dalin, *Religion and State*, 290.

19. Ibid., 291.

20. This has been an ongoing dispute in my hometown of Burlington, Vermont. It appears that all parties wish the entire issue would just quietly disappear. A truce seems to have been reached in which the city, and the former plaintiffs, simply ignore the placement of the menorah each year on public land.

21. *Allegheny County v. Greater Pittsburgh ACLU*, 492 US 573 (1989).

22. Based in part on an interview with Rabbi Levi Shemtov, Washington, D.C., August 2, 2000.

23. Interview with Rabbi Levi Shemtov, June 8, 2001.

24. Transcript, ChaBaD Online, December 17, 2001.

25. Philip Gourevitch, "The Crown Heights Riot and Its Aftermath," *Commentary,* January 1993, 29–34.

26. Michael Specter, "The Oracle of Crown Heights: Rabbi Menachem Schneerson," *New York Times,* March 15, 1992, 32.

27. Gourevitch, "Crown Heights Riot," *Commentary,* 33.

28. Margot Hornblower, "Cultures Clash As Hasidic Jews Compete for Turf; Sect Uses Politics, Law to Overpower Hispanics," *Washington Post,* November 9, 1986, A1.

29. Gourevitch, "Crown Heights Riot," 33.

30. Joe Sexton, "When Work Is Not Enough," *New York Times,* April 21, 1997, B1.

31. Bill Glauber, "Messiah's Flock Prays for Miracle," *Baltimore Sun,* March 22, 1994, 1A.

32. Sam Roberts, "Reflections on the Rebbe and City Politics," *New York Times,* July 3, 1994, 7.

33. "Making It in Brooklyn," *Fortune,* August 6, 1984, 128.

34. Jonathan Rieder, "Crown of Thorns: The Roots of the Black-Jewish Feud," *New Republic,* October 14, 1991, 26.

35. Mintz, *Hasidic People,* 237–42.

36. "In Crown Heights, a Case That Won't Go Away," *New York Times* on the Web, January 9, 2002.

Chapter 4. *Lubavitch and Canadian Politics*

1. Daniel Elazar, *Community and Polity: The Organizational Dynamics of American Jewry* (Philadelphia: Jewish Publication Society, 1995), 33.

2. Harold Troper and Morton Weinfeld, "The Canadian Jews and Canadian Multiculturalism," in *Multiculturalism, Jews, and Identities in Canada,* ed. Howard Adelman and John H. Simpson (Jerusalem: Magnus Press, 1996).

3. Nathan Glazer, "Individual Rights against Group Rights," in *The Rights of Minority Cultures,* ed. Will Kymlicka (Oxford: Oxford University Press, 1995), 135.

4. Ibid.

5. Augie Fleras and Jean Leonard Elliot, *Unequal Relations* (Scarborough, Ontario: Prentice-Hall, 1996), 404.

6. Gary Paul Gershman, *Hamiltonian Ideals and the Bill of Rights* (Ph.D. diss., Duke University, 1992).

7. Morton Weinfeld, "Jews of Quebec: An Overview," in *The Jews of Canada,* ed. Robert Brym, William Shaffir, and Morton Weinfeld (Ontario: Oxford University Press, 1993), 185.

8. Ibid., 172.

9. Interview with Pierre Anctil, agent recherche, Quebec Ministry of Immigration, Montreal, Canada, October 7, 1999.

10. Statistical data comes from the Federation CJA, "Attitudinal Survey of the Montreal Jewish Community," 1996.

11. Janice Arnold, "Landry Urges Jews to Accept Quebec Nationhood," *Canadian Jewish News,* May 18, 2000, 3.

12. Interview with David Sultan, director of the Campagne Sepharade, CJA, September 21, 1999, Montreal, Canada.

13. Pierre Anctil, "Forging a Viable Partnership: The Montreal Jewish Community vis-à-

vis the Quebec State," in *Quebec State and Society,* ed. Alain-G. Gagnon (Toronto: Nelson Canada, 1993), 372–73.

14. Gagnon, *Quebec State and Society,* 2.

15. Anctil, "Forging a Viable Partnership," 384.

16. Janice Arnold, "Quebec Overrides Charters in Education Bill," *Canadian Jewish News,* May 25, 2000, 3–5.

17. Interview with Alexander Werzberger, head of the Coalition d'Organisations Hassidiques d'Outrement, October 22, 1999, Montreal, Canada.

18. Ibid.

19. Interview with Sidney Pfeiffer, city councilor from Outrement, September 16, 1999, Montreal, Canada.

20. Interview with Michel Archambault, former assistant for cultural affairs to Gerald Tremblay, Liberal deputy for Outrement, Montreal, Canada, October 15, 1999.

21. Interview with Alexander Werzberger, head of COHO, October 22, 1999.

22. Interview with Robert Kieffer, député de Groulx, Assemblee Nationale de Quebec, St. Therese, Province of Quebec, October 4, 1999.

23. Interview with Jack Jedwab, director of the Canadian Studies Association, Université du Quebec a Montreal, Montreal, Canada, October 1999.

24. Interview with Rabbi Josef Sputz, principal, Yeshiva Tomche T'mimim, Montreal, Canada, May 10, 2000.

25. Menachem Friedman, "Haredim Confront the Modern City," in *Studies in Contemporary Jewry,* vol. 2, ed. Peter Y. Medding (Bloomington: Indiana University Press, 1986), 93.

26. William Shaffir, *Life in a Religious Community: The Lubavitcher Chassidim in Montreal* (Montreal: Holt, Rinehart & Winston, 1974), 227.

27. Ibid., 178.

28. Interview with Sauli Zajdel, city councilor, District of Victoria, and member of the Montreal Executive Committee, Montreal, Canada, September 23, 1999.

29. Interview with Rabbi Zushi Silberstein, Montreal, Canada, October 14, 1999.

30. Interview with David Sultan, director of the Campagne Sepharade, CJA, Montreal, Canada, September 21, 1999.

31. Interview with Zevi Neuwirth, Montreal, Canada, November 8, 1999.

32. Kate Swoger, "Hasidic Students May Lose Program," *Montreal Gazette,* April 10, 2000.

33. Janice Arnold, "Torah and Vocational Institute Takes UQAM to Court over Cancellation of Program," *Canadian Jewish News,* May 11, 2000, 21.

34. Interview with Eli Meroz, academic director of Torah and Vocational Institute, Montreal, Canada, May 15, 2000.

35. Interview with Rabbi Manis Friedman, Burlington, Vermont, November 14, 1999.

36. Interview with David Sultan, director of the Campagne Sepharade, CJA, Montreal, Canada, September 21, 1999.

37. Interview with Alexander Werzberger, head of COHO, October 22, 1999.

38. Interview with Michel Archambault, former assistant for cultural affairs to Mr. Tremblay, Liberal deputy for Outrement, October 15, 1999.

39. "Lubavitch Week in Canada," *Canadian Jewish News,* June 22, 2000, 5.

Chapter 5. Liberalism

1. John Rawls, *Political Liberalism* (New York: Columbia University Press, 1993); Alasdair MacIntyre, *After Virtue* (Notre Dame, Ind.: University of Notre Dame Press, 1981); Stephen

Macedo, "Liberal Civic Education and Religious Fundamentalism: The Case of God vs. John Rawls?" *Ethics* 105 (April 1995): 468-96.

2. William Galston, *Liberal Purposes* (New York: Cambridge University Press, 1991), 3.

3. Richard Arneson and Ian Shapiro, "Democratic Autonomy and Religious Freedom: A Critique of *Wisconsin v. Yoder*," in *Political Order*, ed. Ian Shapiro and Russell Hardin, Nomos 38 (New York: New York University Press, 1996), 2.

4. John Rawls, "The Priority of Right and Ideas of the Good," *Philosophy and Public Affairs* 17, no. 4 (1988): 263.

5. Ibid., 264.

6. Ibid., 265.

7. Ibid., 268.

8. Stephen Macedo, *Liberal Virtues: Citizenship, Virtue, and Community in Liberal Constitutionalism* (Oxford: Oxford University Press, 1990), 53.

9. Ibid., 60.

10. Ibid., 276.

11. Ibid., 53.

12. Ibid., 253.

13. Ibid., 269.

14. Stephen Macedo, "Charting Liberal Virtues," in *Virtue*, ed. John W. Chapman and William Galston, Nomos 34 (New York: New York University Press, 1992), 215.

15. Ibid., 216.

16. Ibid., 279.

17. Ibid.

18. Ibid., 278.

19. Charles Larmore, "The Limits of Aristotelian Ethics," in *Virtue*, ed. Chapman and Galston, 193.

20. Charles Larmore, "Political Liberalism," *Political Theory* 18 (1990): 339-43.

21. Amy Gutmann, "Civic Education and Social Diversity," *Ethics* 105 (April 1995): 578.

22. Amy Gutmann, "Undemocratic Education," in *Liberalism and the Moral Life*, ed. Nancy Rosenblum (Cambridge: Harvard University Press, 1989).

23. Bruce Ackerman, *Social Justice in the Liberal State* (New Haven: Yale University Press, 1980), 153.

24. Ibid., 148.

25. Will Kymlicka, *Liberalism, Community, and Culture* (New York: Clarendon Press, 1989), 49.

26. Shelley Burtt, "In Defense of *Yoder*: Parental Authority and the Public Schools," in *Political Order*, ed. Shapiro and Hardin, 416.

27. Robert Justin Lipkin, *Liberalism and the Possibility of Multicultural Constitutionalism: The Distinction between Deliberative and Dedicated Cultures*, 29 University of Richmond Law Review 1306 (December 1995).

28. Galston, *Liberal Purposes*, 146.

29. Ibid., 253.

30. Ibid., 254.

31. William Galston, "Two Concepts of Liberalism," *Ethics* 105 (April 1995): 516.

32. Perkei Avot 5:15.

33. Galston, *Liberal Purposes*, 251-52.

34. Arneson and Shapiro, "Democratic Autonomy," 384.

35. Galston, "Two Concepts of Liberalism," 524.

36. Ibid., 523.

37. Arneson and Shapiro, "Democratic Autonomy," 387.

38. Ibid., 367.

39. Macedo, *Liberal Virtues,* 219.

40. David A. Strauss, "The Liberal Virtues," in *Virtue,* ed. Chapman and Galston, 201.

41. Michael J. Sandel, *Liberalism and the Limits of Justice* (Cambridge: Cambridge University Press, 1982), 11.

42. Michael J. Sandel, "Freedom of Conscience or Freedom of Choice," in *Articles of Faith: The Religious Liberty Clauses and the American Public Philosophy,* ed. James David Hunter and Os Guinness (Washington, D.C.: Brookings Institute, 1990), 88–89.

43. Kymlicka, *Liberalism, Community, and Culture,* 12.

44. Ibid., 12–13.

45. Ibid., 52.

46. Ibid., 55.

47. Susan Mendus, *Justifying Toleration: Conceptual and Historical Perspectives* (Cambridge: Cambridge University Press, 1988), 5.

Chapter 6. Lubavitch Reason

1. Stephen L. Carter, *The Culture of Disbelief: How American Law and Politics Trivialize Religious Devotion* (New York: Basic Books, 1993).

2. Joseph Raz, "Facing Diversity: The Case of Epistemic Abstinence," *Philosophy and Public Affairs* 19 (1990): 3.

3. Robert Audi, *The Place of Religious Argument in a Free, Democratic Society,* 30 San Diego Law Review 677 (1993).

4. Edward Foley, *Tillich and Camus: Talking Politics,* 92 Columbia Law Review 954 (1992).

5. Kathleen Sullivan, *Religion and Liberal Democracy,* 59 University of Chicago Law Review 195 (1992).

6. Ronald Theimann, *Religion in Public Life* (Washington, D.C.: Georgetown University Press, 1996).

7. Kent Greenawalt, *Grounds for Political Judgment: The Status of Personal Experience and the Autonomy and Generality of Principles of Restraint,* 30 San Diego Law Review 649 (1993).

8. David Smolin, *Regulating Religious and Cultural Conflict,* 76 Iowa Law Review 1067 (1991).

9. Jeremy Waldron, *Religious Contributions in Public Deliberation,* 30 San Diego Law Review 817 (1993).

10. Richard Neuhaus, *The Naked Public Square: Religion and Democracy in America* (Grand Rapids, Mich.: W. B. Eerdman, 1984).

11. Sanford Levinson, *Religious Language and the Public Square,* 105 Harvard Law Review 206 (1992).

12. *Goldman v. Weinberger,* 475 US 503 (1986).

13. *Bollenbach v. Board of Education of Monroe Woodbury Center School District,* 659 F. Supp. 1450 (1987).

14. Davina D. Cooper, "Talmudic Territory," *Journal of Law and Society* 23, no. 4 (1996): 529–48.

15. Yaakov Brawer, *Something from Nothing* (Montreal: TAV Seminary Publications, 1998), 37–46.

16. HaYom Yom, Adar Sheini 29.

17. Rabbi Emmanuel Feldman, "Orthodox Feminism and Feminist Orthodoxy," *Jewish Action* 60, no. 2 (winter 5760/1999): 13.

18. Ibid.

19. Robert Cover, "Obligation: A Jewish Jurisprudence of the Social Order," in *Narrative, Violence, and the Law: The Essays of Robert Cover,* ed. Martha Minow (Ann Arbor: University of Michigan Press, 1992).

20. Ibid., 241.

21. Interview with Professor Albert Teitelbaum, Montreal, Quebec, October 21, 1999.

22. *The Chassidic Dimension: Talks of the Rebbe, Menachem M. Schneerson,* vol. 1 (Brooklyn, N.Y.: Kehot Publication Society, 5757/1997), 91.

23. Noson Gurary, *Chassidism: Its Development, Theology, and Practice* (Northvale, N.J.: J. Aronson, 1997), 7.

24. *Lessons in Tanya,* chap. 4, 84.

25. Ibid., 80.

26. *Chassidic Dimension,* 192.

27. Yaakov Brawer, *Eyes That See* (Montreal: Bais Menachem Seminary Publications, 1999), 32.

28. Ibid., 23–24.

29. Ibid.

30. Gurary, *Chassidism,* 10.

31. *Lessons in Tanya,* 534.

32. Ibid., 534, n. 2.

33. Erica Goode, "How Culture Molds Habits of Thought," *New York Times* on the Web, "Science and Health" section, August 8, 2000, 1–7.

Chapter 7. Lubavitcher Women and Liberalism

1. Cynthia Ozick, "Notes toward Finding the Right Question," 120–151, and Judith Plaskow, "The Right Question Is Theological," 223–33, both in *On Being a Jewish Feminist,* ed. Susannah Heschel (New York: Schocken Books, 1995).

2. Rita M. Gross, "Steps toward Feminine Imagery of Deity in Jewish Theology," in *On Being a Jewish Feminist,* ed. Heschel, 234–47.

3. Tamar Frankiel, *The Voice of Sarah: Feminine Spirituality and Traditional Judaism* (San Francisco: Harper San Francisco, 1990), xiv.

4. Carol Gilligan, *In a Different Voice: Psychological Theory and Women's Development* (Cambridge: Harvard University Press, 1993).

5. Susan Moller Okin, "Is Multiculturalism Bad for Women?" *Boston Review* 22, no. 5 (October/November 1997): 28.

6. Ibid.

7. Susan Moller Okin, *Justice, Gender, and the Family* (New York: Basic Books, 1989), 172.

8. Ibid., 171.

9. Michael Walzer, *Spheres of Justice* (New York: Basic Books, 1983).

10. Cass Sunstein, "Sexual Equality vs. Religion: What Should the Law Do?" article at Michigan State University Press online, 3.

11. Sander Gilman, "Barbaric Rituals?" a response to "Is Multiculturalism Bad for Women?" by Susan Moller Okin, *Boston Review* 22, no. 5, 34.

12. Robert Post, "Between Norms and Choices," a response to "Is Multiculturalism Bad for Women?" by Susan Moller Okin, *Boston Review* 22, no. 5, 35.

13. Interview with Chantal Pinon, legislative assistant to Robert Kieffer, Députée de Groulx, Assemblee Nationale du Quebec, St. Terese, Quebec, September 4, 1999.

14. Joseph Raz, "Reform or Destroy?" a response to "Is Multiculturalism Bad for Women?" by Susan Moller Okin, *Boston Review* 22, no. 5, 38.

15. Debra Kaufman, *Rachel's Daughters: Newly Orthodox Jewish Women* (New Brunswick, N.J.: Rutgers University Press, 1991).

16. Lanore Weitzman, *The Divorce Revolution: The Unexpected Social and Economic Consequences for Women and Children in America* (New York: Free Press, 1985).

17. Martha Minow, *Making All the Difference: Inclusion, Exclusion, and American Law* (Ithaca: Cornell University Press, 1990), 273.

18. Rabbi Manis Friedman, "How Do Men Become Confident and Nurturing?" *N'shei ChaBaD* newsletter (February 1999), 46–47.

19. Simon Jacobson, ed., *Toward a Meaningful Life: The Wisdom of the Rebbe* (New York: William Morrow, 1995), 178.

20. Rabbi Emmanuel Feldman, "Orthodox Feminism and Feminist Orthodoxy," *Jewish Action* 60, no. 2 (winter 5760/1999): 12–17.

21. Jacobson, *Toward a Meaningful Life,* 185.

22. Wendy Shalit, *A Return to Modesty: Discovering the Lost Virtue* (New York: Free Press, 1999).

23. Jacobson, *Meaningful Life,* 66.

24. Kaufman, *Rachel's Daughters,* 89.

25. Faige Twerski, "Going Home," *Olam* (spring 5760/2000): 33.

26. Debra Kaufman, "Engendering Orthodoxy," in *New World Hasidim: Ethnographic Studies of Hasidic Jews in America,* ed. Janet Belcove-Shalin (Albany: State University of New York Press, 1995), 143.

27. Bonnie Morris, "Agents or Victims of Religious Ideology?" in *New World Hasidim,* ed. Belcove-Shalin, 174–75.

28. Lynn Davidman, *Tradition in a Rootless World: Women Return to Orthodox Judaism* (Berkeley: University of California Press, 1991).

29. Kaufman, *Rachel's Daughters,* 68.

30. Ibid., 86.

31. Ibid., 112.

Chapter 8. Subgroups and Citizenship

1. Robert D. Putnam, *Bowling Alone* (New York: Simon and Schuster, 2000).

2. Benjamin Barber, *A Place for Us: How to Make Society Civil and Democracy Strong* (New York: Hill and Wang, 1998), 54.

3. Stephen J. Whitfield, review of *The Politics and Public Culture of American Jews* by Arthur A. Goren, *Modern Judaism* 20, no. 3 (2000): 315–18.

4. Jonathan Boyarin, *Circumscribing Constitutional Identities in* Kiryas Joel, 106 Yale Law Journal 1537 (1997).

5. Iris Marion Young, *Justice and the Politics of Difference* (Princeton: Princeton University Press, 1990).

6. Shauna van Praagh, *Changing the Lens: Locating Religious Communities within U.S. and Canadian Families and Constitutions,* 15 Arizona Journal of International and Comparative Law 1, 12 (1998).

7. Michael Walzer, *What It Means to Be an American* (New York: Marsilio Press, 1992), 77.

8. Shauna van Praagh, *Chutzpah of the Chassidim,* Canadian Journal of Law and Society 11, no. 2 (fall 1996), 196.

9. Robert M. Cover, *The Supreme Court, 1982 Term-Forward: Nomos and Narrative,* 97 Harvard Law Review 4 (1983).

10. William Shaffir, "Safeguarding a Distinctive Identity: Hasidic Jews in Montreal," in *Re-*

newing Our Days: Montreal Jews in the Twentieth Century, ed. Ira Robinson and Mervin Butovsky (Montreal: Vehicle Press, 1995), 77–78.

11. Cover, *Supreme Court,* 9.

12. Ibid., 13.

13. Ibid., 12.

14. Ibid., 40.

15. Ibid., 43.

16. Ibid., 68.

17. *Board of Education of Kiryas Joel Village School District v. Grumet,* 114 S. Ct. 2481 (1994).

18. Thomas C. Berg, *Slouching towards Secularism,* 44 Emory Law Journal 433 (spring 1995).

19. Martha Minow, *The Constitution and the Subgroup Question,* 71 Indiana Law Journal 1, 4 (winter 1995).

20. Abner S. Greene, Kiryas Joel *and Two Mistakes About Equality,* 96 Columbia Law Review 1 (January 1996).

21. Robert Justin Lipkin, *Liberalism and the Possibility of Multicultural Constitutionalism,* 29 University of Richmond Law Review 1263, 1270 (December 1995).

22. Christopher Eisgruber, *The Constitutional Value of Assimilation,* 96 Columbia Law Review 87 (1996).

23. Jeff Spinner, *The Boundaries of Citizenship: Race, Ethnicity, and Nationality in the Liberal State* (Baltimore: Johns Hopkins University Press, 1994), 110–12.

24. Ibid., 103.

25. Ibid., 108.

26. Ira C. Lupu, *Uncovering the Village of Kiryas Joel,* 96 Columbia Law Review 104, 104–120 (1996).

27. Judith L. Failer, *The Draw and Drawbacks of Religious Enclaves in Constitutional Democracy: Hasidic Public Schools in* Kiryas Joel, 72 Indiana Law Journal 383, 11 (spring 1997).

28. Ibid., 10.

29. These cases and the conflict between the religious and nonreligious residents of these communities are described by Glen O. Robinson, *Communities,* 83 Virginia Law Review 269 (March 1997).

30. Samuel G. Freedman, "The Jewish Tipping Point," *New York Times Magazine,* August 13, 2000, 42–47.

Chapter 9. Normative Citizenship

1. Will Kymlicka and Wayne Norman, "The Return of the Citizen: A Survey of Recent Work on Citizenship Theory," *Ethics* 104 (January 1994): 352–81.

2. Robert Dahl, "Participation and the Problem of Civic Understanding," in *Rights and the Common Good,* ed. Amitai Etzioni (New York: St. Martin's, 1995), 261–70.

3. "Pericles' Funeral Oration," in Thucydides' *Peloponnesian War* 2:34–36.

4. Kymlicka and Norman, "Return of the Citizen," 362.

5. William Galston, *Liberal Purposes: Goods, Virtues, and Diversity in the Liberal State* (Cambridge: Cambridge University Press, 1991).

6. Richard J. Arneson and Ian Shapiro, "Democratic Autonomy and Religious Freedom: A Critique of *Wisconsin v. Yoder,*" in *Political Order,* ed. Ian Shapiro and Russell Hardin, Nomos 38 (New York: New York University Press, 1996).

7. Amy Gutmann, ed., *Charles Taylor and Multiculturalism and the Politics of Recognition* (Princeton: Princeton University Press, 1992).

8. Bhikhu Parekh, cited in *Theorizing Citizenship,* ed. Ronald Beiner (Albany: State University of New York Press, 1995), 7.

9. Vernon van Dyke, "Justice as Fairness: For Groups?" *American Political Science Review* 69, no. 2 (1975): 607–14; and John Tomasi, "Kymlicka, Liberalism, and Respect for Cultural Minorities," *Ethics* 105 (April 1995): 580–603.

10. Nathan Glazer, *Ethnic Dilemmas: 1964–1982* (Cambridge: Harvard University Press, 1983).

11. Michael Walzer, "Pluralism and Social Democracy," *Dissent* (winter 1998): 47.

12. Beiner, *Theorizing Citizenship.*

13. Martha C. Nussbaum, *For Love of Country: Debating the Limits of Patriotism* (Boston: Beacon Press, 1996).

14. Richard E. Flathman, in Beiner, *Theorizing Citizenship,* chap. 4.

15. Interview with Rabbi Manis Friedman, Burlington, Vermont, November 14, 1999.

INDEX

JAN FELDMAN is an Associate Professor of Political Science at the University of Vermont where she teaches political theory, democratic theory, and religion and politics.

Feldman earned her B.A. from Swarthmore College and her M.A. and Ph.D. from Cornell University. She lives with her four children in Shelburne, Vermont.